Service to Sport

Service to Sport

The Story of the CCPR - 1935 - 1972

H. JUSTIN EVANS, O.B.E., M.A.

With a foreword by
H.R.H. The Duke of Edinburgh, K.G., K.T., O.M.

PELHAM BOOKS LTD

in association with

THE SPORTS COUNCIL

1974

ISBN 0 7207 0795 1

Set and printed in Great Britain by
Tonbridge Printers Ltd, Peach Hall Works, Tonbridge, Kent
in Baskerville eleven on twelve point
and bound by Dorstel Press, Harlow

To the Memory of Phyllis Colson

Contents

Foreword by H.R.H. The Duke of Edinburgh, K.G.,
K.T., O.M.   11
Preface by Sir Stanley Rous, C.B.E., J.P.   13
Author's Introduction   15

CONTENTS

Illustrations

Foreword

By H.R.H. The Duke of Edinburgh, K.G. K.T., O.M.
President, The Central Council of Physical Recreation

BUCKINGHAM PALACE

I think it would be fair to say that the CCPR transformed the concept of recreation in Britain. Long before the purposeful use of leisure became a general topic of discussion, Miss Colson and her fellow workers on the Council set about creating recreation centres, training leaders and coaches, encouraging participation and developing new recreational activities.

Ironically, the organisation which Miss Colson created hardly survived her retirement and though it still exists today, its form and purpose have been radically changed. The remarkable thing is that practically all the members of the original Council retained their membership throughout the traumatic events which ended with the entire staff of the CCPR being taken over by the Sports Council and the re-creation of the CCPR in an entirely different form. A display of loyalty, which demonstrates the respect and affection which was built up during the Council's most active days.

I am delighted that this history has been written because I believe the efforts of Miss Colson and the other pioneers in modern recreation should go on record. Their contribution to national health and enjoyment is obvious but their influence on our social development is equally, if not more, important.

It might well be asked whether there is any future for the Council now that the Sports Council has been established. In my opinion, it is absolutely essential for the CCPR to go on simply because it provides an opportunity for all those in the governing bodies of sport and other organisations directly concerned with recreation to voice their opinions on Government and Sports Council policies. The Sports Council has a very important job to do but it does not represent the people it sets out to serve. I think most people would agree that it is a legitimate responsibility of central and local Government to provide facilities for recreation and to support sports in general, but a nominated Council needs to be informed by responsible people who run the organisations for whom the facilities are provided. But that is another story, and I hope the new CCPR will also be worthy of its own history in due course.

Preface

By Sir Stanley Rous, C.B.E., J.P.
Chairman, The CCPR Executive Committee, 1945 to 1972

When the recent major changes in the affairs of the Central Council of Physical Recreation had been completed I felt confident, as a founder-member and later Chairman for twenty-seven years, that its history was important enough to be told and interesting enough to be read and studied.

I am glad that someone so well-equipped for the task as Justin Evans agreed to write it. It seems to me that he has done so with skill and honesty, emphasising the successes without straining credibility by pretending that there were no setbacks or difficulties. I believe that this account of the CCPR's achievements will come as a welcome reminder of the contribution they made to so many people who were connected with it, and that it will be read as a fascinating piece of social history by those whose knowledge of it was less direct.

Among the members of the Executive Committee whose valuable support was always appreciated I should like to thank Arthur Gem, who acted as Vice-Chairman of the Executive and Chairman of the Staff Committee, for his untiring efforts.

On behalf of all associated with the CCPR, I should like to pay tribute to the Sports Council for making the publication of this history possible. It is an essential prelude to its own history, for it is no exaggeration to claim that without the CCPR there could have been no Sports Council. The key word throughout the CCPR's life was 'service' – service with little publicity, often even without recognition, as the History shows. The CCPR sought influence rather than power, to assist rather than to control, and the secret of its successful work lay in the unique combination of the enthusiastic support of many volunteers and the professional skill of a splendid staff. Both sides were led and directed with vision and energy by Phyllis Colson, whose own outstanding contribution to the development of physical recreation is fittingly recorded in the pages that follow.

13

Author's Introduction

The history of an organisation is apt to make much duller reading than the biography of a person. The history of the CCPR may perhaps be redeemed from this fault by the fact that, in large measure, it is the biography of a most remarkable woman, Phyllis Colson. "No great man lives in vain", wrote Carlyle. "The history of the world is but the biography of great men". Phyllis C. Colson (or P.C.C., as we shall hereafter call her) was a great woman and she has left an ineradicable mark upon the development of physical recreation in this country.

Nevertheless, this history, undertaken at the request of the Sports Council, will be no mere eulogy or exercise in hagiography. P.C.C. possessed rare and outstanding abilities and few human weaknesses. But her greatest gift was to secure the collaboration of others, and that is why the story of the CCPR is far richer and more varied than the story of one person, however talented, could be. As will appear in these pages, the work of the CCPR was made possible because she inspired many other people – some over the whole period of the CCPR's existence – to share her vision and to show the same devotion.

The CCPR grew, within thirty-seven years, from a small group of people, setting to work with two donations totalling £300, into a national body spending over £1,250,000 a year, employing a staff of nearly 400 full-time workers, and with capital assets whose real value must be several million pounds. The story of this phenomenal growth and of the kaleidoscopic range of activities and contacts which was the Council's life-blood from its early days cannot be told easily within the covers of a modest volume. If I seem to touch only superficially, or not at all, on certain aspects of the Council's work or on some of the individuals associated with it which some readers may feel deserved more attention, I know that my difficulties will be understood.

Little can be said here about the contribution made by the CCPR to the understanding and solution of technical problems relating to physical recreation and physical education. Quite apart from the Author's lack of any professional qualifications to write about technical matters, it would be invidious, if not impossible, to attempt to separate in technical terms the work done by the CCPR's staff from that done by their professional colleagues working for local education authorities or governing bodies of sport, or teaching in universities, colleges and schools. Further, the CCPR was a body which concentrated almost exclusively on giving practical assistance to other organisations and training leaders and coaches to a non-professional level of technical and teaching skill. It was in no sense an academic body – it was only in its latest years that it had even a single member of its staff free to devote part of his time to any study that could properly be called research.

The historian of the CCPR is not faced with any shortage of material. From its earliest days, its published Annual Reports recorded in meticulous detail the activities and achievements on which it based its claim for continued public support. Few voluntary organisations can have gone to such pains to secure regular reports of the work of its staff, recorded under a vast number of categories, for careful distillation and presentation to Government departments, the Council's committees and sub-committees, and to the general public through its Annual Reports. This was one of the cardinal principles of its founder, which the staff accepted in general with good will. They grumbled and procrastinated at times, but they knew that, in the end, the time and labour they put into their reports were far exceeded by their General Secretary's.

No, the difficulty confronting the historian is the need to explore the vast mass of material in existence so that nothing of real significance is omitted. And a greater difficulty has been to decide how to present it – whether : (1) chronologically, if dully, as the years go by; (2) in terms of service to particular organisations or groups of organisations; (3) as a record of contributions made to the development of particular activities or types of activity; (4) under particular subject-headings, such as "National Recreation Centres"; or, (5) by placing chief emphasis on the gradual, organic, structural development of a body whose very success in getting increasing public recognition and statutory financial support may have planted the seeds for the eventual absorption of its staff and assets by a statutory body. In the end, it seemed best to adopt the last course, telling the CCPR's story in sequences of periods of years, interspersed with chapters* devoted to certain easily separable aspects of its work.

In the interests of historical perspective, it has been thought right to include some references to one or two developments in the field of physical recreation which, strictly, do not fall within the CCPR's own history. For example, though the work of the National Fitness Council from 1937 to 1939 was separate from the CCPR's, the respective fields of work of the two bodies were so close that to speak of one involves the other. Moreover, the story of the National Fitness Campaign seems little known, yet it is of such great historical interest and current relevance that it will, I hope, seem to merit the attention it has been given.

Ideally, a historian should be objective and impersonal. But that ideal is seldom reached by anyone writing about events in which he played some part and I cannot hope to escape some imputations of partiality. But my readers will, I trust, forgive such attempts at comment and interpretation as I shall make; a bare recital of ascertainable facts and statistics would have made an indigestible and not very satisfying meal.

The history of the CCPR is so evidently a 'success story' that there is no need – least of all for someone writing from the comfortable detachment of retirement – for any of its few set-backs or failures to be ignored or minimised. Nor have I sought to exclude mention of controversial issues or of the opposition the Council had occasionally to encounter from some quarters. To have done so would have made its success seem less remarkable than it was.

This history ends with the transfer of the CCPR's principal assets to the statutory Sports Council in June 1972. To avoid overburdening the text with too many names and statistics, certain material vital in an historical record has been relegated to Appendices. These contain some published tributes to Phyllis Colson; the names of the Council's Honorary Officers and Committee Chairmen whose invaluable voluntary service might otherwise have gone unchronicled; the membership of the Executive Committee in 1972; the names and dates of service of long-serving members of the staff; the organisations represented on the Council and the individual members with their dates

*For instance, chapters 7, 8, 11 and 12.

of election; and lists of the Council's publications and of sources consulted.

In addition to drawing on the Council's records and my own memories, I have had the advantage of being able to discuss various sections of this history, not only with some of my former colleagues but with many friends who have been closely associated with the CCPR's work. Among them, I record my particular thanks to The Baroness Burton of Coventry, Sir Robin Brook, Sylvia Buzzard, Kathleen Colson, Arthur Gem, Sir Reginald Goodwin, R. E. Griffith, Sir George Haynes, Denis Howell, M. P., Lord Hunt, Sir Jack Longland, P. B. Lucas, Peter McIntosh, Ernest Major, B. L. Pearson, Sir Stanley Rous, H. Sagar, Lesley Sewell, Phyllis Spafford and Lord Wolfenden. Though they have given me both advice and encouragement, they bear no responsibility for the opinions and reflections contained in the pages that follow.

Finally, I wish to acknowledge my great debt to my wife for her forbearance and interest throughout the writing of this book.

CHAPTER ONE

The Early 'Thirties:
Some Relevant Factors

The formation in 1935 of the Central Council of Recreative Physical Training – for that was its title until 1944 – can only be understood in the light of the social, educational, economic and international situation of the years immediately preceding. The nation was passing through a series of financial and industrial crises. The financial position had seemed so grave in 1931 that a National Government was formed, a cut of ten per cent imposed on the salaries of teachers and other employees in the statutory services, and other drastic economies made in public expenditure. The number of registered unemployed varied between two and three million, and unemployment was particularly high among juveniles.

The school-leaving age was 14, and less than ten per cent of the nation's boys and girls went on from elementary to secondary schools. Of that percentage fewer than one third remained at school after 16. For those who got work at 14, wages were low, apprenticeships rare, and 'blind-alley' jobs, leading to dismissal at 16, a common form of employment. Until 1934, those under 16 were covered by no compulsory insurance scheme against either sickness or unemployment, and there was no restriction upon the hours worked by shop boys or factory hands. A large proportion had no holiday whatever except at Bank Holidays, for which they had to work especially hard beforehand.

No 'dole' or unemployment pay was received until after the age of 16 was reached, and, then, a condition of receiving it was attendance at what were called Junior Instruction Centres, which met in makeshift premises and offered physical training (often without any changing from ordinary clothing), handicrafts and some games. It was a grim and ghastly time for many young people, which they bore with astonishing fortitude and cheerfulness.

That there was great physical and moral deterioration in the nation's youth during their first years after leaving school was gradually being driven into the general conscience. Youth organisations (or juvenile organisations as they were then called), had had some statutory recognition in the Education Act of 1921 but not much practical assistance from either central or local government – the relevant clause in the Act was permissive rather than mandatory. They were struggling hard in their various ways to deal with problems of young people's leisure. They were also becoming more aware of each other's existence, a process fostered in some areas by the Juvenile Organisations Committees which had been set up during the previous war with statutory support. But the problems to be faced, including the evils arising from unemployment, went far beyond their combined resources.

A not dissimilar situation existed in the adult world, and there was great and growing concern about the continued high rate of unemployment, particularly in what were designated the 'Special Areas'. Social service agencies such as University and Educational Settlements were devoting much time to organising clubs and 'occupation centres' which attempted to provide on a voluntary basis the sort of activities for men which Junior Instruction Centres and youth organisations offered to young people. Here again, premises were poor, and trained leadership and other facilities extremely scarce. The National Council of Social Service did much to focus public attention on this work by appointing special staff to co-ordinate it and provide advisory services. They also arranged a series of tours by the then Prince of Wales 'to see what was being done for the unemployed'.

In the elementary and secondary schools, the quality of the physical education given was rapidly improving as a result of the influences so graphically described in Peter McIntosh's book, Physical Education in England since 1800. Colleges for specialist women teachers of physical education had grown from one in 1895 to six by 1905, but there had been no comparable development on the men's side and there were few full-time men specialists teaching boys in the schools. Many teaching in secondary and public schools had received their training in the Services. Helped by the Carnegie United Kingdom Trust, Carnegie College of Physical Education was opened by Leeds Education Authority in 1933, offering a one-year course in physical education to sixty men students who were either trained teachers

or University graduates. Loughborough College started a similar
one-year course in 1935, and the products of these two colleges
have made a great impact on the physical education of boys
and men in this country.

But the end of the 'drill in the classroom or playground'
stage at school only served to emphasise the complete inadequacy of the provision for the health, physical education and
recreation of adolescent boys and girls in their first years of
working life. There was an acute shortage of facilities and
trained leadership – or, indeed, of any leadership – not to mention the lack of organisation and incentives.

On the facilities side, a positive and valuable forward move
had been the establishment in 1925, at a meeting addressed by
H.R.H. The Duke of York (later King George VI), of the
National Playing Fields Association. Public subscription raised
£100,000 initially, a sum augmented by a grant of £200,000
from the Carnegie Trust in 1927. Since that date the NPFA
has raised and distributed large sums by way of grants and loans
for playing fields and playground schemes, and, as will be seen,
gave invaluable support to the CCRPT in its early days.

In terms of organisation and outlook, the world of sport was
largely an adult world, even though in some youth organisations activities such as football, cricket, boxing, basketball, swimming, athletics, gymnastics, table tennis, and, by girls, netball
and hockey, were popular and widely practised. But though
most sports had their own governing body, the concern of most
of these bodies, run almost entirely by voluntary officials, lay
in regulating and running competitions rather than in coaching
and development. For Olympic Games purposes most of them
came together under the auspices of the British Olympic Association (formed in 1905) but, otherwise, each governing body
did its work in isolation from other governing bodies and guarded
its autonomy jealously.

In non-competitive outdoor activities, the Youth Hostels Association, formed in this country in 1930 after the German prototype, was probably the best-known body and it was growing
rapidly, although its membership came more from the middle
than from the working classes. There were smaller national
bodies promoting camping, canoeing, cycling and rambling.
Also noteworthy in this context is the growth of women's keep-
fit movements from 1929, notably in Sunderland, Glasgow,

Lancashire and South Wales, and the Women's League of Health and Beauty, initiated by Mrs. Bagot Stack in London in 1929, which by 1933 was strong enough to take the Royal Albert Hall for a demonstration of its work.

As one step to meet public concern about the effects of unemployment among young people (Mr. Malcolm Stewart, Commissioner for the Special Areas, had drawn attention in his report to "the low medical standard of boys and young men") the Government were to propose in 1936 legislation to raise the school-leaving age to 15 in 1939, "with exemption for beneficial employment". There was hot opposition to the exemption clause and very wide advocacy of the 'day continuation school' movement, in which Cadbury's of Bournville had been a notable pioneer, with 'physical culture' as an essential item in the curriculum. The Government got their way and the Act was passed. But it never took effect and nothing more was heard about "exemption for beneficial employment".

But whatever solutions were advocated, public concern about the welfare of young people was increasing, one factor in the situation being undoubtedly a growing apprehension that aggressive Nazism and Fascism in European countries might lead us into a large-scale war for which we were physically ill-prepared. Comparisons were drawn between the apparent listlessness and lack of patriotic idealism which were thought to mark so large a proportion of British boys, on the one hand, and the well-drilled Hitler Youth with their motto "I was born to die for Germany", the faces of Italian boys "lit up with an almost ecstatic expression of devotion to the ideal of an all-dominant Italy to which every citizen owed unquestioning loyalty" and the no less fanatical willingness of Russia's young communists to sacrifice their all for the glory of their country, on the other.

Though motives were mixed and many gloomy prophecies were to prove hopelessly wrong, the feeling was general that 'something must be done' about the fitness of the nation's youth. The recovery of King George V from a serious illness led to an outburst of loyal fervour, and in 1935, the Jubilee of his accession to the throne was marked by a national appeal as a thank-offering for His Majesty's reign, the proceeds to be devoted to advancing "the physical, mental and spiritual welfare of the younger generation". The King George's Jubilee Trust was established in March 1935 and Lord Portal, vice-chairman of the Trust, was soon to write of "large numbers of boys and girls who are approaching the age of full citizenship ill-equipped for the responsibilities which face them – and this at a time when it is clear that the manhood and womanhood of this nation may yet be tested as never before".

Apart from the work of a few forward-looking local authorities, the after-school welfare of young people largely depended upon the work of voluntary youth organisations – Scouts, Guides, Brigades, Boys' Clubs, Girls' Clubs, YMCA, YWCA, Urdd Gobaith Cymru (Welsh League of Youth), and so on – all deeply attached to their own principles, methods and techniques, not least in matters of physical training, camping and other activities. In general, there was little co-operation between them; they were far too busy trying to keep their own movements going on inadequate resources. In spite of Section 86 of the 1921 Education Act, they received virtually no help from local authorities. The limited help that came from the Carnegie and Pilgrim Trusts was mainly given for conducting experiments.

The youth organisations were much cheered by the prospect of financial help from the Jubilee Trust. This helped to create a desire for greater co-operation, so that there was a ready response to the move made by the National Council of Social Service in 1936 to establish a Standing Conference of National Voluntary Juvenile Organisations, a consultative body which has remained in being to this day, in recent years under the name of National Council for Voluntary Youth Services.

In November 1934, the then Minister of Health, Sir Hilton Young (later Lord Kennet), asked at a Dinner of the British Medical Association whether something could not be done "to bring home the benefits of physical culture, which was a culture of mind as well as of muscle". He hoped that the medical profession would tell him how some advance might be made in that direction. The challenge was accepted. The BMA set up a Physical Education Committee, with a very high-powered membership under the chairmanship of E. Kay le Fleming, Chairman of the BMA Council, and numbering among its members, in addition to distinguished medical experts, Phyllis Spafford, Secretary of the Ling Association of Teachers of Swedish Gymnastics, H. E. Naylor, Vice-Chairman of the

British Association for Physical Training and National Physical Director of the YMCA, and Captain S. J. Parker, Staff Inspector for Physical Training at the Board of Education. The report of this committee will be referred to later.

So a combination of four factors created a favourable climate for some new initiative in the field of 'physical and mental culture' – the progress of thought about physical education; concern about the nation's health and morale, particularly of its young people; the scourge of unemployment; and a growing recognition on the part of voluntary bodies which had hitherto worked in isolation that they needed the additional strength that could come from co-operation.

But *what* new initiative? To get the medical profession more closely linked with physical educationists? To harness the technical knowledge of the physical education profession in the service of the voluntary youth organisations? To promote some co-operation between the governing bodies of sport and other specialist bodies and to get them to do more for younger people? To recruit and train more voluntary leaders for various forms of recreation? To persuade local authorities to be far more active in using their powers to provide facilities for physical recreation? To get the Board of Education more deeply involved in what people were trying to do for those who had left school and for unemployed men and women? To ensure that all those working in this amorphous field of post-school physical recreation at least knew each other and that none of the scarce resources available ran to waste through duplication of effort or inefficient organisation?

Though *all* these things needed doing, it was an original and imaginative conception of the highest order – almost amounting to genius – to think of creating one single organisation which could attempt to tackle them all. Yet this, no less, was the "vision splendid" which led Phyllis Colson to propose to her colleagues in the physical education profession that a completely new body should be formed which might set to work upon all these considerable tasks.

CHAPTER TWO

Formation and Early Activities:
1935 - 1937

The personality and unique abilities of P.C.C. played so dominant a part in the creation, growth and functioning of the CCPR that her name will keep cropping up in this history. Later, some attempt must be made to give a picture of what sort of a person she really was, but, at this stage, a few biographical facts are called for. Born in London in 1904, she attended Liverpool College for Girls at Huyton as a boarder before going to Bedford College of Physical Education in 1923. She was an outstanding student and described as "a brilliant teacher". After teaching at girls' secondary schools from 1926–1930, she accepted an oppointment as assistant to Phyllis Spafford, organising physical education within what was then known as the National Council of Girls' Clubs. In 1931, Miss Spafford left to become Secretary of the Ling Association of Teachers of Swedish Gymnastics (at that time mainly a feminine body, but which has now become the Physical Education Association) of which both she and P.C.C. were members. P.C.C. continued to work for the NCGC, getting to know everyone 'who mattered' nationally in youth work and physical education, including those in charge of physical training at the Board of Education.

While working for Girls' Clubs she meditated on the recreational needs of young people and of the country as a whole. She was well aware of the prospects of financial and moral support for youth work engendered by the formation of the King George's Jubilee Trust, and by the BMA Inquiry. She kept closely in touch with other physical educationists through the two professional bodies, the Ling Association and the National Association of Organisers of Physical Education. From 1934–1937, she was the Ling Association's Press Officer and the Editor of both its *News Letter* and quarterly *Journal*. In 1935, she became a member of its Executive Committee, so she had direct access to all its officers and members, and a ready-made line of communication with all physical educationists. "Nominally", she recalled in a private paper written after her retirement, "the Ling Association acted; in fact, it supported and gave a platform to one of its members".

In an article entitled 'Some Birthday Reminiscences' which she wrote for the April 1956 issue of the CCPR's journal *Physical Recreation* commemorating the Council's twenty-first birthday, P.C.C. describes the day when "winding my way down Upper Woburn Place, I suddenly pictured a Great Britain in which every youngster had a chance to take part in enjoyable and health-giving physical activity and in which all the people and associations with something to offer to that end – teachers and organisers, sports bodies and youth organisations, education authorities and industrial firms, and many others – worked *together,* pooling their knowledge, experience and resources, helping each other and tackling their problems by joint effort. Facilities would be first class; classes of various kinds would be available in every area, rural as well as urban; in the bigger cities, comprehensive centres would provide for youth organisations as well as physical activity bodies; and there would be a plentiful supply of voluntary leaders, men and women who were more than teachers of technique. Yes, it *could* happen if there were a really active 'umbrella' body with provincial branches but no vested interests!"

"I cannot pretend", she continued, "that the 'flash' was the outcome of reasoning. But perhaps a long period off work had, unbeknown to me, allowed time for two things to become linked in my mind – concern about the bad effect which the unhappy economic position of the country was having on the well-being of young people, and the impressions about the value of physical recreation which I had gained from serving as an Organiser of Physical Education to the NAGC and from watching the quick growth of keep-fit movements."

This was her vision. She 'dashed home' and drafted a memorandum – she had no idea for whom! – advocating the formation of a co-ordinating council. Things moved quickly. To continue the story in her own words: "Miss Spafford of the Ling Association and Mr. Henry Cole, Honorary Secretary of the NAOPE expressed keen interest and immediately enlisted the support of their organisations. Together we visited the Board of Education, where, to our gratified surprise, the idea was received with enthusiasm – though not, of course, with any offer of financial support.

"On the afternoon of Easter Sunday I sat in the Ling Association's office and laboriously typed (with two fingers!) letters to prospective members. Rather surprisingly, nearly all of them agreed to serve. Among them were some who have been stalwarts of the Council for the whole twenty-one years – Sir Stanley Rous, Mr. A. H. Gem, Lord Aberdare, Lord Hampton, Professor Winifred Cullis, Mr. D. Kennedy, Mr. E. Major and Dr. Anna Broman, for example".

Much of the distinguished support recruited for the new Council must be attributed to the enthusiasm and influence of the Board of Education – not least that of Herwald Ramsbotham, M.P., then Parliamentary Secretary to the Board (later Lord Soulbury). Sir George Newman, its Chief Medical Officer, and Captain S. J. Parker, H.M.I. It was probably their combined influence that persuaded the King and Queen to be the new Council's Patrons, the Prince of Wales its Vice-Patron, and Lord Astor its President.

On 18th June, the Board of Education in a Press statement announced the formation of the Central Council of Recreative Physical Training, under Royal Patronage and with the Board's cordial co-operation. It urged all those interested in the welfare of the youth of the country to give it their active co-operation. The Press gave the announcement wide national and local coverage.

An Inaugural Meeting followed, held in the Conference Room of the Board of Education, Whitehall, S.W. on Thursday afternoon, 4th July 1935. Viscount Astor took the chair and twenty-seven attended, there being a number of apologies for absence. Lord Halifax, President of the Board, welcomed those present, emphasising that the Board had no official concern with the Council's activities but had full sympathy with its aims and objects.

After a few preliminary words about the new Council's aims, which made it clear that the term "physical training" in its title was used in a wide sense to include every form of indoor and outdoor recreative activity, Lord Astor announced that forty-five men and women had accepted invitations to join the Council. He proposed that a Provisional Executive Committee should be appointed under the chairmanship of Sir George Newman, with power to co-opt, to appoint a Secretary, secure premises, and draw up a simple constitution. Lord Derby, who was Chairman of the National Playing Fields Association, Lord Dawson of Penn and others supported the proposal, and a Committee of seventeen, whose names were put forward by Lord Astor was appointed. These included three who in 1972 were still active in the Council's service – Stanley Rous, Arthur Gem and Ernest Major. Captain Parker was made Liaison Officer with the Board of Education.

It was considered important to establish a clear demarcation between the functions of the NPFA and the CCRPT, and in October 1935, the Provisional Executive initiated discussions with representatives of the NPFA on the subject. First conclusions were that an immediate amalgamation of the two bodies was desirable, the body so formed to be called the National Playing Fields and Physical Recreation Association. But after further discussions this step was rejected in favour of close co-operation, and a Joint Advisory Committee was set up between the two bodies under the chairmanship of the Earl of Athlone.

To meet the initial expenses of forming the new Council, the Ling Association contributed £240 and the NAOPE £60. There was no other source of income, and for some time P.C.C. worked without any salary and was looked upon as an Honorary Officer. A tiny office was rented in Doughty Street, and Brenda Mortiboy, a volunteer keep-fit leader, joined P.C.C. as her secretary. Several women teachers of physical education gave the CCRPT voluntary full-time or part-time help. To avoid an exclusively feminine look about the staff, Henry Cole accepted the office of Honorary Secretary of the organisation, though his role was mainly titular, as he was still in the full-time post of Superintendent of Physical Training to Sheffield Education Committee, which he had held since 1913.

Hopes of financial support had rested mainly on an approach to the new King George's Jubilee Trust, but their grant of £1,000 in February 1936 was far less generous than had been hoped. It was given, moreover, on the understanding that the Council would not mount a separate public appeal of its own. In May 1936, the National Playing Fields Association came to the rescue with a donation of £1,000 and the additional welcome offer of the free use of an office in Eccleston Square. Lord Astor had given £125 in 1935, and by August 1936 a number of small donations totalling over £300 had been elicited from other individuals and industrial firms. Among them were £40 from the Bergman Osterberg College and £20 from Miss Spafford herself. The first statutory help was not to come until February 1937 – £1,000 from the Board of Education.

P.C.C.'s first intention had been that the CCRPT should be composed of "influential and widely-experienced men and women", but so many national organisations wished to be associated with the new body that, at a meeting of the Council held on 27th September 1935, it was decided to invite all interested national organisations to appoint one representative each to serve on the permanent Council. By December 1935, the Council consisted of the representatives of eighty-two national bodies and thirty-four individual members.

The national bodies fell into three main categories :
(1) those concerned exclusively with physical activity, like the governing bodies of sport and those promoting dancing and keep-fit work (whatever happened to the Legion of Health and Happiness?);
(2) those which included physical recreation within a wider programme, particularly the national voluntary youth organisations; and
(3) "other interested national organisations", for example The British Medical Association, the National Union of Teachers, and the Chartered Society of Massage and Medical Gymnastics. The Amateur Athletic Association, MCC, the Football Association, the Rugby Football Union and the Amateur Swimming Association were among the important national governing bodies of sport which joined the Council in its first year.

It is indicative of the grave concern current at that period about the physical health of the community that of the thirty-four original individual members of the Council no fewer than fourteen were members of the medical profession, including Sir Henry Brackenbury, Sir Farquhar Buzzard, Dame Janet Campbell, Dr. R. Cove-Smith, Lord Dawson of Penn, Lord Horder, Sir William Arbuthnot Lane, Lord Moyniham and Sir George Newman. There were seven physical educationists, including some of those mentioned earlier, three prominent politicians – the Earl of Derby, Herbert Morrison, M.P., and Sir Archibald Sinclair, M.P. – and two educationists with a national reputation – Dr. L. P. Jacks and Dr. (later Sir) Cyril Norwood.

In addition to a Provisional Executive Committee a Technical Advisory Sub-Committee was set up under the chairmanship of S. F. Rous, "in order to establish the closest link between the Council and those responsible for physical activities in voluntary organisations and to investigate the best methods of placing the specialised knowledge of the physical training associations at the service of the population". Mr. Rous, who had gained a national reputation for his interest in sport and physical training while on the staff of Watford Grammar School, had been Secretary of the Football Association since 1934. Twelve national youth organisations, the Ling Association, the NAOPE, and the British Association for Physical Training were represented on the sub-committee, together with five independent members: Dr. Anna Broman, Major W. K. Garnier, A. H. Gem, E. Major and Edith Thompson.

A *First News Leaflet* was published in December 1935, which stated clearly the origin, aims and policy of the Council. The Ling Association and the NAOPE had realised, it was said, that more organised effort was needed on the part of expert bodies to give their services to voluntary organisations working in the field of post-school physical training. They had therefore initiated this new central body, national and all-embracing in its aims, "to help to improve the physical and mental health of the community through physical recreation, by developing existing facilities for recreative physical activities of all kinds, and also by making provision for the thousands not yet associated with any organisation". Co-operation was to be the accepted basis of the Central Council and, from its very nature, it could not supersede any independent organisation. There would be no dogmatism about methods and no attempt to impose 'a system'. "Who can say", it asked, "that one system or method is definitely right or wrong for another group? Such a policy would be presumptuous and entirely foreign to the aims of a voluntary national body which hopes to be of use to all.'

Even at this early date it was possible to report an impressive list of activities initiated by the Council: a Register of Leaders started, various courses arranged, many public classes and demonstrations held, and contacts made with hundreds of individuals, voluntary bodies and industrial concerns. After such a wealth of activity in so short a time, it is almost ironic to read in the leaflet that "it has been constantly borne in mind that an organisation of the magnitude of the Central Council and especially one which aims at co-ordination and elimination of overlapping must, of necessity, develop slowly".

A *Second News Leaflet,* published in April 1936, recorded the confirmation in office of the Provisional Excutive Committee at a meeting of the Council the previous month, the important additions to its membership of the Association of Education Committees, the Association of Directors and Secretaries for Education, the National Federation of Women's Institutes, and the National Union of Townswomen's Guilds, and drew attention to the issue by the Board of Education of the unusually forceful Circular 1445, on *Physical Education,* on 13th January 1936. This had urged local education authorities to make more adequate provision for the physical development of young people, including helping voluntary bodies in their work, reminded them of their powers under the 1921 Education Act, and expressed regret that only 124 of the 316 local education authorities in England and Wales had yet seen fit to appoint organisers of physical training. One effect of the Circular which the Council was right to foresee was an increased demand for its services.

But a publication with even more long-term influence was the Report of the BMA's Physical Education Committee referred to in the previous chapter, which appeared in April 1936. Its terms of reference had been "to consider and report upon the necessity for the cultivation of the physical development of the civilian population and the methods to be pursued for this object", and its Report was full, uncompromising and far-reaching – a landmark in physical education.

Its opening words were : 'The aim of physical education is to obtain and maintain the best possible development and functioning of the body, and thereby to aid the development of mental capacity and of character. The mind and body are so essentially one, that the divorce between them in what is commonly called education appears as unscientific as it is pronounced. However brilliant the intellect, a neglected body hinders the attainment of the highest capacity possible to an individual; and, conversely, the maintenance of the best possible functioning of the body must react as a beneficial mental stimulus ... The absence of adequate education in the care of the body has led many to accept without thought the deformity of their bodies as something beyond their control.'

There followed paragraphs, still relevant today, on the relation to physical fitness of such factors as exercise, fresh air, sun-bathing, nutrition and diet, clothing, posture, alcohol and tobacco. The Report found the existing provision for the physical education of adolescents and adults gravely inadequate – even of the young people in voluntary organisations only twenty-five per cent took part in physical activity. There was a lack of accommodation, equipment, funds, and, above all, of suitably trained leaders.

From the point of view of the CCRPT, a number of whose members and P.C.C. had supplied evidence, the Committee's most telling recommendations were that "training courses for leaders of recreative physical training throughout the country should be co-ordinated by some central body such as the Central Council of Recreative Physical Training" and "voluntary organisations for young people between the ages of 14 and 18 should be encouraged in each area to make use of the recently formed CCRPT...A branch of the CCRPT or an active Juvenile Organisations Committee could, and should, by uniting the force and experience of all the juvenile organisations, achieve results beyond the power of a single organisation acting alone".

As evidence that the connotation of the phrase "recreative physical training" at that time was very wide, one may quote the Report's definition of it as "including organised games, athletic sports, swimming, boxing and fencing, and other physical activities, such as dancing, which help to produce a healthy constitution and impart a true physical culture". But the Report adds the caveat: "The Committee is unable to accept the view that field games and athletics provide a sufficient means of maintaining physical fitness. It regards gymnastic exercises as an essential and fundamental part of physical education", and it goes on to say why.

At that time, one of the most stimulating and well-informed writers about the general welfare of young people was W. McG. Eagar. His full-time post was that of Secretary-General of the National Institute for the Blind, but his real interests were physical education and social work with boys. His combative editorials in *The Boy*, the quarterly journal of the National Association of Boys' Clubs, are one of the best sources of information for current thinking about the welfare of the adolescent. Writing of the BMA Report, he said, "Wisely, I think, the NABC is attaching itself for guidance to the newly-formed Central Council of Recreative Physical Training. If any agreement between experts is possible at all, the CCRPT are most likely to secure it. The physical training world is so riven with sectarian jealousies, that the inexpert club leader may safely discount the extremists and devote himself to finding the right teacher rather than the ideal system ... Women have gone a long way ahead of us. They started in a clear field. They did not have to clear the ground of the debris of the old Army and German gymnastic systems, intended to make strong men stronger. They have much to teach us in the science of making young bodies fitter."

Encouraged by its recognition in the BMA Report, the Council in May 1936 appointed at very modest salaries its first two full-time Technical Representatives, K. Caister (now Mrs.Latto) and F. Knibbs, who worked valiantly to try to meet the ever-increasing demands for their services. Hitherto, virtually all the work undertaken by the Council had been done by volunteers, and it should be remembered that, though its professional staff grew in numbers over the years, it was the source of recruitment of thousands of voluntary workers, not only as demonstrators but also as teachers and lecturers at leaders' training courses.

The first Annual Report of the CCRPT covered the period from 4th July 1935 to 31st August 1936, and was presented to a meeting of the Council held in September 1936. King Edward VIII had accepted his late father's position as Patron of the Council; ninety-four national bodies were now represented on the Council. Lord Hampden had been appointed chairman of the Executive in January 1936, succeeding the temporary chairman, Sir George Newman, and a General Purposes Committee had been set up consisting of Lord Hampden (chairman), Miss M. Fountain (Principal of Chelsea College of Physical Education who represented the Ling Association on the Council), A. H. Gem and S. F. Rous. Close working relations had in particular been established with the Central Council for Health Education, the Industrial Welfare Society, the National Federation of Women's Institutes and the National Playing Fields Association. Work had already been done in twenty-nine English and four Welsh counties. Hopes were expressed that it might prove possible "to extend operations to Scotland at an early date".

Clearly the solid achievements of the Council in its first year greatly impressed those in touch with it and, in the Autumn of 1936, the Council was invited by the Board of Education to submit in confidence a memorandum on the national development of post-school physical recreation. According to a handwritten note by P.C.C., this memorandum was in due course presented to the Cabinet by the Hon. Oliver Stanley, who had succeeded Lord Halifax as President of the Board. It was, she wrote, so well accepted that it played a part in the processes that were to lead to the establishment of the National Fitness Council in the following year.

From the Council's *Third News Leaflet* in January 1937, it was evident that something was already 'in the wind'. It was noted that the previous few months had been "ones of eager anticipation". But, it was added, "the hoped-for 'awakening' is not so meteoric as it appears; it has sound foundations, for it is the outcome of the untiring work of organisations and individuals during the past thirty or more years".

"In order that the present drive may bring about lasting progress", the leaflet continued, "physical training must not be treated as a separate entity : it must be linked up with other pursuits and developed in proper conjunction with all general factors such as nutrition and hygiene ... The future is full of hopeful signs but it is certain that the problem can only be met adequately by concerted national action. Co-operation and co-ordination of effort are essential. It is in the knowledge that these are the fundamentals of its policy that the Central Council hopes that it be allowed to play an active part in whatever national policy is adopted by His Majesty's Government."

By the time the CCRPT's second Annual Report – that for 1936–1937 – was published, the National Fitness Council, as it quickly came to be called, was an established fact. The work of that Council and its effect upon the activities and policy of the CCRPT will be considered in the next chapter.

CHAPTER THREE

The National Fitness Campaign:
1937 - 1939

Chapter One gave some of the evidence that led informed opinion to conclude that the provision for the continued education – physical, mental and moral – of the nation's young people after they had left school was gravely inadequate. No doubt, an additional factor for concern in the minds of some people was the poor showing made by Great Britain at the 1936 Olympic Games, held in Berlin, and so stage-managed as to glorify the achievements of the National Socialist régime in Germany.

The Government's view was that any solution to the problem along compulsory lines was neither practicable nor desirable; above all, they were anxious to rebut in advance any charge that they were endeavouring to imitate the regimentation of youth practised in Nazi Germany and elsewhere. The solution, it felt, had to be based on voluntary action : strengthening the whole work, not just the physical work, of the voluntary youth organisations; financing the provision of more and better facilities for physical recreation; and encouraging local education authorities to make more use of their powers under the 1921 Act to provide facilities for social and physical training. It was hoped that adult sports bodies could be helped at the same time but they were not the primary object of the campaign.

Something new and dynamic was felt to be needed which would capture the nation's imagination and be backed by adequate finance from the State. So, in January 1937, the Government issued a White Paper, *Physical Training and Recreation,* outlining its plans for physical fitness, largely conceived in terms of the development and expansion of existing facilities and organisations. The standard of school provision, it said, was already being raised, but there was need for it to be supplemented by arrangements "for those whose daily environment of the office or the workshop makes the provision for physical improvement particularly desirable". Local authorities had a variety of powers for aiding physical training and recreation, and voluntary organisations made some provision in practically every part of the country for promoting the social and physical welfare of youth. There were also a number of central organisations whose primary function was to promote and stimulate local effort. It had to be recognised, however, that "many might desire opportunities for physical exercise and recreation not solely as such but as part of a fuller club or community life, and the scheme would accordingly extend to combined provision of that character'.

A National Advisory Council for England and Wales was to be established "to survey the field and advise on needs and methods" with a similar provision for Scotland. A small Grants Committee of three would make recommendations to the Board of Education. Area Committees, each with a paid secretary, would be set up "to raise public interest, encourage assistance from voluntary sources, and be channels for grant applications". Capital grants would be given in aid of projects for the provision of gymnasia and gymnastic equipment, and would also be made for the provision of swimming baths, camping sites and other facilities for physical recreation.

Grants would help national organisations to stimulate and encourage local effort. The Grants Committee "would also have powers to recommend grants to the Central Council of Recreative Physical Training for providing training classes, giving expert advice and aiding the provision of adequate salaries for teachers and leaders, and expenses involved by the above duties". The National Playing Fields Association would receive grants for work done in connection with the provision of playing fields.

A National College of Physical Training was to be established, "provided and maintained by the Government, to train leaders and do research work into some of the many outstanding problems connected with the physiology of physical training". (Concurrently with the issue of the White Paper, the Board of Education published *Recreation and Physical Fitness for Youths and Young Men,* and *Recreation and Physical Fitness for Girls and Women,* technical hand-books that had great value for the recreative field. The CCRPT took a half-page of advertising space in each!)

It was estimated that £2,400,000, a figure subsequently amended to £4,000,000 (the latter perhaps £30,000,000 by today's standards) would be required over three years for capital

36

grants for facilities, and that a continuing annual charge of about £50,000 would be required for maintaining the work of the Advisory Council.

Captain Lionel F. Ellis, C.V.O., C.B.E., D.S.O., M.C., Secretary of the National Council of Social Service since 1919, was chosen to be secretary. He was 52. He set up the Fitness Council's office in Tothill Street S.W.1, in March 1937. Its Chairman was Lord Aberdare, well-known to the sporting world as the former Hon. C. N. Bruce, the distinguished cricketer and tennis player, the British Olympic Committee's representative on the CCRPT, a member of the International Olympic Committee, and Honorary Treasurer of the National Association of Boys' Clubs. The Vice-chairman was the Hon. Edward Cadogan, C.B. (Knighted in 1939), elder brother of Sir Alexander Cadogan, at that time Deputy Under-Secretary of State for Foreign Affairs. Among the twenty-nine other members of the Council were Philip Noel-Baker, M.P., Lord Burghley, M.P. (now the Marquess of Exeter), Chairman of the Amateur Athletic Association, Sir Noel Curtis Bennett, Lord Dawson of Penn, W. McG. Eagar, H. E. Fern of the Amateur Swimming Association. A. H. Gem, S. F. Rous, Phyllis Spafford, Prunella Stack of the League of Health and Beauty, and W. W. Wakefield, M.P. (now Lord Wakefield of Kendal) of the Rugby Football Union. Eighteen of the thirty-one members of the NFC were either individual or representative members of the CCRPT A. H. Gem, who had been Senior Inspector of Physical Education to the LCC since 1919, and Miss Spafford were the only professional physical educationists on it.

Bright young men and women were recruited from outside the Civil Service to help staff the NFC, including people who attained distinction in other fields later in life, such as Elaine Burton (now Baroness Burton), Anthony Greenwood (now Lord Greenwood), the late Sir John Newsom and Eirene Jones (now Baroness White). Secretaries of the twenty-two Area Committees set up under the Act were appointed at salaries that had the effect of attracting candidates who were on the staffs of voluntary social service bodies, education authorities and universities. When their jobs were terminated abruptly on the outbreak of war less than two years after their appointment many of these Area Secretaries wished they had stayed where they were!

It is quite evident from the files that, early in its life, the officers of the NFC, both officially and unofficially, urged that the NFC should absorb the CCRPT. This suggestion was strongly resisted by the latter, both in memoranda and at the private meetings which took place between representatives of the two bodies. The CCRPT felt that the cause of 'national fitness' would be best served if both bodies worked according to the terms of the White Paper, the function of the NFC being purely advisory and grant-recommending, and that of the CCRPT, grant-aided by the Board on the recommendation of the NFC Grants Committee, being "to provide, or aid the provision of, courses designed to improve the qualifications of teachers and leaders, and to provide expert advice as to forms of physical training and recreation". The General Purposes Committee – of which Dr. (later Sir) Percival Sharp, the Council's Hon. Treasurer and the influential Secretary of the Association of Education Committees, was a prominent and vocal member – felt strongly that the CCRPT should retain its name and identity as a voluntary organisation. At a meeting with Sir Henry Pelham, Chairman of the Grants Committee and Captain Ellis, they pressed for, and obtained, an assurance that the National Fitness Council would remain purely advisory and that no further suggestions for absorbing the CCRPT would be made. They claimed that such an assurance would dispel the confusion that was already growing in the public mind as to the respective functions of the two bodies.

The Physical Training and Recreation Act, 1937, which established the National Fitness Council, became law in July 1937. Though hotly opposed by some members of the Opposition in the House of Commons, it was, as Peter McIntosh records, welcomed by the physical education profession and the country at large. Many local bodies, especially the voluntary youth organisations, got busy with schemes for clubs, gymnasia, playing fields and so on. It took a long time for these to be scrutinised and processed – there had, of course, to be adequate safeguards that there was security of tenure, that the balance of capital was forthcoming and that future maintenance was assured. But nearly two million pounds was offered in grants and nearly £500,000 paid out (about two thirds to local authorities and one third to voluntary bodies) before the scheme abruptly ended on the outbreak of war. Many fine permanent facilities for physical recreation-community centres, youth hostels, youth clubs, village halls, swimming baths and playing fields – remain as memorials to the short-lived national fitness campaign.

A good deal was spent on publicity and there was a wide circulation of attractive posters, with the slogans "Fitness Wins" and "Get Fit – Keep Fit" labelling individuals or groups of people engaged in physical recreation. There was a good deal of other propaganda material, including films, "daily dozen" charts, and leaflets about how to apply for grants under the scheme. Many of the national voluntary youth organisations and some of the governing bodies of sport (for athletics, rowing, cycling, swimming and women's team games) received grants to appoint full time organisers or coaches.

The CCRPT received a first grant of £1,000 from the Board of Education in February 1937 to help it to play the part assigned to it by the White Paper, and its work continued on the lines previously followed. It was given the specific responsibility of approving the qualifications of those appointed by the youth organisations to develop physical recreation and later worked closely with them. The Council's second Annual Report (for 1936–1937) showed the appointments of Bruce Campbell, B.Sc., A. Mulford, B.A. and Millicent Adair Jackson as new Representatives, and Dorothea M. Vaughan A.C.A. as part-time Accountant. H. A. Cole, awarded the O.B.E. on his retirement from Sheffield at the age of 60, had become full-time Technical Adviser. C. Wreford Brown, who represented the Football Association on the Council, was made its Honorary Legal Adviser. A 'Physical Recreation in Industry' Sub-Committee had been formed under the chairmanship of Capt. J. G. Paterson of the Industrial Welfare Society. He was best known in the country for his part in promoting the 'Duke of York's Camps', at which Public School boys spent a week under canvas with boys from industry year by year, generally in the company of the Duke of York. The Duke, on becoming King George VI in 1936, had accepted office as Patron of the CCRPT. The number of bodies in membership had increased to 104, and Dr. Peter Innes, Director of Education for Birmingham, Douglas Kennedy, Director of the English Folk Dance and Song Society, and Phyllis Spafford were among the new members of the Executive.

The Council's offices had been moved from 71 Eccleston

Square to Abbey House, Victoria Street, and among Council's publications noted were *1937 Daily Dozen for Girls and Women, 1937 Daily Dozen for Boys and Men, Play Leadership, Twelve Simple Dances, The Use of Music in Recreative Gymnastic Classes,* and the report of an investigation into *Recreative Gymnastics for Older Women* which had been carried out by Dr. Anna Broman and Miss M. Vulliamy.

An event of special interest was The Festival of Youth at Wembley Stadium on 3rd July 1937, staged by the British Sports and Games Association (a small body set up in 1935 – with Lord Hampden as chairman and S. F. Rous as secretary – to raise funds for the Jubilee Trust) with the assistance of the CCRPT. It was the first function of its kind in England and aroused great enthusiasm, being honoured by the attendance of the King and Queen and the young Princesses Elizabeth and Margaret. The Festival provided the clearest proof, commented the Annual Report, that "the co-ordination of many organisations results in a pleasing emphasis of their individuality, rather than that subordination to uniformity which is sometimes so acutely feared".

The Annual Report also gave the text of the Council's first Constitution, which remained effective until 1949 when the CCPR was incorporated as "a company limited by guarantee and not having a share capital" with its own Memorandum and Articles of Association and enjoying charitable status. Its stated aim remained: "to promote the physical and mental health of the community through physical recreation".

The following year, 1937–1938, appears to have been a time of slow growth and solid achievement rather than of any spectacular advance. The Annual Report declared that "an interim period for the formulation and development of large-scale schemes was unavoidable, and preparation has, perhaps, been the feature of 1938. In view of the foundations being laid by the National Fitness Council, 1939 can surely be anticipated with confidence, in that careful groundwork should ensure impressive results." Those who know the pace at which P.C.C. liked to work may see in those two sentences a barely-concealed note of frustration and impatience that progress had, after all, been so slow. But it was never her way in public, and very seldom indeed even in private, to criticize the action and inaction of any other body or individual.

"But", the Report continued, "to its declared policy of active co-operation and co-ordination, without interference with the individual character of any of its 109 constituent organisations, the Council has most faithfully adhered . . . Every opportunity has been taken of co-operating, in an executive or advisory capacity, with the Area Committees formed early in 1938. Contact has been established with all the 22 Committees and practical work has been or will be carried out in the very near future for fifteen of them". Work in co-operation with local education authorities ("reinforcing the fine work of the physical training organisers employed by them and avoiding at all costs, any action which would overlap with or detract from it") and all types of voluntary organisations and industrial concerns had continued.

Mr. Rous had become deputy chairman of the Executive, Mr. Gem was now chairman of the Technical Advisory Committee and Councillor J. W. Catlow of the Finance Committee.

A new grants committee had been set up to deal with applications from organisations and individuals in respect of training, a function deputed to the Council by the NFC. A total grant of £8,800 was received during the financial year from the Board of Education. In conjunction with the CCRPT, Anstey College and Loughborough College had arranged and conducted three three-months' courses for women and men respectively in 1938 and 1939. These courses were intended to give those trained to teach physical training in schools or in the Services "an insight into the type of work suitable for voluntary recreative classes, so that they may be better fitted to fill full-time posts if and when they are created". It was also hoped that local education authorities would release some of those teaching in evening classes and doing similar work to attend the courses. Though the courses were well attended, they did not in fact lead to any full-time specialists' posts.

Three most successful one-week training camps for men in recreative physical training had been held for men at sites provided by the Boy Scouts Association, the National Association of Boys' Clubs and the Association for Jewish Youth – 147 attended. A Summer School had been held at Milton Mount College, Crawley, Sussex which had attracted 130 students and a waiting list of nearly as many. The value of *national* events was stressed : "the fact that these students return to their respective centres feeling that they are taking part in a national campaign and have also become linked to a central organisation from which they can at any time seek support and guidance, is of inestimable importance".

About 3,500 names were now on the National Register of Leaders. The number of Representatives had been increased to nine (five women and four men), including Jane Solkhon (later Mrs. Madders) and Mrs. L. Blanckenberg (now Mrs. Medlicott) who was to remain with the Council until 1949. Though, there was no mention in the Report, P.C.C. had been appointed O.B.E. in the 1937 New Year's Honours.

The following Annual Report recorded a staff of thirteen representatives in 1939, among them A. L. Colbeck, E. Doxford (killed at Dunkirk), Margaret Holmes (later Mrs. Mulford), Max Madders, C. Sayer, M.A., H. B. T. Schwabe and Mrs. H. M. Watt. The number of national bodies represented on the Council had risen to 113, which might be classified as follows: governing bodies of sport, 23; outdoor activity associations 5; dancing, movement and gymnastic bodies, 12; youth organisations, 24; physical education 7; general education, 16; school and Civil Service sport, 4; Armed Services, 7; medical, 4; industrial, 3; comprehensive and miscellaneous, 8.

The Report gave impressive statistics of progress during the Council's first four years:

	1936	1937	1938	1939
Training courses	10	40	125	247
Lecture-demonstrations and 'open' classes	25	155	350	825
Visits to factories, shops, etc.	10	50	300	523
Talks and lectures	15	52	200	532

There were many innovations and experiments during this year – all faithfully recorded – including classes taken at seaside resorts by Representatives at the request of Area Fitness Committees, of which two striking photographs were included in the Report. The Board of Education's grant to the Council had gone up to £14,312 and other income, including £217 in donations, totalled £5,199.

The voluntary youth organisations, some governing bodies

and outdoor activity associations, and many local education authorities were doing their best to profit from the new opportunities offered but there was a general feeling that the National Fitness Campaign was hanging fire somewhat. The international skies were growing steadily more menacing and the country's thoughts and energies had to be directed more urgently toward precautions against possible air raids and plans for evacuating school children from industrial areas.

It was a time of agonising soul-searching about the nature of democracy and the limits of individual freedom. Early in 1938, Eagar wrote in *The Boy* that "the establishment of the National Fitness Council means much more than erecting a piece of machinery for giving grants to juvenile organisations and local education authorities. It signifies the advance of the educational army into the 'no man's land' of adolescence". But later he was to write : "The National Fitness Movement is not yet a national movement in the full sense of that term – it is so far little more than a campaign for increasing the opportunities for personal fitness. The desire for personal fitness is a fine thing. Many of our boys possess it – but not most, still less all. 'The contentedly unfit youth of today', 'the sloth of modern adolescence' – those phrases of Kurt Hahn sting, but none of us can honestly reject or resent them. So long as they are even partly true, National Fitness is not achieved and even Personal Fitness is not generally desired."

Disillusionment and scepticism about the results of the National Fitness Campaign were widespread. They continued until war was declared when experience was to show that whatever might be true about the physical fitness of the population, many had been mistaken about the fundamental moral fitness of the nation to face the challenge of the next five years.

In July 1939, shortly before the War broke out, the Lingiad was held at Stockholm, a festival in honour of P. H. Ling, regarded as the father of modern physical education. Teams of boys, girls, men and women from Great Britain – 250 in all – aided by the NFC, took part in the opening ceremony and the demonstrations as well as in the conference and international camp which concluded the Lingiad. The pleasant informality of the British teams contrasted strongly with the massed uniformity of the huge contingents from Germany, Denmark and Sweden. The varied displays they gave left the impression that

Great Britain still possessed a wealth of talent and originality, and led people to conclude that perhaps there was more myth than reality behind the rumours of our national decadence.

The National Fitness Council was one of the first casualties of the War. It died, it has been said, "unhonoured and unsung, without an inquest, with scarcely an obituary notice". It had to work with limited powers and in times of peculiar difficulty. It is impossible to say whether, given more time, it would have achieved its full objectives, but there is no disguising the fact that, in some quarters at least, there were hearty sighs of relief when the outbreak of war brought its operations to an abrupt end. Indeed it is credibly reported that with the closure of all its offices at the beginning of September 1939, the order was given for its records and surveys to be destroyed.

The side of the NFC's work that attracted the strongest criticism was the establishment of an area bureaucracy of its own – committees covering an area of two or three counties as a rule, and purporting to represent wide voluntary and statutory knowledge and interests. But local authorities felt strongly that there was an unnecessary duplication of organisation and that they could have done the job themselves more efficiently and at less expense. The reply given to this criticism was that the Area Committees were in a position to stimulate development in areas where the local authorities had shown themselves laggard or parsimonious, and that they were in a better position to promote co-operation between the voluntary and statutory sides. The Board of Education did its utmost to involve local education authorities in the Fitness Campaign and, in an Administrative Memorandum to them (No. 172, 25th November 1937), it emphasised that the Physical Training and Recreation Act could be fully effective only if they were "prepared to take an active part in the task of extending and improving facilities for young people and adults in their areas". The Memorandum suggested that leaders might be found from among those who had taken courses organised by the CCRPT; "for the future, it was hoped that the National College of Physical Training would ensure a sufficient supply of suitable candidates".

Though a site for the proposed college had been selected at Merstham in Surrey, and plans showing accommodation and layout had been formally approved at an estimated cost of £450,000, the project never materialised, and the CCRPT went on with its work of training leaders. There were many doubts about the feasibility of the whole project, and by 1939, more urgent priorities were evident. Perhaps, also, there were second thoughts about the statement that the grant given to the CCRPT for its training work was an "interim" one!

It would be neglectful for a historian not to draw attention to certain parallels between the National Fitness Council of thirty-seven years ago and the Advisory Sports Council set up by the Government in 1965. Both Councils followed important reports produced by non-statutory committees – the BMA Report on 'Physical Education' and the Wolfenden Report on 'Sport and the Community'. One of their principal functions was to recommend the distribution of grants for the promotion of physical recreation among the post-school population, though obviously each did so according to the needs and circumstances of their times. In each case there was a National Advisory Committee appointed by Government nomination and a secretary or director appointed from an outside voluntary organisation. Each set up some form of regional organisation which did not coincide with the areas of local government.

But there are striking differences, some of which will emerge later. Here it is sufficient to observe that, in the National Fitness Campaign, the approach emphasised was that of health and social welfare; the focus was on the younger age group and there was no determined effort to involve the adult sports bodies in the campaign; the Secretary's background was of the Army and the social services not of sport or physical education; the Area Committees did not make the direct use of officers of local authorities that the Regional Sports Councils did (there were no County Planning Officers then); and the Regional Sports Councils had the advantage of securing the administrative services of the CCPR's staff, all of whom were well-known in and fully familiar with the areas in which they were working. Another important difference was that there was a non-political chairman of the Fitness Council who though personally a very charming man was not very forceful, whereas the chairman of the Advisory Sports Council was a Minister in the Government.

The files and Minutes available for study show that cordial or even effective relations were never established between the CCRPT and the Fitness Council. The latter did little to make it possible for the CCRPT to respond to the requests for the services of Representatives, which were being received not only from local authorities and voluntary organisations but from its own Area Fitness Committees. For example, a request from the London and Middlesex Area Committee, fully supported by the London Juvenile Organisations Committee, that two CCRPT Representatives should be appointed to work in their area was rejected by the NFC. Those in a position to speak with inside knowledge of the situation at the time are emphatic that the fault did not lie with the CCRPT or with P.C.C. Attempts by the CCRPT to co-operate fully in the national campaign received rebuff after rebuff. In spite of the value her knowledge and experience would have been, P.C.C. was never invited to serve on the Council – a member of it has suggested that her ability might have overshadowed Ellis's! Happily the Advisory Sports Council of the sixties was not jealous of the CCPR, but used its experience, staff and machinery to the full.

But whatever the defects, inherent or adventitious, of the NFC, the CCRPT did its utmost to serve it loyally and well. In the process, it immensely strengthened its own reputation as an efficient, hard-working and impartial body, with a staff of men and women who were unrivalled in understanding the needs and characteristics of the many organisations they worked for.

CHAPTER FOUR

War Years:
1939 - 1954

War was declared on 3rd September 1939. The previous day, the CCRPT had received a letter from an official of the National Fitness Council instructing it to terminate the lease of its office accommodation immediately and to end the contracts of all members of its staff. On 5th September, this letter was considered by the General Purposes Sub-Committee which appointed Lord Hampden, Sir Percival Sharp, S. F. Rous, J. W. Catlow and P.C.C. as a deputation to see the President and Permanent Secretary of the Board of Education. A meeting took place on 7th September, and a Minute records that "the Deputation was favourably received". The letter from the National Fitness Council was to be ignored, and the CCRPT was asked "to submit to the Board a programme of work together with a statement of personnel required to carry out such work and two Budgets, one for the remaining five months of the current financial year, and one for 1940/1".

Such was the dramatic reprieve received by the CCRPT which ensured its continued existence. On 3rd October, the President of the Board announced that the Government had decided to make itself more responsible for juvenile welfare and had set up a special Branch of the Board for the purpose. In charge of that Branch was B. L. Pearson.

This was followed up on 27th November by the issue to local education authorities of *The Service of Youth,* the far-reaching Circular 1486, which started with the words, "The social and physical development of boys and girls between the ages of 14 and 20 who have ceased full-time education has for long been neglected in this country". It continued with the declaration: "The Government are determined to prevent the recurrence during this war of the social problem which arose during the last. They have accordingly decided that the Board of Education shall undertake a direct responsibility for youth welfare". A National Youth Committee was appointed, under the chairmanship of Kenneth Lindsay, M.P., Parliamentary

Secretary to the Board, to advise the President. Among its members were "those competent to speak on behalf of industry, medicine and physical training". A separate Youth Committee was set up for Wales.

Among other steps announced in the Circular was that "financial assistance was being provided which would include grant-aid to the Central Council of Recreative Physical Training for carrying on the Council's valuable work in maintaining and developing the supply of trained leadership in all forms of recreational activity". "The Council", it added, "will be happy to cooperate with any local authority, voluntary body, industrial or other organisation that requests them to do so". The Circular ended by calling for "a new initiative", urged all local authorities to set up Youth Committees in their areas, and gave suggestions as to how these should be constituted.

Apart from the effect of the Circular in establishing "the Service of Youth" as "having an equal status with the other educational services conducted by the local authority", it obviously greatly strengthened the position and influence of the CCRPT as a body grant-aided by the Board of Education to undertake specific services. Though still a voluntary body it was also an agency of the State. An interesting contemporary sidelight is a reference in *Young Citizen,* the war-time 'Penguin Special' edition of Dr. A. E. Morgan's classic *The Needs of Youth,* a prewar study of youth work carried out for the Jubilee Trust. "Like the Fitness Council", it reads, "the new Youth Committees show a tendency to concentrate their efforts on physical activities. It is possible to attend conferences of youth leaders and find that they are nearly all teachers, or would-be teachers, of physical training and athletics. It is to the credit of such a body as the Central Council of Recreative Physical Training that it has acquired considerable standing in the work. It is doing most admirable service and deserves encouragement and help to extend its activities. It recognises that youth needs more than physical training and is at pains to emphasise the necessity of a full development of personality. But its primary function, as its name implies, is to encourage development on the physical side, and if other agencies do not supplement its activities, the Central Council is not to blame."

Apart from continuing its work on behalf of the 14–20 age group, in cooperation with local education authorities and youth organisations, the Council undertook many new forms of work during the War. The first was a 'Fitness for Service' campaign, organised from June 1940, in conjunction with the Football Association, for youths and men, whether employed in essential industry, in Home Defence or waiting to be called up for the Services. The Board of Education, the Ministry of Labour, the Ministry of Home Security and the three Armed Services co-operated, and by the end of July, 230 'Fitness for Service' centres had been organised on local football and recreation grounds and some 35,000 had taken part in the activities offered – physical training, games, boxing and some pre-military training. The scheme continued into the winter with groups meeting in indoor halls. Over £2,000, including £1,000 from the FA, was received in donations for the scheme.

In addition, some special courses were run for selected Civil Defence Workers, with instruction in activities designed to improve general health, endurance, and physical and mental alertness. A special tribute was paid by the Minister of Home Security to the value of the courses. Another piece of wartime work was the administration of the Civil Defence Sports Committee. Representatives worked hard to develop physical recreation within the Civil Defence Services, including the National Fire Service, through appropriate courses for leaders, arranging regional and national competitions, and demonstrating activities suitable for stations and posts with limited space and facilities.

Early in the war the Council's offices were moved to 58 Victoria Street, S.W.1, and the technical staff were dispersed according to the country's Civil Defence Regions. The Council's regional offices remained in Durham, Leeds, Manchester (and, later in Salford), Nottingham, Bedford, Birmingham, Crewkerne, Reading and London, with a Welsh office in Cardiff (and a sub-office in Wrexham from 1958). By January 1941, the technical staff numbered 42 (26 women and 16 men); a year later it was 64 (42 women and 22 men); and by the end of the war it was 70. Among the Representatives joining during the war who stayed with the Council for many years were Grace Bartram, Eve Clarkson, Berenice Davis, Madge Docking, Kay Evans, Ruth Keeble, Catherine Loader, Ivy Price, Brenda Salkeld, Eleanor Scott, Ivy West, Kay Withers and Muriel Wyness, and J. Barry, W. L. Latto, H. Littlewood, W. S. Mackenzie, G. Richards and C. E. Wiggins.

The first of six successive CCRPT Summer Schools was held in 1940 at Lowther College, a girls' boarding school near Abergele in North Wales. These Summer Schools had an atmosphere and flavour all their own – not only were they a series of vigorous and hard-working courses but, for many, they afforded a welcome relief from the endless tensions of bomb-stricken industrial areas. Though inevitably the majority of the adult students were women, to help to make good the shortage of adult leaders in wartime a new type of course for 'sub-leaders' or 'junior leaders' was developed which surprised even those who started them by the vast reserve of ability they revealed, actual as well as potential. Hundreds of these courses for 'junior leaders' were arranged by the CCRPT during the war – weekend, sessional and lasting a week – some for members of youth service bodies sent by local education authorities, others for the members of particular youth organisations in cooperation with the bodies concerned. Summer Schools were also organised at other centres. To give some idea of their scale the 1942 Annual Report records that there had been 1,350 applications for the 750 places available at Lowther College that year.

Since its formation, the Council's staff had given specialist instruction and advice at the general courses for leaders or senior members organised by both uniformed and non-uniformed youth organisations, but from September 1940 onwards the Board itself entered the field of youth leadership training and ran a number of fortnight courses in the general principles of youth work at various universities and colleges in England and Wales, and called upon the CCRPT to run sessions within most of them on practical and theoretical aspects of physical and social recreation.

One feature of the war years was that many men and women were engaged on forms of industrial and armaments work which imposed severe and unaccustomed physical strains on them. This led the Ministry of Labour and National Service to invoke the Council's aid and, from October 1940, to give grants to enable it to appoint a number of men and women Representatives to work on the special problems of applying physical training and recreation to industrial situations. Though some of these Representatives did not possess the full professional qualifications normally looked for in the Council's technical staff, all were men and women with a good deal of experience of leadership and the right personalities for work in industry. Some had been in industry themselves.

This was not an entirely new departure, as the Council had done a good deal of work with industrial firms before the war, but the scale was increased and many new problems had to be tackled by what were called 'Industrial Reps.' There are many references to this work in the wartime Annual Reports. For instance : "To find out the needs and desires of employees, Representatives have visited some 1,300 factories and firms during the year, where possible discussing the matter with the workers themselves, for only with their intelligent cooperation can the problem . . . be satisfactorily tackled. In addition to the provision made by many firms on their own premises, thousands of workers have been stimulated to use local facilities. The oft-expressed view that industrial workers neither need nor desire physical recreation because their working hours are long and tiring is gradually disappearing. With perseverance, Representatives have introduced many workers to many new forms of healthful and enjoyable activity.'

Again : "The Council is also interested in the application of dexterity exercises to safety in industrial work; even in modern factories there remain possibilities of injury due to faulty methods of lifting and carrying, or to wrong habits of carriage and posture. Recreative exercises for and practices in lifting, manipulating, carrying and holding heavy objects may well be found to be a successful means of 'short-circuiting' the painful empirical way in which the workman generally has to learn." And, yet again : "The main preoccupation of undertakings engaged on war work is to obtain maximum output. As the war progresses, production will be increasingly governed by the stamina of the workers . . . A director of a factory which allows its women employees to take part in keep-fit classes during working hours writes that the classes, though short, have already proved valuable to women sitting all day at benches."

As part of its work in industry, the CCRPT ran many holiday camps, generally under canvas, which were well appreciated and towards which a number of generous donations were received from the British War Relief Society of America, the Football Association, ICI and many other firms. Some firms wanted full-time workers to promote physical recreation for their workers and grant-aided the Council to enable them to make special appointments to their staff; others asked the Council to recommend suitable candidates, which they were generally able to do.

CCPR headquarters maintained its interest in this type of industrial work for many years after the war, and special sub-committees advised the Council on the subject under the successive chairmanships of Lord Bridgeman and T. G. Bedwell. Towards the end of the war, Mrs. H. M. Watt, who was then Senior Representative in the Yorkshire Region, was seconded to headquarters for a year to make a special study of this aspect of CCPR work. Later George Hickling, who had been an 'Industrial Rep.' in the North Midlands and who had almost a genius for teaching industrial workers how to lift and handle heavy weights, became a headquarters specialist in the subject, until the Industrial Welfare Society, with whom the Council had been working closely, took responsibility to his work.

In 1940 the Council instituted the 'National Test for Leaders of Physical Recreation', as an incentive to leaders to improve their qualifications and to reach a recognised standard of competence. By the end of the war, a thousand men and women had qualified by examination or exemption. Many local National Leaders' Associations sprang up and did useful work in helping to keep each other up to date and in finding leaders for youth work. The CCRPT ran many courses for them, and also kept in touch with them by producing a periodical bulletin, at first cyclostyled and then printed, which passed on much useful information and included many expert technical and semi-technical articles, and book reviews. Among the articles was one on 'The Presentation of Displays', by Eileen Fowler, M.I.S.T.D., herself a National Leader and then at the beginning of her exciting career. This bulletin continued for eighteen issues until it was incorporated in the CCPR/NPFA joint journal in 1947.

The National Test was administered by a special sub-committee set up in 1940, and not the least of Arthur Gem's long and outstanding services to the Council was his chairmanship of that committee for eighteen years. His technical knowledge and tactful guidance were among the chief factors in the National Test scheme, which did so much to increase the supply of, and set high standards for, part-time leaders in many branches of physical recreation, and which operated until the end of 1958 when it was superseded by the development of the governing bodies' own coaching schemes.

Early in August 1940, Herwald Ramsbotham, who had become President of the Board of Education, announced in the House of Commons that a small Directorate of Physical Recreation was being formed "to work in close association with the Youth Branch of the Board and in cooperation with the War Office", the purpose of which was "to help the development of physical recreation among the 14–20 group and thereby to help to raise the national standard of health and efficiency".

On 19th August, Mr. Ramsbotham wrote a confidential letter to Lord Hampden, parts of which must be quoted for the light they cast on the regard in which both P.C.C. and the CCRPT were held at the Board. Referring to the new Directorate, Mr. Ramsbotham said, "I feel it most essential that if this Directorate is to do its work at all efficiently we should have the services of an experienced and competent Woman Officer to to look after the girls' and women's side, and after very careful thought I am convinced that there is no one who could fill this post better than Miss Colson. On the other hand, I also feel it of great importance that the close link which already exists between the Central Council of Recreative Physical Training and the Board should not only be maintained but considerably increased if this new movement is to succeed; the Central Council have experience and prestige in the country which it would be folly not to use to the full. The obvious conclusion seems to be that we should, if possible, use the services of Miss Colson part-time at the Board for the present, leaving her a substantial part of her time to devote to the work of the Central Council and to train up a competent deputy to relieve her of the very heavy burden and to take her place if in the future it were found desirable to make further demands upon her time . . . I would emphasise the fact that for the success of the Direcorate we require both the whole-hearted cooperation of your Council and also its goodwill in releasing the services of Miss Colson for part-time work.'

The Committee agreed to the President's request, and P.C.C. joined the Directorate, the other members of which were B. L. Pearson, Capt S. J. Parker, H.M.I. and Colonel T. H. Wand-Tetley, Inspector of Physical Training at the War Office. In spite of its somewhat sinister and misleading title, the real purpose of establishing this group seems to have been to enable four intelligent and influential officials to make rapid decisions and to take action without having to seek the authority of any outside body such as the National Youth Committee or any committee at the War Office or the CCRPT – an extremely sensible measure in war time. The Directorate's functions were to draft the contents of Circular 1529, *Youth, Physical Recreation and Service,* issued in November 1940; to secure the release from the Army of men suitably qualified and willing to return to civilian life to help with physical recreation for young people; to facilitate the use for youth work of premises that could be spared from military or civil defence purposes; to investigate physical training in the ATS (the women's Auxiliary Territorial Service); to promote the publication by the CCRPT of pamphlets giving suggestions about developing physical recreation among boys and men, girls and women; and to inquire into the desirability of instituting some form of youth fitness badge.

According to an article P.C.C. wrote about the Directorate in the first National Leaders' Bulletin in April 1941, its terms of reference were later enlarged to include "building for the future by taking action which will assist with post-war reconstruction". Circular 1529 commended the CCRPT's National Test Scheme and commented on the Youth Service Corps which had been formed in some areas. The Directorate did useful work with premises and in getting men released for work with local education authorities, youth organisations and the CCRPT itself. In July 1941, Mr. Ramsbotham wrote to Lord Hampden to say that the practical work of the Directorate was almost completed, but he hoped that P.C.C. could remain on it when it was retained as an advisory body. This was agreed. The Directorate does not appear to have published anything about fitness badges, but at this point some comment on Badge Schemes is called for.

Both before and during National Fitness Council days, the subject of standard tests for physical achievements like running, throwing and jumping was much discussed by people concerned with the fitness of the young. In 1939, Eagar, wrote in *The Boy* that the Fitness Council (of which he was, of course, a member) was likely to announce a plan soon for

awarding personal badges for fitness. There were a number of
persistent advocates of such incentives, none with greater effect
than Kurt Hahn. Dr. Hahn was a German who, after an Oxford education, became headmaster of a school at Salem in
Germany which attained a high reputation. In 1936, disagree-
ing with Hitler's policies, he left Germany and became headmaster of Gordonstoun School in Morayshire, Scotland. There,
as part of his work to promote the all-round fitness of his boys,
he established the Moray County Badge as a standard of
achievement in physical ability and community service. The
war made it necessary for him to transfer his school to Plas
Dinam, Lord Davies' home in Montgomeryshire, and while
there he cooperated with Lawrence Holt, a Liverpool ship-
owner (married, incidentally, to the daughter of Dr. L. P. Jacks,
mentioned in Chapter Two) in establishing the Outward Bound
Sea School at Aberdovey in 1941, (the first of the Outward
Bound Schools), which owed much to Dr. Hahn's methods and
active cooperation.

The topic of fitness tests and badges was hotly debated
within the youth service. Scouts, Guides and Boys' and Girls'
Brigades had their own badge systems. Some work on standard
tests took place within the pre-Service units but the club movements had divided views on the practicability and advisability
of individual badge schemes, especially for boys in industry. The
NABC instituted a 'fitness plaque' as a group award to individual clubs reaching prescribed standards and the CCRPT's
staff acted as advisers and judges. As was its practice, the
CCRPT took no public stand in the controversy over 'standard
tests' and 'badge schemes', but kept in touch with all developments, ventilated the subject frequently in its journal, and discussed it at conferences with youth organisations and at its
various sub-committees.

The formation in 1940 of the County Badge Experimental
Committee was an important move. It was composed of a
number of distinguished educationists under the chairmanship
of the Dr. A. D. Lindsay (later Lord Lindsay), Master of Bal-
liol; the secretary was Jim Hogan, a schoolmaster who became
the first Warden of the Outward Bound Sea School and, later,
Deputy Education Officer in the West Riding. It published a
small booklet in 1941 entitled, *The County Badge or the Fourfold Achievement,* to publicise the scheme and encourage ex-

periments. In 1942, the CCRPT accepted an invitation to nominate two technical experts to serve on the committee – one was
A. H. Gem, the other P.C.C. In 1943 the Executive appointed
a special sub-committee to consider fitness test schemes but no
conclusive recommendations emerged. Hertfordshire was one of
the education authorities to try to get the scheme going but
the war years were not propitious for effective experiments and
no large-scale advances were made until 1956, when the Duke
of Edinburgh's Award Scheme was established under the best
possible auspices (see Chapter Six).

Statutory grants to the CCRPT inevitably increased with the
scale of its work. In seven successive years from 1939/40 to
1945/46 grants from the Board of Education were: £17,334,
£27,213, £36,785, £40,847, £41,416, £42,007, £45,275.
From 1940/41 on, the grants from the Ministry of Labour and
National Service were: £4,200, £10,800, £10,500, £10,000,
£10,000, £8,578.

In 1943, Kay Evans, a Representative working in the North
West Region, was appointed Woman Technical Adviser at
Headquarters as H. A. Cole's colleague, and remained in that
post until her retirement in 1966. Miss Evans made a distinctive
and valuable contribution to the Council's work, particularly
on the women's and girls' side. Never completely happy in a
large conference, she was at her best in small informal groups,
giving sound technical advice as well as much wise guidance to
her women colleagues in the Regions, Wales, Scotland and N.
Ireland. She travelled all over the country, doing good by
stealth and never seeking the limelight. On her retirement, she
was awarded the M.B.E. and elected an individual member of
the Council, and, since then, has worked indefatigably for the
welfare of mentally and physically handicapped people.

In the same year, the Technical Advisory Sub-committee was
replaced by three new sub-committees: (1) Games and Sports
– Chairman, Alderman H. E. Fern. (2) Outdoor Activities –
Chairman, Wing Commander J. G. Paterson and (3) Recreative Gymnastics and Dancing – Chairman, A. H. Gem. S. F.
Rous was Chairman of a panel set up to advise the BBC on the
broadcasting of early morning exercises – it was estimated that
a million and a half people responded to the call of "Up in
the Morning Early" from Coleman Smith and May Brown.
Many and varied publications poured out from Headquarters

including, *Get Fit! Keep Fit! – Daily Exercises for Youths and Men, Ballroom Dancing in Youth Clubs, Physical Recreation for Mixed Groups, Films about Movement and Health, Keep Fit and Recreative Gymnastics for Girls and Women*, and *Books on Physical Recreation – a list for leaders,* the last being an annotated catalogue produced by R. E. Roper, M.A., M.Ed., that remarkable if unorthodox scholar who had been described as "one of the few British thinkers of real vision as to the possibilities within physical education". His unusual career included periods on the staffs of Eton and of Bedales, and he showed a real devotion in his later years to the work of the CCPR of which he was made an individual member. The fascinating story of his life had been told by P. Smithells and Gerald Murray in *Nine Pioneers in Physical Education,* published by the Physical Education Association in 1964.

In January 1944, the Council held its first Annual General Meeting since 1938, at the Middlesex Guildhall. Lord Astor presided, the report was presented by Lord Hampden as Chairman of the Executive, and the new title of Central Council of Physical Recreation was adopted, a measure which had been long contemplated but which required the sanction of an AGM. After the Meeting, an address on 'The Youth Service After the War' was given by J. F. Wolfenden, (later Sir John, and created a Life Peer in 1974) Chairman of the Youth Advisory Council, the body appointed in 1942 to replace the National Youth Committee. Shortly afterwards, Sir Percival Sharp resigned as Honorary Treasurer and was succeeded by Sir John Catlow.

In March 1944, H. A. Cole retired from his full-time job as Technical Adviser though he continued for some months to work part-time. Henry Cole played a distinguished part in the history of physical education in this country, and an appreciation of his work is also given in 'Nine Pioneers'. He was a founder member with Miss Grant Clark of the NAOPE and its Chairman. He served the CCRPT splendidly in its earliest years and was an admirable partner for P.C.C. Straight and honourable in all his dealings, possessing ripe wisdom founded on years of extensive experience, there was a solidity and strength about his character that made him a much-loved and respected leader of the technical staff.

In the following month, the Author was appointed to a new post of Administrative Assistant, one of his duties being to act as the General Secretary's deputy – the title Deputy Secretary came a little later. After four years reading 'Mods.' and 'Greats' at Oxford, he had done Settlement and Boys' Club work in Liverpool before becoming Secretary for Training to the National Association of Boys' Clubs in 1936. He had formed a high regard for the CCRPT from the excellent cooperation the NABC had enjoyed from its staff in training matters, from his experience attending its courses and as a member of its Technical Advisory Sub-Committee since 1936. Above all, he had a warm admiration for the ideals and abilities of P.C.C.

In November 1944, the Scottish Education Office, in the words of the Annual Report for 1943–45, "acting upon the representations of certain physical education associations and with the full concurrence of Scottish local authorities and voluntary organisations, invited the CCPR to extend its activities to Scotland, with financial assistance from the Department. The Council gladly accepted the invitation, and, in consultation with the Secretary of State for Scotland, set up a provisional Scottish Committee, of which Mr. W. J. Stuart is Chairman. A Scottish Secretary, Mrs. May Brown, and Technical Representatives have been appointed and a Scottish Section will be formed." The CCPR's Scottish Section flourished from the start and more details of its distinctive achievements are given in Chapter Eight.

By the end of 1944, the end of the war was in sight but its effects were felt everywhere. Two extracts from the December 1944 issue of the *National Leaders' Bulletin* effectively illustrate the circumstances and difficulties of the period :

(1) "The course for women teachers which was to have been held in London in September had to be postponed owing to flying bomb attacks. It will now take place at the Central YWCA, London, from December 28th to January 1st."

(2) "Physical Recreation Clothing – as a result of negotiations between the Ministry of Education and the Board of Trade, following a visit to the Ministry of a CCPR deputation in April last, the Ministry announced in Circular 3A that 'where an allocation of plimsolls has been made, local education authorities, schools, and youth organisations may also supply on loan and coupon-free an equal number of pairs of shorts, where the pupils or members of youth organisations cannot provide the shorts themselves'."

In spite of many and formidable obstacles, the CCRPT had

prospered well during the war and made the most of the opportunities for service that the circumstances of the time presented. There had been a marked expansion in all branches of its work and important developments along many new lines. There was a well-tried regional organisation throughout England and Wales and a recent extension to Scotland.

What is hard to convey through the written word is the 'spirit' of the Council's work during the war. The staff worked with endless zest and never-failing good humour, in spite of the most intimidating conditions, to promote the gospel of 'physical and mental health through physical recreation'. They travelled far and wide, through the black-out, to take classes and run demonstrations and courses. Each Region worked as a team of comrades as well as colleagues. "I can well remember the freshness of the Council's impact in the early days", wrote a Director of Education to the Author recently. Ballroom dancing, indoor team games, keep-fit, athletic training, outdoor sports, stick work, 'applied' physical training, holiday camps for workers under canvas – nothing came amiss and all was tackled with vigour and enthusiasm, but without loss of professional or other standards. Not for the CCPR were the sort of courses where people could turn up for meals after sessions without being spruce and 'properly dressed'.

The value of the Council's war-time work had been fully recognised, not least by Government Departments. The last Annual Report for the war years foresaw an even more testing time in the first years of peace. When the intenser urges of the war-time struggle were removed, would the atmosphere, it asked, be one of vigour or of enervation? The answer would depend, said the Report, as much upon voluntary effort as upon statutory provision, and the Council stressed that, in spite of the generous support it received from public funds, it enjoyed freedom from arbitrary control, and, as a voluntary body, had an advantage in those fields where progress must largely depend on experiment, initiative and personal contact. "To be a propagandist for a cause is an alien role for a statutory body, but it is the *raison d'être* of a voluntary organisation".

CHAPTER FIVE

Post-war Plans and Achievements:
1945 - 1950

Much hard thinking had been going on in the last years of the war about the problems and opportunities of reconstruction. The Youth Advisory Council had issued its report on *The Youth Service after the War* in 1943, and the McNair Report on *Teachers and Youth Leaders* was published in 1944. Both of these as well as the 1944 Education Act had wide implications for the provision of facilities and leadership for leisure-time physical recreation.

But the CCPR was also busy on its own account. At the end of 1944, it published *Facilities for Physical Recreation – Some Suggestions for Local Authorities,* a small pamphlet full of practical information designed to help local authorities to discharge their new responsibilities under the Education Act, including authoritative details of the needs and requirements of the national bodies for about fifty different physical activities.

The forward-looking mind of P.C.C. had produced in September 1944 – primarily for consideration by the Ministry of Education – a memorandum on *The Post-War Work of the Central Council of Physical Recreation,* including the following ambitious plans: (1) Acting on behalf of the British Council to promote international fellowship through physical recreation; (2) Arranging a variety of courses to meet the needs of different sections of the public, including industrial workers, and even students at agricultural and theological colleges; (3) Organising a National Health and Fitness Week in 1947 on behalf of the Ministry of Education; (4) Setting up one or two residential National Physical Recreation Centres in accessible but beautiful parts of the country, "where adolescents and young adults will be able to spend a week or ten days receiving personal training in one or more forms of physical activity"; and (5) Publishing a weekly *Journal of Physical Recreation,* aiming at an eventual circulation of 50,000.

These outline plans in the memorandum were followed by a five-year scheme of development, an estimate of the additional staff required by the CCPR to carry it out, and a request that the Officers of the Council should be allowed to discuss the proposals with the Ministry before submitting a detailed estimate of expenditure, both capital and annual.

A meeting duly took place, at which the Ministry made it clear that : (1) they were prepared to continue to grant-aid the Council; (2) they could not finance so ambitious a programme as had been suggested; (3) because of the obligations imposed by the Education Act on local authorities, they expected the CCPR gradually to withdraw from purely local activities and concentrate on regional and national work; (4) if the Council wished to establish and maintain one or more National Physical Recreation Centres, it must do so at its own expense; and (5) the Ministry could not grant-aid any overseas work.

A more serious issue of financial policy was raised in 1946. A newcomer to the Branch of the Ministry concerned with the CCPR's affairs suggested that "some charge should be made to local education authorities requesting the services of the Council". This seemed to introduce so fundamental a change in the relations between the Council and local education authorities that the whole future of the organisation was affected. An emergency meeting of the Executive was called, which had the help of the written advice of Sir Percival Sharp, the Council's former Honorary Treasurer, that "unless certain officials of the Ministry of Education had been charged with authority to decide the Ministry's policy with regard to the CCPR, some further inquiry might be advisable from the Minister herself" (then Miss Ellen Wilkinson). Fortified with this influential advice, the Executive decided to resist. At the next meeting, it was happily reported that "after further consideration the Ministry had decided that for the present it would be wiser not to ask local education authorities to pay for the services of representatives of the Council", a not unimportant tactical victory for the CCPR.

With the return of men and women to civilian life from their wartime occupations, the circumstances were ripe for a great expansion in the work of national bodies concerned with adult physical recreation – the governing bodies of sport and the outdoor activity associations. The CCPR played an important part in encouraging the governing bodies to turn their minds towards establishing coaching and development schemes, a considerable innovation in the work of many of them. At that time, only a small minority of them had as much as a single paid or full-time official in any capacity, and their administrative work of running competitions was in the hands of honorary officers, working from their own homes or places of business. There was, therefore, a big field of missionary work here, into which the CCPR's staff made a gradual, tactful, and, in the end, effective entry.

So, apart from continuing with its normal advisory and training commitments to its constituent bodies, the four main new preoccupations of the Council in the immediate post-war years were :

(a) To withdraw as much as possible from purely local work, even at the risk of disappointing some of the voluntary youth organisations who had come to look upon help from the Representatives as something they could call upon for rather minor events, often at very short notice,

(b) To give the men's and women's governing bodies of sport technical advice as well as national and regional administrative assistance to enable them to expand their coaching schemes and development work,

(c) To raise sufficient money from voluntary sources to enable it to undertake new and experimental work, including the establishment of a National Recreation Centre,

(d) To press on with promoting contacts with overseas countries, as far as funds permitted.

The wartime grant from the Ministry of Labour came to an end in March 1946. Some of the 'Industrial Reps.' went to other posts, one or two within industry; the remainder were absorbed into the Council's normal staff. After the war, it naturally became easier to recruit suitably qualified men Representatives but it was less easy to recruit women, a situation that continued until 1972, in spite of every effort to maintain a balance between the sexes.

In December 1945, G. A. McPartlin was appointed to succeed H. A. Cole. He served as Man Technical Adviser, and later as Technical Director. On his retirement from the CCPR in 1969 he received the O.B.E. and took up the post of Secretary of the Golf Development Council. George McPartlin served during the war as Squadron Leader in charge of physical fitness in RAF Bomber Command. He had received his professional training at Dunfermline College of Physical Education. After some years' teaching, he was successively organiser of physical education to West Hartlepool and Huddersfield Local Education Authorities. He brought to his new work with the Council, therefore, a wide experience as well as strong convictions about the lines along which its work should develop, and his outlook and attitudes about physical recreation, as well as his technical knowledge, were to have great influence on the Council's work during its later years.

At the A.G.M. in July 1945, Lord Astor's resignation from the Presidency was announced and Lord Hampden was elected to succeed him, a position he retained until 1951. At the same meeting, Ernest Watkins was appointed to succeed Wreford Brown as the Council's Honorary Legal Adviser, and gave invaluable help in that capacity until he went to live in Canada in 1954.

He was succeeded by Geoffrey Rickman, who gave similar good service until 1961. By that time the Council's legal work had become too extensive to be carried out by honorary advisers. At the first meeting of the Executive following the A.G.M., S. F. Rous and A. H. Gem were elected Chairman and Deputy Chairman respectively and remained in those offices until 1972, a record of continuous service which must surely be without parallel in any voluntary organisation. Great pleasure was given by the Honours conferred on them for their services to sport and physical education – Mr. Rous, made C.B.E. during the war, was Knighted in 1948, and Mr. Gem was created O.B.E. in 1955 and C.B.E. in 1967. Sir John Catlow, the CCPR's Honorary Treasurer, died in 1947, and was succeeded by Sir Clarence Sadd, C.B.E.

A feature of 1945 was the organisation of twelve one-week training courses for leaders of organised camps in May. They attracted 288 students and particular help with sites and staffing was given by the Scout and Girl Guide Associations. The courses met an evident need and were repeated the following year, after which the Ministry of Education took a direct interest in the subject of organised camping. They set up a Camping Advisory Committee, on which the CCPR were represented and which still meets. The Ministry published a handbook on the subject, *Organised Camping*, in whose production the CCPR had some share, and ran for some years a series of courses as part of their contribution to the youth service. Fashions and needs changed, and the standing camps which had been such a beneficent feature of some youth organisations' early camping became less common as the emphasis turned to light-weight, mobile camping.

In cooperation with HM Prison Commission, Representatives had undertaken pieces of work at various times in HM Prisons and Borstal Institutions, and in 1946 the Council was invited to make a thorough investigation into the provision made for the physical recreation of boys and men in penal institutions. The report and recommendations were well received and led to close and fruitful contact between the CCPR and the Commission which continued until 1972. The Commission appointed its own full-time officer for physical recreation and many residential courses for Prison Officers have been held at various National Recreation Centres, with excellent results. Experimental work was also undertaken in some mental hospitals, and for a time the Council had two full-time members of its staff devoting themselves exclusively to this work.

Another tribute to the Council's growing reputation was the invitation to organise the civilian section of the Lord Mayor's Show procession in London in November 1946. P.C.C.'s account written at the time records that, "thanks to the cooperation of Ministries, industrial concerns, voluntary organisations, governing bodies of games and sports and outdoor activities, and many leaders and young people, the various civilian tableaux and marching columns were colourful, attractive and excellently presented." Among many items in the procession was "a most realistic ballroom dancing tableau – complete with band, dancers in evening dress, and even a meal being served by waiters". Truly a treat for glamour-starved Londoners who had not seen a Lord Mayor's Show since 1938. Jack Barry was the brain behind the organisation of the procession.

An even more important event in 1946 was the National Festival of Youth at Wembley Stadium on July 6th which the CCPR organised. It was attended by the Duchess of Kent and 35,000 spectators. Over 8,000 young people from Scotland, Wales, Northern Ireland and all parts of England, representing seventy organisations, took part at their own expense, and showed, in the words of the Annual Report, that "the austerities of six years of war had not deadened the spirits of the younger generation".

In the same year, the CCPR presented to the Chancellor of the Exchequer a very strong case on behalf of the governing bodies for the remission or reduction of entertainments duty charged on admission to games and sports events. The rate was reduced and later the duty was abolished altogether. The Council also made regular representations protesting against the high rate of purchase tax charged on items of sports equipment, which led to some concessions. It also obtained some kudos in canoeing circles for successfully negotiating an agreement with the Railway Clearing House that folding canoes should be allowed to fall within the category of passengers' personal luggage – a modest achievement but of much importance to those concerned, and quoted here as an indication of the sort of service the CCPR gave.

There was some post-war disillusionment. The Annual Report for 1946 said: 'Many playing fields are still under cultivation as part of the battle for food or given over to housing; games equipment is scarce and expensive; there are no cheap travel facilities; and the prior claims of housing and industry make it likely that some years must elapse before labour and materials can be spared for building gymnasia, swimming baths, and other facilities so desperately needed". Grounds for hope were found in the increase in the number of physical education organisers being appointed by local education authorities, and the promise of better planned cities and of National Parks.

A threatened increase in rents made it necessary to move the headquarters office from Victoria Street and, with the help of the Ministry of Works, new offices were found in December 1946 at 6 Bedford Square, where the CCPR remained happily, apart from increasing overcrowding, until 1964, when the move to 26 Park Crescent was made. An event in 1946, which vitally affected the whole course of the CCPR's history was the establishment of Bisham Abbey as a National Recreation Centre, the first of seven such centres set up by the CCPR between 1946 and 1972. Their story is told in Chapter Seven.

At this stage some attention must be paid to the Council's finances. Apart from fees received from students attending courses, its main income came from statutory grants, and the balance, from profits on the sale of publications, the occasional surplus from a demonstration or display, a few fees from industrial firms for services rendered, and a small number of donations, of which the most substantial continued to come from the Football Association. Its independent income as a national voluntary organisation was comparatively small.

For a less ambitious organisation, it would have been easy to continue in this way but some of the Council's post-war plans could only be realised if a substantial income from some non-statutory source could be obtained. The staff set to work to examine the problem. The obstacles were formidable. The post-war years were a period of financial stringency and few public appeals did well. It was well known that the Council was in receipt of considerable grant-aid and it was difficult to convince anyone that it really needed money. The objects for which it needed it were somewhat vague, and, moreover, quite devoid of the emotional ingredient which is the basis of most successful appeals for money.

The British Council could not respond to the CCPR's approaches, though the Rhodes Trust made a grant of £250 towards overseas work. The Jubilee Trust too, were also deaf to CCPR appeals – they felt, no doubt with some justice, that others had stronger claims upon them. A somewhat amateurish appeal was launched for donations or subscriptions to a "Special Purposes Fund" for "certain experimental and research work which the Council is hoping to undertake in the near future". Not surprisingly, the response was hardly overwhelming! But some friends of the Council responded and one encouraging feature was the number of National Leaders and others who, having trained at the Council's courses, put on displays and demonstrations for its benefit. Students of Bedford and I.M. Marsh Colleges made a collection, and Anstey College gave the proceeds from their annual students' display. The Council's staff in several regions arranged special events or made collections in aid of the appeal.

With the acceptance of the lease of Bisham Abbey in 1946, the need for raising funds became more urgent. The appeal for the "Special Purposes Fund" was prosecuted more widely and with greater success now that the specific object of establishing Bisham Abbey could be included. The 'Big Five' Banks between them contributed £670 (not quite what had been hoped for!), some industrial firms for whom the Council had worked helped, and, to their credit, the Boys' Brigade and the All-England Ladies' Lacrosse Association gave £50 and £23.10.0 respectively.

In the Autumn of 1946, 'out of the blue', a firm offered to act as the Council's "public relations officers" at an annual fee of £2,000. The reply had to be given that their services could be welcome but there was no money to pay for them. The firm then offered to combine public relations work with running an appeal, without charging for the former until they had raised a substantial sum from the appeal. As there seemed nothing to lose, the offer was accepted, but, in case the governing bodies of sport might feel that a big national appeal for sport on behalf of the CCPR might prejudice their own independent efforts to raise money, the CCPR undertook that fifty per cent of any sum in excess of £25,000 raised in the first year of the appeal would be distributed in grants to governing bodies.

And so the National Sports Development Fund was launched with high hopes and a target of £100,000. Much literature was produced and some local appeal committees were set up, notably on Merseyside and Tyneside and in Manchester. Sir Bracewell Smith, a good friend of Mr. Rous in the world of football, happened to be Lord Mayor of London that year, and, to inaugurate the NSDF Appeal, gave a Dinner at the Mansion House on 18th April 1947, as well as a personal donation of £1,000. Invitations to attend were accepted by the Lord Mayors of eleven provincial cities and by the Lords Provost of Edinburgh and Glasgow. It was a distinguished gathering. The speakers at the Dinner were The Duke of Gloucester, the Lord Mayor of London, the Speaker of the House of Commons, George Tomlinson, M.P., Minister of Education, S. F. Rous, Sir Clarence Sadd, and two of the CCPR's junior leaders, Sydney Burrows and Beryl Merwood. As a social occasion the Dinner was memorable but its financial success was ruined by its unfortunate coincidence with an emergency National Flood Disaster Appeal, which made a much more successful call on the public's generosity.

The Annual Report for 1947-48 gave £11,394 as the total raised for the NSDF in the first year, a disappointing result. But, though it was not possible to offer any grants to the governing bodies, at least the CCPR had a little of the financial 'headroom' which it had previously lacked – enough to provide for the short-term maintenance of Bisham Abbey and for a little overseas work.

The arrangement with the public relations firm proved far from satisfactory in practice. It was brought to an end in July 1947 and Roy Eveleigh was appointed as the Council's National Appeal Organiser. In spite of his efforts, the success of the appeal did not justify the cost of a whole-time appeals officer, and after 1948 the Council relied for its voluntary income upon the efforts of its own supporters and staff.

Various special appeal events have been held from time to time, such as the Royal Performance of Bertram Mills Circus at Olympia on behalf of the CCPR and NPFA jointly on 18th December 1952, attended by her Majesty the Queen and the Duke of Edinburgh; a Gala Performance of the Ice Musical *Wildfire* at Empress Hall on 28th June 1955 in the presence of Princess Alice and the Earl of Athlone; and a number of 'five-a-side' football tournaments sponsored by the *Evening Standard*. For many years the CCPR enjoyed the financial support of the Football Association. It gave direct donations and also encouraged its clubs to make grants to the NSDF from the proceeds of their public practice matches. For example, in 1948, £1,643 came from that source. The help received through the FA was of crucial importance in some of the CCPR's most difficult years. By June 1972, when the Council's assets were transferred to the Sports Council, a total of £215,000 had been raised for the NSDF since its inception, a sum primarily though not exclusively raised to provide capital and meet the deficits on running the National Recreation Centres.

The year 1946 saw the appointment of D. G. Ross, M.C., as the Council's first – and last – Officer for Overseas Work. David Ross, who had lately come out of the Army and was an enthusiastic steeplechaser and cross-country runner, secured the appointment initially by his own persuasive fervour as well as by his willingness to work for a small salary, drawn from the NSDF. He worked hard and successfully in his chosen field. There were exchanges of students at courses. The British Council arranged for twenty-six leaders from France to attend the CCPR's Christmas Courses in 1946, and the French Ministry of Education invited the CCPR to send a party of fifty men and women to attend a fortnight's course in physical education and training methods in Strasbourg as their guests in April 1947.

Relations with other countries were cultivated, and a printed quarterly bulletin was circulated widely overseas between 1947 and 1949, when it was incorporated in the Council's own *Journal*. Many individual students from abroad were accepted for the Council's courses, and a number of the staff had opportunities to make brief visits to study facilities and methods in various European countries, notably France, Sweden and Germany. During the following few years the Council was represented at certain European conferences, including a Western European Union's conference on sport and youth work in Paris and several conferences of 'non-governmental' organisations concerned with sport convened by the Council of Europe in Strasbourg, and similarly pleasant and profitable gatherings. But the pressure on staff time and the limits on the funds available imposed severe restriction on what could be undertaken in this field. Visitors from overseas (including the Dominions and Colonies) who wanted to learn about how the CCPR worked and to exchange ideas generally about physical recreation were almost embarrassingly numerous at Bedford Square, but the value of the contacts made was beyond question.

From the 23rd to 26th July 1948, just before the first Olympic Games since 1936, an important International Congress on 'Physical Education, Recreation and Rehabilitation' was held in London under the aegis of the Ministry of Education. It was attended by 400 delegates, 200 of whom came from seventy-four overseas countries, and the success of the event was considerable. Seven national bodies combined to arrange the programme and P.C.C. was General Secretary of the Organising Committee. The whole administration of the Congress was in the hands of the CCPR's staff and the papers on the file show the brilliance of P.C.C.'s powers of organisation.

The CCPR was not directly concerned with the Olympic Games, held at Wembley Stadium and other centres from 29th July to 14th August though some members of its staff acted as officials, judges and commentators at various centres.

It was the activity of skiing that led to especially close contacts between the CCPR and Norway and France, and very many parties went from this country under the CCPR's auspices for skiing holidays in Norway which were generally pre-

ceded by sessional courses in 'dry-ski training' centres, centres
which were the subject of an amusing article by J. B. Boothroyd
in *Punch* with the title 'Ustaoset, Norway, W.C.1'. They were
organised by the CCPR at various regional centres in cooperation with the Ski Club of Great Britain. Later, the scheme
was extended to France in cooperation, with the Union
Nationale des Centres de Montagne, with which the Council
established close relations as the result of friendly contacts made
with officials of the French Ministry of Youth and Sport. These
skiing holidays were arranged by the CCPR from 1950 to
1972, profits or losses going to the NSDF.

Easily the most spectacular and paradoxical event arranged
by the CCPR was the Ski Jumping Competition in March
1950 at Hampstead Heath, with outstanding help from the
London County Council. It is estimated that 80,000 people
must have made their first acquaintance with ski-jumping that
Friday evening and Saturday afternoon. Not only did the Nor-
wegians send twenty-five of their most brilliant jumpers to
compete with members of British University teams but they
sent the snow as well – 45 tons of it, packed in insulated crates.
H.M. Customs and Excise Officers wanted to charge duty on it
on its arrival in Harwich until someone at a high level was
persuaded to intervene. The resulting publicity did much to
ensure the huge attendance. A photograph of this unique event
adorned the cover of the Annual Report for 1949–50. The
event was repeated in Hampstead the following year and in the
Braid Hills, Edinburgh, but the weather was bad and the at-
tendances disappointing. The first rapture was never recaptured!

Also in the international field, mention must be made of
the 1949 Lingiad, again in Stockholm, at which Britain had
over 1,000 representatives, including 700 demonstrators. On
behalf of the Ling PEA, the CCPR combined with the
National Association of Organisers and Lecturers in Physical
Education to prepare the British teams of 192 men and 192
women for their mass display item. P.C.C. wrote an amusing
description of it: 'The demonstrations began on the second
day – so did the rain! The British team was one of the first to
perform. Inspired by their leaders, Norah Reed and Jack Barry,
first the women and then the men defied the appalling conditions and gave a performance of which Britain can be justly

proud. Barefoot and wearing their attractive blue dresses, the women cheerfully sat and lay in pools of water, wallowed in mud, and slithered here, there and everywhere, while they went through their table of rhythmical exercises to music. As they made their exit at one end of the stadium, the men in immaculate shorts and singlets appeared at the other, to be covered in mud from head to foot within a few minutes. But one and all entered into the spirit of the occasion and gave an outstandingly good display. Press reports paid high tribute to both sections of the team, and expressed particular interest in the men's game-like exercises, partner contests, and agilities with human support and sticks – it was evident that such a recreative approach to physical training was new to many... The fifteen British elite teams also acquitted themselves well.'

With the departure of David Ross for a post in the travel business in 1953, the CCPR's International Service Department came to an end officially, but contacts with other countries were maintained so far as resources permitted.

The Council was constantly feeling the need for more specialists on its headquarters staff. Reference was made in the previous chapter to Mrs. Watt's secondment to Headquarters to advise on work in industry. She continued in that capacity until 1948, when George McPartlin took over responsibility for the Council's industrial work. But another specialist was appointed at the end of the war – Barbara Dummett, M.I.S.T.D., a ballroom dancing specialist. Her primary job was to promote good relations between the CCPR and the ballroom dancing profession and to improve the standard of ballroom dancing in youth organisations. She succeeded well in both tasks and was much helped by the splendid co-operation given by Phyllis Haylor of the Imperial Society of Teachers of Dancing and a leading figure in the ballroom dancing world. A special test was set up by the ISTD for class teachers, the CCPR published *Ballroom Dancing in Youth Clubs,* and Barbara Dummett travelled widely, holding courses, giving demonstrations, visiting youth clubs and colleges, and examining for the award. She remained with the Council until 1953.

But the most significant and far-reaching development on the part of the CCPR during the early post-war years was the contribution the technical staff were able to make to the adoption and growth of organised coaching schemes by many governing bodies of men's and women's sport. Any systematic account would take too long. Briefly, more and more of the governing bodies became willing to take advantage of the 80 per cent grants which the Ministry of Education offered from 1947 towards the salaries of properly qualified national coaches, and to work out national, regional and local schemes of training and examining coaches for a recognised qualification. Each body had its own distinctive methods and requirements, and it fell to the CCPR's national and regional staff to make their professional knowledge as teachers of physical education tactfully available in working out the various schemes and helping with their administration, generally in cooperation with the physical education organisers employed by local education authorities.

The pressure on the staff's services became very heavy. Since the war there had been a substantial reduction in the size of the technical staff – seventy-four in 1945 had become forty-eight by 1952, and the regional establishment became fairly constant at two men and two women Representatives in each Region, with more in London and the South East. The headquarters staff was strengthened in 1948 by the appointment of two Assistant Technical Advisers – W. L. Latto, who was Senior Representative in the North Midlands and had married his colleague, Miss Caister, the Council's first representative, and Christine Tayler, who left a post at Liverpool University to join the staff. Bill Latto remained until 1951, when he was succeeded as Assistant Technical Adviser by Emlyn Jones, a representative in North Wales since 1947. Miss Tayler remained with the CCPR until her retirement in 1963, making a valuable contribution to the development of women's sport as well as to the CCPR's production of large-scale national displays of movement and dance.

One other prominent feature of the staff's post-war work was the presentation of a series of public displays with both an entertainment and an instructional value. They acted as an incentive to individuals and to classes to reach high standards of technical skill, they brought many sports organisations together in cooperative efforts, they enabled the public to see 'star' performers as well as teams, they gave publicity to many lesser-known activities, and they raised much-needed funds for the NSDF. The interest and value of the displays was greatly enhanced by the expert commentaries given by Bill Latto,

Emlyn Jones and other members of the staff. The Lord Mayor's Show has already been mentioned. From a plethora of displays only one or two can be picked out – Spotlight on Sport, created in the North Midlands Region, was outstanding enough to be a feature of the 1947 AGM and to be given other London, performances. There was 'Recreation Roundabout', 'Sportlight', 'Action', 'Sports Parade', and 'Recreation Revue', produced by various Regions and in Wales. From 1949, two shows that had outstanding instructional value and which travelled throughout the country were 'Focus on Lawn Tennis', with Dan Maskell and Fred Perry and 'Focus on Table Tennis' with Victor Barna, Jack Carrington and Johnny Leach, Emlyn Jones acting as manager and commentator in each case and the organisation being handled by the regional staff. The main emphasis was on coaching methods. The first 'Focus on Lawn Tennis' gave twenty-three performances in seventeen days, travelled 1,500 miles, was seen by 22,000 spectators, and raised £1,200 for the NSDF.

The 1946 'National Festival of Youth' at Wembley Stadium had won such acclaim that the demands for a 'repeat' were irresistible. On 8th June 1948 two performances of a 'National Festival of Youth and Sport' were given at the Empire Pool, Wembley, before 15,000 spectators with Marshal of the Royal Air Force Lord Tedder in the afternoon, and Princess Elizabeth and Prince Philip in the evening, as honoured guests.

Once again, the Festival, produced and directed imaginatively by George McPartlin and his technical colleagues, was an outstanding success. Twenty-six voluntary youth organisations and twenty-four governing bodies of sport contributed to an impressive opening parade, and the programme included displays of archery, gymnastics, basketball, formation ballroom dancing, and indoor football. Keep-fit was demonstrated colourfully by 800 young women from all parts of the country, 250 displayed rhythmic dancing, and seventy-two students from Bedford and Dartford Colleges of Physical Education gave a classic and beautiful exhibition of educational gymnastics. The stick exercises for which 120 young men had been trained by the CCPR Regions drew great applause and were the subject of many humorous recollections at subsequent CCPR staff conferences! The three Services closed the Festival with an item of traditional polish, ending by drawing up their demonstrators to form the letters 'E' and 'P', in an affectionate tribute to their Royal Highnesses.

These, as well as other large-scale Festivals organised by the CCPR, engendered a nation-wide spirit of collaboration; they will not be forgotten by those who saw them.

In the following year, the 'Festival of Football' at the Empress Hall on the 4th June, concentrated on one sport and 10,000 spectators saw brilliant exhibitions of the skills of the game by prominent players, and a demonstration of coaching methods presented by Walter Winterbottom, the FA's Director of Coaching, later to be the CCPR's General Secretary.

In 1947, the CCPR and the NPFA reached an agreement to publish a joint quarterly journal called *Recreation Review* under the editorship of Marjorie Pollard. The publication served the needs of both bodies well but, after eight issues, they agreed that they both needed the freedom and space of their own journal. From 1949 until 1972, the CCPR had its own quarterly, first *Physical Recreation,* later *Sport and Recreation.* The Author was the editor for the first nine years, after which Robert MacKinnon was appointed part-time editor and publicity officer, to be succeeded in 1966 by Reginald Moore in a full-time post. It is thought that the journal played a valuable part in promoting the CCPR's purposes, in encouraging public discussion of important issues, and in spreading knowledge and information. Its circulation was about 7,000. Much of the history both of the CCPR and of physical recreation is recorded in its successive issues. One of its editorials on 'Sport and National Prestige' had the honour of being reprinted in the quarterly *Bulletin of the International Olympic Committee.*

A few final points must be included in the history of this period. Well-attended Summer Schools were held each year, some at Lowther College, Dartford College, Carnegie College and St. Andrew's University. The CCPR through its headquarters staff took an active part on many important national committees, including the Research Board for the Correlation of Medical Science and Physical Education (established in 1943), the Royal Society for the Prevention of Accidents, the Central Council for Health Education, the Chartered Society of Physiotherapy, the Central Committee on Camping Legislation, MCC's Cricket Inquiry Committee, the Standing Conference of National Voluntary Youth Organisations, as well as on the committees of many national youth organisations, governing bodies of sport and dancing organisations.

At the 1948 Annual General Meeting, Philip Noel-Baker M.P., gave an address on 'The Lessons of the XIV Olympiad' and Lord Aberdare, a member of the International Olympic Committee and chairman of the Games and Sport Sub-Committee, presented the Coubertin Coup to the Council, the CCPR having been adjudged by the IOC as the voluntary organisation which had made the greatest contribution to the development of sport since the previous Olympic Games in 1936.

In 1948, came the news that the Council's application to the South African 'Aid to Britain' Fund for a grant to establish a second National Recreation Centre in the North of England had been successful and the long search for suitable premises started, as recorded in Chapter Seven. In the same year an invitation from the Ministry of Education for Northern Ireland for the CCPR to work there was gladly accepted.

In 1949, the Council sustained a grievous loss in the sudden death of Colonel S. J. Parker, O.B.E., H.M.I., who had been one of the Council's earliest and keenest supporters and its liaison officer with the Ministry of Education since 1935. He was succeeded by Ernest Major, M.B.E., H.M.I., who remained in that capacity until his retirement at the end of 1958, after which he continued to serve the Council devotedly in many other ways as an individual member. His successor as the Ministry's liaison officer was H. (Bill) Sagar, H.M.I., who served until 1972. The work of these three staff inspectors was necessarily unobtrusive and 'off-stage' but a warm tribute is due to the invariably helpful way in which they used their experience and influence for the Council's benefit – their constructive support for the CCPR was a crucial and continuing element in its progress and development. The Council's gratitude cannot be overstated.

In 1950, an important whole-day conference was held at Holborn Town Hall, at which, under the chairmanship of Mr. Gem, seventy representatives of twenty-seven national youth organisations met members of the Council's staff for a fruitful discussion about the CCPR's services to them. They also heard a talk by Spencer Summers, M.P., on the work of the Outward

Bound Trust, which that year had opened its second Centre, the Mountain Centre at Eskdale.

The volume of the CCPR's activities and courses was becoming so considerable that in 1948 an Information Service was started, subscribers to which, for 7s. 6d. a year, received details of the Council's national and regional activities, as well as the Annual Report and the Journals. The Service caught on immediately and continued until 1972 when it was taken over by the Sports Council.

Grants from the Ministry of Education during the period were: 1946–47, £53,999; 1947–48, £60,000; 1948–49, £64,524; 1949–50, £66,000; 1950–51, £66,000. From the Scottish Education Department they were: 1946–47, £7,523; 1947–48, £12,028; 1948–49, £10,718; 1949–50, £13,065; 1950–51, £13,825.

The shadow of economic stringency was hanging over the nation at the end of the decade, and, following the devaluation of the pound, there was a policy of retrenchment. The Treasury would make no grants to help teams attend the Lingiad. In October 1949, local education authorities were told that they were spending too much on "recreation and social and physical training" under the Education Act, which provoked *Physical Recreation* to ask in an editorial, 'Must the Axe fall on '53'?", and to plead that, as County Colleges (the somewhat inept name given to the proposed institutions for compulsory part-time education for young workers between 15 and 18) had had to be postponed, parsimony should not invade the youth service and neighbouring territory. But it did, and capital grants were also severely curtailed.

CHAPTER SIX

Growing Strength and Maturity: 1951 - 1960

The CCPR's next ten years was a period of immense activity and constant growth, of fruitful experiment and of an unending battle to secure the finance necessary to carry out its ambitious plans – some of its own; others thrust upon it. There was never any plateau in its affairs. Its life was one of continuous ascent to new achievements.

By now it was an established and well-accepted body, with no vested interests except to give efficient and appropriate service to its constituent bodies and to use every device of experiment and stimulation to promote all forms of physical activity among the general public. Its programme of national and regional training courses, both for leaders and coaches as well as in personal performance, was extended year by year. The professional experience of its technical staff, aided by the increase in the number and quality of residential facilities afforded by the National Recreation Centres, enabled it to help the specialist bodies to increase their own coaching and development work.

The decade saw the Patronage of a new Sovereign and the enthusiastic encouragement of a new and Royal President. It also saw the establishment of two new National Recreation Centres – Lilleshall Hall and Plas y Brenin – and the promise of a third, at Crystal Palace. During it, the Council fittingly celebrated its own twenty-first birthday, emerged triumphant from the searching investigations of a House of Commons Select Committee, and set up the Wolfenden Committee on Sport, an action which was to have a far-reaching effect upon its own future. A fuller account of these events is given later.

The year 1951 was 'Festival of Britain Year', the principal aim of which was to demonstrate to the world that Great Britain had recovered, both economically and culturally, from the privations and sacrifices imposed by the war. There was the new Festival Hall on the South Bank Site to display the lively, creative imagination of British architects and designers, and the extravaganzas of the Battersea Fun Fair to show that we had not lost our national gaiety.

The CCPR's own contribution to the Festival of Britain was two-fold. It accepted responsibility for planning and coordinating an almost continuous series of sports demonstrations in an exiguous arena on the South Bank Site. Nearly 500 displays were given, involving 44 governing bodies and youth organisations, between May and September, and they were seen by about a million people, excluding television viewers. Jim Lewis was seconded from his job in the Region to organise the event and his work was warmly appreciated. It was a good example of the Council's coordinating role and technical function.

The second special contribution was a Festival of Sport, given two performances at the Empire Pool, Wembley, on Whit-Friday and Saturday before 20,000 spectators. It brought together athletes, cricketers, footballers, swimmers, lawn tennis players and boxers, and included displays of formation ballroom dancing, skipping, Scottish country dancing and 'fun and fitness with ladders' by NABC boys. Among the sporting celebrities of the day who took part were Maureen Gardner, Arthur Wint, Learie Constantine, Molly Hide, Ted Ditchburn, Randolf Turpin and Eileen Fenton, and commentators were the renowned Raymond Glendenning and Richard Dimbleby.

At the Council's annual Meeting held in September 1951, Lord Hampden resigned the Presidency which he had held with such distinction. He had been MCC's representative on the Council and an Honorary Officer since its earliest days, and his influence had been of unique value. He was the embodiment of the traditional English gentleman – modest, courteous, friendly, and imbued with the highest ideals of public service. Two years before his death in 1958, he passed over to the Council the gift of £500 which had been made to him in recognition of his fifty years as a Director of the County Fire Office.

The very genuine sorrow at losing Lord Hampden was tempered by the knowledge that H.R.H. Prince Philip had agreed to succeed him as President. Prince Philip has remained the Council's President since 1951, and has not only showed the liveliest personal interest in its progress but, also as will be seen, helped its work in many significant ways.

The official inauguration of the Festival of Britain was one of the last official ceremonies performed by King George VI, and his death in February 1952 deprived the Council of a valued friend. The new Queen quickly showed her support for the Council by succeeding her father as Patron.

But in spite of the optimistic front assumed by the Festival of Britain, the succeeding years were a time of great national economy – the air was full of words like 'cuts in grant', 'moratorium' and 'restrictions on capital expenditure'. Many hopes had to be deferred and a deaf ear was again turned to the resolution, moved by Lord Hampton and carried at the Council's A.G.M. in 1951, uging the Government to remove, or at least to reduce, the heavy rate of purchase tax carried by articles of sports equipment, which in the Council's view was a tax on the instruments of fitness and seriously handicapped the development of physical recreation.

From 1951 to 1954, the CCPR's own grants remained static but there was a modest improvement for 1954/55. In October 1954 the then Prime Minister had said in the House of Commons that "it is the declared policy of Her Majesty's Government to encourage the development of sport and physical fitness". Wanting a more specific undertaking, Norman Dodds, M.P., moved a resolution calling for more facilities and for more money to be spent on sport. Of the CCPR he said "it has done an amazing job on a budget of £100,000 of which probably £75,000 is provided by the State", and in replying to the Debate, Dennis Vosper, Parliamentary Secretary to the Ministry of Education, said, "I should like to endorse everything Mr. Dodds has said about the CCPR. If it does nothing else, I hope this Debate will emphasise the important work which this body has been doing. It is a quasi-official body in that, when the Physical Training and Recreation Act, 1937, went through this House, the CCPR was the body which was expected to see that the work was carried out. It is a body which was financed last year, as to 47 per cent of its money, by the Ministry of Education. The remainder of its contributions come from voluntary subscriptions, from local education authorities which make use of its services, and, indeed, from the fees of those who attend its courses. It does not organise games so much as train leaders, and help and advise local authorities. In the words of its own report, '. . . it serves to stimulate and, where appropriate, to coordinate but not to compete'." Mr. Vosper said that in the current year its grant would be £80,000, adding,

"I have no doubt at all that the Council, which we look upon as the principal body in this field, could spend more money". Though perhaps not every word said about the CCPR in the Debate was strictly accurate, the Council very much welcomed this public declaration of confidence.

Though the Council's work continued to move forward along a very broad front, this period may be chiefly remembered for a remarkable surge of interest nationally in adventurous non-competitive outdoor activity, and the next few pages will be devoted to the part played by the CCPR in promoting and assisting this movement.

Many social, economic and other factors combined to induce young people – and many older ones, too – to seek new outlets for leisure-time recreation in the open countryside, on the mountains, and on all forms of water – sea, estuary, river, lake, canal and reservoir. After the war, many habits and attitudes changed. Through serving in the Forces, many town-bred men and women had gained wider vistas of what life and greater leisure could offer them. For many, the possession of cars and caravans made for greater mobility; for the less well-off, Youth Hostels or the acquisition of light-weight camping equipment (in which there had been great technical improvements) opened wide possibilities of adventurous exploring. Class consciousness was slowly disappearing from the world of mountaineering and rock climbing. Physical education in the schools was rapidly moving beyond the conventional games and sports for which so many youngsters had no real aptitude, and the work of most voluntary youth organisations and of local authorities' youth organisers helped to infect young people with the joy and excitement to be gained in the open country.

Nearly all the national bodies concerned with rambling and youth-hostelling, camping, canoeing, riding, sailing and cycling were in existence before the CCPR was formed, and most were among its earliest members. As briefly mentioned earlier, they came together with the main non-profit making holiday-providing bodies and some of the national youth organisations to form the CCPR's Outdoor Activities Advisory Committee in 1943, of which the quietly influential chairman from 1945–1960 was J. B. Henderson of the Holiday Fellowship. There was more natural common ground and less rivalry among these bodies than among the governing bodies for particular sports, and they and the CCPR's staff learnt much from each other during their meetings. Outdoor activity featured far less in the training offered by the specialist physical education colleges in the thirties and forties than it does today and not many of the CCPR's staff had had any professional training in it. But some had gained personal expertise in angling, camping, climbing, canoeing, gliding, skiing, sailing and so on, and many had learnt much from the Scout and Guide Movements and in the Services. The rest, with that ready adaptability which is one of the most valuable characteristics of those who have trained for the physical education profession, learnt quickly, with the result that the CCPR was able to play a constructive part in this new development of outdoor activity.

The Committee concerned itself with legislation affecting camping, access to facilities, cheap travel arrangements, safety on the mountains and on the water, and similar matters, and discussed how the CCPR could best help its members. The Committee had induced the Executive to submit a resolution in July 1948 uging the Government to implement the recommendations of the Hobhouse Report, particularly that relating to the setting up of a Central National Parks Committee. This was part of the pressure leading to the passing of the National Parks and Access to the Countryside Act of 1949.

The Ministry's action mentioned in the previous chapter gave a great stimulus to camping, and many local education authorities, some of whose physical education organisers had attended Ministry's courses, gave much encouragement to the activity, including the provision of camp sites. Water sports, particularly canoeing and sailing, made great headway, and the CCPR played a prominent part here, with especially close cooperation with the British Canoe Union. Very many courses in canoeing, sailing and boat building were held at Bisham Abbey and at numerous other centres in England, Scotland and Wales, notably Hayling Island, the Norfolk Broads, Salcombe Bay and on the Clyde. Glenmore Lodge, the CCPR's Scottish Centre of Outdoor Training in the Cairngorms which had operated since 1948, became a focus for mountaineering courses of high standard, and many of the staff organised mountain activity courses in the Lake and Peak Districts, Snowdonia and N. Ireland. Scotland led the way in pony-trekking holidays, to be effectively followed by Wales, and, in cooperation with various professional riding schools, the CCPR entered increasingly into more sophisticated forms of equitation, organising in 1957, for example, 52 courses in riding and horse management with the approval of the British Horse Society.

The Outdoor Activities Committee gained a considerable access of strength from the membership of the British Mountaineering Council, the British Gliding Association, and the Outward Bound Trust who joined the Council between 1951 and 1953, and the interest of local education authorities in this field was shown by the representation on the committee of the National Association of Youth Service Officers who joined the Council in 1952. The Royal Yachting Association followed with membership in 1958.

The hazards as well as the attractions of mountaineering were becoming so evident, as well as the need for all bodies offering any form of mountain training to meet together to discuss standards, that in May 1953, on the advice of the Outdoor Activities Committee, the CCPR convened a conference at the Alpine Club in London under the chairmanship of Jack Longland. Forty-six attended, representing a score of bodies, including the British Mountaineering Council, the Mountaineering Association and the Ramblers' Association, and among those who spoke were Eric Shipton, then Warden of the Outward Bound Trust's Eskdale Centre, and Peter Mosedale, Warden of White Hall, the Open Country Pursuits Centre in Derbyshire established in 1951 by Jack Longland, when Director of Education there.

This conference on the then virtually uncharted subject of mountain training was one of the most important and significant ever organised by the CCPR, and the report of it in the Council's journal makes interesting reading in the light of the great achievements in that field during the twenty years following. Some of these will be touched on later in the story of Plas y Brenin Mountaineering Centre, but, though outside the decade, it is relevant to make mention here of the two no less important and fruitful conferences held in 1962 and 1964 at Plas y Brenin for those responsible for running residential centres for mountain activities, also under Jack Longland's experienced chairmanship. Hitherto these centres, nearly all established by local authorities or voluntary bodies in the 'fifties, had had no common meeting ground nor any opportunity of discussing together, or setting standards for, the very important work on which they were engaged.

Harrison's Rocks, an outcrop on the Kent/Sussex border and a favourite resort for climbers in the south-east of England, came into the CCPR's possession somewhat curiously in 1954. The Rocks were on the land of the Forestry Commission, which found the presence of hundreds of climbers, many of whom arrived by uncovenanted routes, highly embarrassing and were ready to dispose of the rocks for a modest price. For the good of the climbing fraternity, the British Mountaineering Council were anxious to acquire them, but, not having the legal status to own property, persuaded the CCPR to become the owners and make some contribution to maintenance costs and supervision. The BMC raised the purchase price of £50, plus £10 for standing timber, and the CCPR assumed ownership. Since that time, the Rocks have been administered by a joint BMC/ CCPR committee and, though the intervening years have not been without problems of trespass and litter, the Rocks have been of great service to climbers for training and recreation.

Early in 1960, as part of its work of promoting outdoor activity, the CCPR organised a series of nine whole-day conferences at various centres in England and in Cardiff. Without being spectacularly successful, they were useful in promoting closer working relations between the national outdoor organisations on the one hand, and local authorities and youth organisations on the other. Notable speakers at the conferences were Arthur Blenkinsop, M.P., Sir John Hunt, Jack Longland, Peter Scott and Tom Stephenson.

One of the most pleasant benefactions ever to come the way of the CCPR was the setting up of the Whitbread Sports Fund by Col. W. H. Whitbread in 1954, and from which the CCPR benefited until 1972. The annual income from the fund, starting at about £2,000 a year, was devoted to promoting outdoor activities, in which Col. Whitbread was specially interested, and most of it was spent on the advice of the CCPR. This gift, administered by the trustees with great understanding, enabled the Council to make films, build riding stables at Plas y Brenin, buy much-needed camping, canoeing and other outdoor equipment for the Regions and Centres, and above all, to establish various bursary schemes to help students and youth leaders to attend training courses in outdoor activities. It also met many other needs for which no statutory help was available, for instance providing fences at Harrison's Rocks and meeting part of the cost of the conferences just referred to.

The success of the Outward Bound Courses for boys at Aberdovey and Eskdale made many of those concerned with the welfare of girls in commerce and industry eager for girls to enjoy similar experiences. The Outward Bound Trust were ready to experiment, but turned to the CCPR for advice about the differing needs of girls. After discussions it was agreed that Ruth Keeble, one of the Council's Senior Representatives, should direct an experimental four-week course at Eskdale in October 1951. This course showed that girls could gain as much from the mountains as boys could. Incidentally, of the 54 girls between 16 and 19 who attended, half had never had a country holiday before – a sad reflection on the nation's social and educational provision at that time. Demands for further girls' courses could not be resisted and as the Trust had no accommodation to spare, a number of them were run during the 'fifties by the CCPR for the Trust at Bisham Abbey and Plas y Brenin, until the Trust decided to establish its own Centre for girls, at Rhowniar, Merioneth, with a representative of the CCPR on the management committee.

A reference to these courses is contained in *A Woman's Reach*, by Nea Morin, the distinguished woman climber and mother and mother-in-law of two other distinguished climbers. She describes her work as a voluntary instructor for several years at the Outward Bound girls' courses at Plas y Brenin. In the same book, she refers to having run with Evelyn Leach in 1948 what she believed – rightly – to have been the first CCPR mountaineering courses in Snowdonia.

The wartime controversies about the merits of 'fitness badge' schemes lingered on. In 1948 the CCPR had invited a group of men and women, all authorities in their own sphere, to meet to discuss the appropriateness of launching such a scheme as an incentive to personal fitness. Of the rightness of the aim there were no doubts, but few who attended felt that a badge based on tests of speed or strength would make any notable contribution towards achieving it. Powerful advocates, however, continued to press for fitness badge schemes, including Brigadier Michael Wardell of the Beaverbrook Press, who argued his case in the pages of *Physical Recreation* and quoted numerous European precedents. On many occasions the topic was raised at the Council's Committees, including the Games and Sports Committee, but there was no decisive following, though the effect on boys and girls of the training and testing at Outward Bound courses was noted with a good deal of admiration.

Further speculations came to an end in February 1956, when it was publicly announced that a new Award Scheme was to be launched on an experimental basis, bearing the name of the Duke of Edinburgh and with Sir John Hunt as its Secretary (later Director), under which certificates would be given to young people under 18 achieving certain standards in four separate sections – 'Fitness', 'Adventure', 'Public Service', and 'Pursuits'. (Ten years later, about 150,000 Awards had been gained, over 10,000 of them 'Gold' Awards).

From the start the Council's General Technical Committee agreed that the CCPR should do all in its power to help. The members of the Outdoor Activities Committee also discussed the Scheme and offered their help. The staff were represented at the two conferences at Ashridge and in London called to discuss cooperation between 'the operating organisations' and 'the assisting bodies', and advised on facilities and opportunities for training. The regional staff arranged a number of conferences for representatives of local 'operating authorities' to re-appraise the Scheme and discuss problems, and full reports of these were sent to the Award Office by Emlyn Jones, who was the first of a series of the CCPR's very active liaison officers with the Award Scheme. The CCPR was asked to suggest requirements for the sailing award in the 'pursuits' section, and to prepare a modification of the 'Fitness' section to meet the special needs of handicapped boys – the latter was carried out in consultation with the BAOLPE, PEA and NABC.

The CCPR was also involved in the meetings called to discuss the possible institution of an Award for girls, and Ruth Keeble served on the small 'ad hoc' group set up to present firm proposals. On the basis of these, a 'pilot scheme' for girls started in 1958.

The first course of training for leaders of the Award's 'Expedition' section was provided by the staff of Plas y Brenin in June 1959 under the direction of Sir John Hunt, attended by 46 men nominated by industry, local authorities and youth organisations. In the next few years, many further courses were held at

Plas y Brenin for the Award scheme – for 'Expedition' leaders, both men and women, for both leaders and boys in mountain activities and canoeing, and for boys preparing for the 'Gold Expedition' tests. The Award was regularly discussed at the staff's conferences so that the CCPR might make its maximum contribution to its success, and it was given prominence in the Journal through articles and news items. Members of CCPR headquarters staff served as chairman of a number of Award committees.

The fact that no mention of the manifold ways in which the CCPR was able to be of direct service to the Award Scheme found its way into the volume recording the story of the Award's first ten years should perhaps be regarded as an illustration of the amount of unacknowledged background service the CCPR was able to give to many forms of physical recreation during its history. As it did not want to be looked upon as a new 'national organisation', the Award Scheme did not seek representation on the CCPR Council until 1971.

On 30th April 1956, the CCPR celebrated the twenty-first Anniversary of its formation in a singularly successful way – credit for the idea goes to George McPartlin. Sir Bracewell Smith gave a reception for 400 CCPR guests at the Park Lane Hotel in London, and, during it, Prince Philip as the Council's President gave a half-hour's televised broadcast on 'Active Leisure', illustrated by film, which, apart from the general public, was watched by those invited to twelve simultaneous CCPR functions at Belfast, Cardiff, Exeter, Leeds, Manchester, Newcastle-upon-Tyne, Norwich, Nottingham, County Hall, London, and the three National Recreation Centres.

The broadcast, seen by an estimated ten million viewers, evoked great praise, some welcome donations, and much interesting correspondence. Prince Philip put into pithy and simple language the philosophy the CCPR had held for twenty-one years: "The CCPR does two things – it introduces all forms of physical recreation to people and it introduces people to all forms of physical recreation ... We believe that a very large proportion of the people of this country like taking some sort of exercise and that they feel better and happier for it ... I don't think leisure is any problem, and if people like doing nothing, I have no objection. All I am concerned about is that people should not be forced to do nothing because there is no opportunity for them to do something in their leisure time."

Prince Philip ended his broadcast by saying, "My last word ought to be addressed to all the people attending the various CCPR receptions. Those of you who work for the CCPR are doing a very worthwhile job. I hope that the very happy relations which exist between the CCPR and the people who give their time to the governing bodies of different sports and activities will long continue to the benefit of both."

After the broadcast, Sir David Eccles, then Minister of Education (now Lord Eccles), addressing the Park Lane reception, said that he considered no grant awarded by his Ministry was put to better use than that given to the CCPR – in fact, his colleagues were surprised at the amount the Council was able to do on its grant.

A special edition of *Physical Recreation* included not only P.C.C.'s reminiscences referred to in Chapter Three, but an article on 'The First Twenty-One Years' by Arthur Gem, in which he paid tribute to the vision, zeal and energy of the men and women staff who had built up the CCPR's reputation, and another on 'The Next Twenty-one Years' by Sir Stanley Rous, many of the hopes and predictions in which have since been realised.

We must now turn to consider a field of the Council's work into which a great deal of thought and effort had been put but which produced disappointment and, indeed, an acute sense of failure – namely, the field of service to the voluntary youth organisations. It is not possible to treat the subject in great depth here; at the same time, facile and superficial generalisations must be avoided for the sphere of the youth service is so wide and covers so great a range both of age and activity that any generalisation is liable to be misleading. Moreover, even within a single national youth organisation, the nature and quality of work done varies to such an extent that what would be true of one part of that organisation might be quite untrue of another part.

As has been seen, the first ten years of the CCPR's life were closely linked with youth work, and its services to the voluntary youth organisations were given freely and received with appreciation. Though the CCPR was only concerned with part of the programme of a youth organisation, it was both an important and a popular part, and probably more youngsters joined their units in order to take part in physical recreation – broadly defined – than for any other reason.

After the war, as the provisions of the Education Act came into effect, the responsibility for much that the CCPR had been trying to do for local youth organisations was carried – at least in theory – by local education authorities and came within the field of the physical education organisers and youth officers they employed in increasing numbers. The CCPR, moreover, had been enjoined by the Ministry which grant-aided it, to detach itself from purely local services, and particularly from undertaking work for individual units of organisations. Yet this was precisely the sort of work which youth organisations had most welcomed from the CCPR, and they felt aggrieved by its withdrawal, especially in areas where local authorities were not showing themselves very sympathetic or helpful to their work. So there was some local disappointment that the CCPR could no longer do what the youth bodies had become used to expect.

On the wider national and regional front, the CCPR felt they had an important coordinating role to play in serving the youth organisations – that of promoting closer and more effective working relations between them, and between them and the adult specialist bodies for games, sports and outdoor activities. Success in this field, it was hoped would help members of youth organisations to develop greater skills or wider interests in physical recreation, something that would serve them well in later life. It was also hoped that the first-class residential training facilities for so many activities which the Council was now able to offer at National Recreation Centres would be of great practical value to youth organisations.

These hopes were never fully realised. In general, efforts made to provide special courses at NRC's or elsewhere to meet the training needs of leaders and senior members in youth organisations met with little response, and though some youth organisations made occasional reservations at NRC's for their own members' events, the wider opportunities failed to appeal and the CCPR was able to do little for the youth service as a combined or coordinated whole. It was claimed that finance was a barrier but this was only a marginal factor, for, when the CCPR offered reduced rates for members of youth organisations at NRC's and even free bursaries at courses from funds provided by the London Parochial Charities or the Whitbread Sports Fund, the response was only a little less disappointing.

In brief, the CCPR found itself unable to erect more than a very narrow bridge over the gulf which seems to exist between organised sport and youth work in this country, which does not seem to be paralleled in Europe. The reasons for this comparative failure do not necessarily reflect discredit on anyone : they are probably inherent in the way that the country's youth service had grown and developed. A very large proportion of the membership of the voluntary youth organisations – probably a larger proportion than would be admitted publicly – was drawn from youngsters still in full-time attendance at school, whose talents and interests in physical recreation were met with varying degrees of comprehensiveness by official education provision, and who were anyway outside the age limits of the CCPR's responsibility. Next, each youth organisation had its own special 'ethos' or uniting principle, and physical recreation, however attractive, could never be allowed to become the dominant part of the programme. And, as most youth organisations are engaged in an endless struggle to retain their older members as a source of leadership within their own movements, it was natural for such bodies to be reluctant to take any action which might have the result, directly or indirectly, of tempting their members to join specialist bodies for physical recreation, which could not offer these members, it was felt, the all-round training which the organisations tried to offer themselves.

And there was a further important factor. Financially, the fifteen post-war years was a time of great stringency for most youth organisations, and there was a 'backs to the wall' atmosphere within the youth service which was a sad disillusionment after the brave promises of statutory partnership expressed in the wartime Circular 1486. Many of the youth organisations had found no difficulty in securing capital grants from charitable trusts or private benefactors to acquire their own national centres for training, camping or holidays – after the war, substantial properties were easy and cheap to be had. But to finance their maintenance was a very different problem, and it was natural that the organisations' first efforts had to be directed towards making full use of their own centres rather than sending their members to courses run by other bodies, however good the facilities and training they provided.

Though these factors came to be fully appreciated, it was nevertheless a disappointment to the staff of the CCPR that, although their work with adult bodies was prospering, that on behalf of the youth service in any generic sense was at a low ebb. Determined efforts were made to make the services of the Council of greater use to the voluntary youth organisations, and the subject was discussed at many staff conferences, often in the presence of senior officers from those organisations. But the progress made was meagre and it was natural that the staff should come to feel that their efforts would have to be used in more productive ways.

It should be emphasised that the personal relations existing between the staffs of the youth organisations and the CCPR were never anything but uniformly pleasant, and there was a good deal of helpful cross-representation on each others' committees. The nearest thing the Author can recall to anything approaching discord was when his friend and former colleague Reg. Goodwin, General Secretary of the NABC (now Sir Reginald Goodwin, Leader of the GLC), took exception to certain strictures that had been made in an editorial in *Physical Recreation* in 1957 against what was considered to be the increasing 'juvenility' of the youth service. Mr. Goodwin had a talk with P.C.C. about it and the hand-written notes she prepared for herself in advance of the interview in which she tried to pacify the critic without letting down the editor are still extant – a good example of the tactful way in which she handled potentially difficult situations.

No, the barrier was just that some bodies did not feel that they needed or could use what the CCPR had to offer – and it must be remembered that youth organisations were never in a position to make their leaders or members do anything they did not want to do. Comparisons are somewhat invidious, but the Boys' Brigade might perhaps be singled out as a body which made more consistent use of the CCPR than most others. The CCPR helped to staff the courses at its training centre, Felden Lodge, and for some years the CCPR had responsibility for bringing out successive issues of the BB Tables of physical exercises for their Companies, a task discharged in the main by Jack Barry.

Since 1939, nearly all the national voluntary youth organisations received annual grants for their headquarters administrative and training expenditure under the Social and Physical Training Grant Regulations. The amount received was never more than a fraction of their total expenditure and there was much bitterness when, as an act of national economy, their grants were cut by from ten per cent to fifteen per cent for the year 1952/53. They contrasted their position enviously with that of the CCPR, who had not suffered similarly.

The criticism of the Ministry's apparently lukewarm policy about the youth service in the early 'fifties was brought to a head by the publication in 1955 by King George's Jubilee Trust of *Citizens of Tomorrow*. This consisted of a series of reports and recommendations by working parties on different aspects of youth welfare, and one of the strongest recommendations was that there should be a substantial increase in the funds made available by the nation for the youth service.

Parliamentary concern about the condition of the youth service found expression in the reference to the Select Committee on Estimates for 1956–57 of the Government's expenditure on the youth employment service and the youth service. The dissatisfaction of the youth organisations with their grants had been brought to the notice of this Committee, together with their fear that the amount of grant received by the CCPR was at the expense of their own share of what was available.

The Select Committee, under the chairmanship of Miss Elaine Burton, M.P., saw representatives of the Ministry of Education, the Association of Education Committees, King George's Jubilee Trust, the Standing Conference of National Voluntary Youth Organisations, and the CCPR. At the session at which the CCPR appeared, Miss Burton declared her interest as a member of the CCPR's Executive Committee, and, of the three other members of the Select Committee present, Sir Ian Horobin, M.P., took the most prominent part in questioning the CCPR's representatives – P.C.C., George Reynolds, the CCPR's very new part-time accountant, and the Author. Sir Ian was well known as the Warden of Mansfield House University Settlement and its somewhat unorthodox satellite Boys' Club, Fairbairn House, in the East End.

After P.C.C. had made a very clear initial statement about the Council's activities and financial position, Sir Ian at once assumed the rôle of a prosecuting counsel, and asked a series of challenging questions that were designed to demonstrate that the CCPR was not a youth organisation; that it did not train leaders in the youth service sense but only coaches and instructors for physical activities which were not the most important part of the youth service; that most of the people the CCPR was working with had nothing to do with the youth service; that in the matter of grants it was far more generously treated than the youth organisations who were doing far more important work; and that it could quite easily get its income from local education authorities, instead of relying for its finances on the Ministry of Education and so depriving youth organisations of the money they needed so desperately.

Under this withering attack, P.C.C. stood up magnificently – candid in her facts, clear in her reasoning, and impassive in her demeanour. (Some readers might enjoy studying the verbatim report published in July 1957.) Her answers made it clear that the CCPR's grants were negotiated independently, and that their total had no effect whatever on the amount available for youth organisations.

For the historical record, her explanation to Sir Ian as to why Kent was the only education authority to give the CCPR a grant should be mentioned here. Early in the Council's existence, Kent Education Authority had been so grateful for the work of Kay Caister, who lived in Kent and who was on the Council's small staff (at first as a volunteer), that they asked whether, if the County gave grant-aid for the purpose, a CCRPT Representative could be allocated for work in Kent. The Council was so pressed for funds at the time that a chance to increase the staff was welcomed, and M. Adair Jackson was appointed a full-time Representative to work in Kent for some years. The arrangement with Kent continued until 1967. But there were conclusive administrative reasons why the scheme could not be repeated elsewhere – indeed, when he gave evidence to the Select Committee, Sir William Alexander* of the AEC was emphatic in his view that the statutory grant to enable the CCPR to provide its services should come solely from the Ministry, even if, indeed, there was a debit *pro rata* to all authorities in the country.

In due course, the Select Committee issued its report. So far as the CCPR was concerned the following emerged :

(1) The CCPR was not, and had never claimed to be, a youth organisation.

*Created a Life Peer in 1974.

CCPR Staff Conferences
Above: at Birmingham University, summer 1945

Below: at Lilleshall, January 1953

Staff Conference at Crystal Palace, 1964

Boys' Brigade instructors in training, 1945

George Hickling giving a lifting and handling demonstration

Athletes at a men's training camp, 1939

The National Festival of Youth and Sport, Empire Pool, Wembley, June
1948

Plas y Brenin

Right: an instructor demonstrating rock climbing

Plas y Brenin. A course on the artificial ski slope

Bisham Abbey

The river at Bisham

Bisham Abbey. H.R.H. Prince Philip on a visit to the centre

Two views of Lilleshall

Lilleshall Hall – its official opening as a national recreation centre in June 1951 – H.R.H. Princess Elizabeth on a tour of the grounds with Sir Stanley Rous and party

Above: Crystal Palace from the air
Right: Prince Philip by the swimming pool during the official opening ceremony in 1964
Below: tennis in the indoor arena

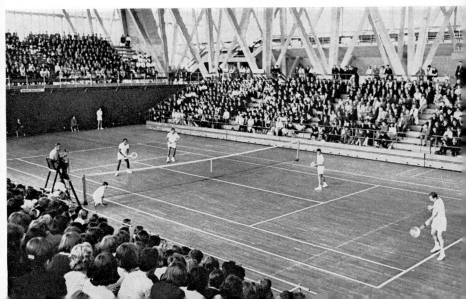

The National Sailing Centre, Cowes, I.O.W. Prince Philip declares the centre officially open

National Sports Centre for Wales

The Wolfenden Committee. From right end of table clockwise: Sir John Wolfenden (chairman), The Bishop of Chester, Mrs. G. Allen, Miss E. B. Clarke, J. L. Longland, Sir Arthur Porritt, A. D. Munrow, H. A. Pawson and Justin Evans (secretary). Absent abroad: Sir Godfrey Ince
(*photo P.A. Reuter*)

Ski jumping
competition at
Hampstead Heath

Visit of Members of Parliament to Lilleshall, July 1963 – J. P. W.
Mallalieu tries his hand at archery, watched by Lord Aberdare,
Capt. Fred Bellenger, the Warden and the Deputy Warden

Presentation to Miss Colson on her retirement, by CCPR chairman Sir Stanley Rous

Sir Stanley Rous and Arthur Gem, on their retirement as CCPR
chairman and vice-chairman respectively, were honoured by a
reception at Fishmongers Hall in July 1973. H.R.H. Prince Philip,
CCPR president, is at the microphone and, to his right, Denis Howell,
MP, the new chairman, and Dr. Roger Bannister, chairman of the
Sports Council

The 1972 Executive Committee of the CCPR

The author with Miss Phyllis Spafford

(2) No criticism of its services had come from any quarter examined, statutory or voluntary – indeed, the youth organisations were at pains to pay high tribute to its work and to say that it was regarded by them as a friend and ally.

(3) The amount of grant paid to the CCPR had no effect on the amount available for or paid to the voluntary youth organisations.

(4) The Select Committee did not recommend any reduction in the CCPR's grants, but, to avoid any further misconceptions on the subject, thought that the whole of the CCPR's grant should be paid under the Physical Training and Recreation Act, not a fraction as hitherto, whereas the youth organisations' grants should continue to be paid under the Social and Physical Training Grant Regulations of 1939. This recommendation was accepted and put into effect.

This report cleared the air considerably and was much welcomed by the Council. But it also gave considerable publicity to the adverse criticism about the Ministry's youth service policy, as enshrined in the Ministry's own evidence that "the youth service was one of the educational services which it had been definite policy for some time not to advance". The Select Committee added its own comment that "the impression gained from the inquiry is that the Ministry is little interested in the present state of the youth service and apathetic about its future". The setting-up of the Albemarle Committee on the youth service which will be referred to in a later Chapter was undoubtedly an outcome of the Select Committee's report.

But youth service was not the only sphere in which feeling was growing that more vigorous and generous statutory action was needed to meet the circumstances of the day. *Britain in the World of Sport*, a short pamphlet but one of outstanding importance, written by members of the staff of the Physical Education Department of Birmingham University and published in 1956 by the PEA, drew attention to the handicaps suffered by sports bodies and amateur sportsmen and sportswomen in trying to prepare for any form of international competition, and gave a searching analysis of many of the factors affecting sport in Great Britain. The pamphlet, the subject of review and editorial comment in *Physical Recreation*, prompted A. L. Colbeck one of the most able and experienced members of the CCPR's regional technical staff, to propose a resolution at the staff's

Annual Conference in January 1957 calling on the Council's Executive Committee to respond to the challenge contained in the last chapter of the pamphlet. The resolution was carried and referred to the Council's committees, where it was clear that there was general agreement that the time had come for the whole subject of the development of physical recreation to be referred to an impartial body, "qualified to hear evidence and reach conclusions". In the Summer of 1957 the appointment was announced by the CCPR of the Wolfenden Committee, whose work and its far-reaching consequences will be considered in later Chapters.

Before turning to the National Recreation Centres, the next major topic to be examined in this history, a few points must be added here to round off our survey of the CCPR in the 'fifties. This Chapter's preoccupation with the CCPR's work in outdoor activities and the youth service should not be taken as implying that the Council was not at the same time devoting much attention to its two other main divisions of work – that of assisting the bodies concerned with movement and dance, and those controlling competitive games and sports. Grant aid through the Ministry had enabled more of the latter to appoint their own National Coaches and create new coaching schemes, and the Council's technical staff were closely involved in this work, both with individual bodies and in arranging for those working for the governing bodies – coaches and administrators alike – to meet together for consultation and conference, usually at National Recreation Centres.

Film-lectures and lecture-demonstrations continued on a wider scale as features of regional work, with titles such as 'Lessons of Helsinki', 'The Way to Wimbledon', 'The Key to Gold', and 'Focus on Mountaineering'. The lecturers and demonstrators included such famous sportsmen as Cyril Tolley, Dai Rees, Bill Cox, Alex and Eric Bedser, the Choong Brothers, and R. C. F. Nichols.

The Council's women staff were active in the field of movement and dance, advising, encouraging and stimulating the bodies concerned. A large-scale Festival of Movement and Dance at the Empire Pool, Wembley in March 1955 enabled a public of 8,000 to watch demonstrations by 1,100 performers in a colourful and varied programme of keep-fit, skipping, national dancing, Medau rhythmic movement by a team from

Germany, and items by Margaret Morris Movement, Laban Art of Movement Guild, Women's League of Health and Beauty, English Folk Dance and Song Society, Scottish Country Dance Society, Imperial Society of Teachers of Dancing, the Women's Section of the Amateur Gymnastic Association, and a solo display by Eileen Fowler. It was again a triumphant manifestation of feminine effort and enthusiasm, which added a much-needed £750 to the NSDF. A similar Festival was held at Wembley in March 1958, with two performances and 13,000 spectators.

The growth of keep-fit in various areas of the country, helped by the staff and some organisers of physical education, had been striking, and a conference called at Bisham Abbey agreed that the time was ripe for the formation of a national body for keep-fit work. At a meeting in Coventry, attended by over 400 people in Coventry in September 1956, the Keep-Fit Association was inaugurated, which soon became represented on the Council and has had a successful life. Its first chairman was Norah Reed.

In the international field, the CCPR had the main responsibility for organising the Third Congress of the International Association of Physical Education and Sports for Women and Girls, held in London in July 1957, and with the active help of a Welsh Advisory Committee organised the Second Empire and Commonwealth Physical Education Conference, held at Barry from 11th to 17th July, before the Commonwealth Games of 1958. Both conferences were grant-aided by the Ministry of Education.

It was with a sense of deprivation that the CCPR learnt in 1953 of the decision of the Committee of its Scottish Section to seek autonomy as the Scottish Council of Physical Recreation. The national sentiments and aspirations of Scotland were fully recognised, but the Council had hoped that they would be met by the great measure of freedom enjoyed by the Section to manage its own affairs. The hope that the CCPR, which, successively and at the invitations of the countries concerned, had extended to Scotland in 1946 and to Northern Ireland in 1948, could speak for the whole United Kingdom in matters of physical recreation could be held no longer. So it was with regret but with as much good grace as the circumstances permitted that the Executive accepted the inevitable, wished the new body 'God speed', and agreed to maintain close relations. But things were never quite the same, and the CCPR was saddened by the loss of a healthy limb which had grown so recently.

The sudden death in a car accident abroad of the third Lord Aberdare, chairman of the Games and Sports Committee, in 1957 was a great personal loss to the Council. He had been an enthusiastic supporter of its work since its formation. His son, the fourth Lord Aberdare, was welcomed as an individual member in 1961 and continued his father's interest.

A final comment should be made in this Chapter. In any history of the CCPR it is hard to do justice to the achievements of the staff who worked from the regional offices and in Wales and Northern Ireland. They inevitably had less publicity than Headquarters, but few of the Council's services could have been given or major events organised without the hard and efficient work of the regional staff. Their work was essential in the staging of national demonstrations and displays, in channelling technical, administrative and advisory help to the local units and associations of the Council's constituent bodies, and in seeing that NRC's were put to the fullest possible use. Above all, the CCPR's reputation as a body existing to serve, and to give that service with efficiency, enthusiasm and good humour, rested as much on the technical and secretarial staff in the regions as on any other factor. They did not enjoy – or suffer from! – the advantages of having their own regional advisory committees. But their activities were reported fully both orally and on paper to the Council's committees and the Ministry.

The title "Central Council of Physical Recreation" was not universally liked, and some committee members and some of the staff, including P.C.C. herself, often canvassed the possibility of changing it. It was a regular target for the caustic remarks of journalists, who naturally disliked its length. But in spite of the wider connotation that the word 'sport' was acquiring, officials of the Ministry, consulted privately, were nervous about the wisdom of substituting it for 'physical recreation'. The matter was eventually referred to the Executive in 1954, who rejected any suggestion for a change almost unanimously – one of the rare occasions when a vote was taken at that Committee. So "CCPR" it remained.

CHAPTER SEVEN

The National Recreation Centre Story: 1946 - 1972

No more important contribution was made to the nation by the CCPR in its thirty-seven years' history than the establishment of seven National Recreation Centres, each with its own distinctive origin, character and achievements, as well as problems. Once again it is the story of an initial vision, reinforced by faith and determination to surmount all obstacles. The original conception was vindicated in the most satisfying way possible – a pattern set by voluntary pioneers was recognised as good, and in due course was adopted or imitated by statutory bodies, in cooperation with the pioneers and building on their experience.

Without the CCPR, it is reasonable to assert that no National Recreation Centre would have been, or could have been, started. P.C.C. was well justified in saying in her valedictory address to the Council on her retirement in 1962 : "The country might still be without National Recreation Centres had we looked longer and leapt less quickly when the idea of Centres first came to us late in 1945"

Apart from the unifying, generic idea of a National Recreation Centre as being an institution set up to provide first-class residential facilities for participation and training in a wide variety of physical activities, the story of the Centres is marked more by the elements that distinguish them from each other than by those common to all. Each one has a history worth telling at some length, but here we must be content to pick out only the main threads in a very complex tapestry.

In the first ten years of its life, the CCPR had run numerous residential courses, using facilities of varying standards and in every type of accommodation, ranging from tented and hutment camps, public schools, training colleges and university halls of residence. Immense experience was gained in the process, and those early training camps and vacation courses played a vital part in building up CCPR traditions as well as in producing badly-needed coaches and leaders. But they led to an overwhelming desire for 'a place of one's own' which could be used all the year round, not only when it could be spared from its primary purpose. The setting up of one or two National Physical Recreation Centres "in accessible but beautiful parts of the country" was, as had already been mentioned, one of P.C.C.'s first post-war aims. As the Council had been told firmly by the Ministry of Education that no financial help could be expected from them for such Centres, the only hope lay in approaching voluntary sources.

Bisham Abbey

A letter from Lord Astor and Lord Hampden published in *The Times* in June 1945 produced the offer from Miss Phyllis Vansittart-Neale, its owner, of the lease at a peppercorn rent of Bisham Abbey for use as a National Physical Recreation Centre. This was a former house of the Knights Templar, on the Berkshire bank of the Thames, a mile from Marlow, parts of which dated back to the twelfth century. In an article in *Country Life* in 1941, E. T. Long had written of Bisham Abbey : "Few ancient houses in this country have a lovelier or more characteristically English setting. Among the buttercups of water meadows and tall enclosing trees, the old rose and silvery grey of its walls reflect the colours of the May trees in the fields beside the peaceful river. The building itself is in every sense worthy of its exquisite surroundings."

The prospect of possessing so lovely and historic a house as Bisham Abbey was so exciting that it tended to obscure the hard financial realities implied by the acceptance of a 'full repairing lease' for an ancient structure. The terms were held later to include liability for restoring the ravages of death watch beetles as well as responsibility, set out in a full 'schedule of plight and condition', for many vulnerable pieces of antique furniture. But the house had a unique charm and character, and fears that vigorous young students of physical activity might be careless or destructive proved groundless. Its mellow antiquity imposed its own discipline.

The Abbey had been used as an officers' convalescent home during the war, so was reasonably well furnished for its new use, though the cooking and domestic arrangements were inconvenient and the sleeping accommodation – for about fifty in all – mainly in dormitories for six or more people. There was an historic dining hall and good common room, but the only other indoor facility was a fine ballroom, which could be used for other suitable activities. With some difficulty – at this time, any new building was virtually out of the question – permission was obtained to have a prefabricated gymnasium erected, size 60 ft. by 25 ft. in the old kitchen garden. Outside, there were playing fields and two grass lawn tennis courts with space for more, but the chief glory was the wide and gently-flowing Thames alongside, admirable for canoeing and elementary sailing.

In establishing Bisham Abbey in April 1946 as the first National Recreation Centre, there were four unfamiliar problems to be faced – to finance it, to improve its facilities, to staff it, and to make full use of it.

How part of the financial problem was tackled has been covered in Chapter Five. The policy of the CCPR about facilities at all its Centres was, as the commercial companies say, 'one of continuous improvement'. Accommodation for students and resident staff was made more comfortable and attractive, arrangements for cooking and serving meals improved and simplified, facilities for indoor and outdoor activities extended and modernised, particular care being taken to see that the provision was in accordance with the needs and requirements of the governing bodies of sport and the other associations concerned.

The initial task of equipping Bisham Abbey for its new purpose was made easier by a timely and generous grant of £2,500 from the Carnegie UK Trust. A special gift of £1,000 was made by the Football Association. Over the years, the improvements to Bisham's facilities have included a new boat house and better landing stage, five hard 'Tennisquick' lawn tennis courts (three of them flood-lit), a hard porous training pitch, a paved area for basketball, netball and volley ball, three hard cricket practice wickets (a gift from the NPFA's Lord's Taverners' Fund), a nine-hole 'pitch and putt' golf course, and many additions to make comprehensive athletics training more possible. There was also an agreement for golf and squash rackets to be played at the nearby Temple Golf Club.

More ambitious plans for improving and enlarging the residential and sporting facilities were drawn up and discussed by committees and staff, and with the Government Departments concerned, for well over a decade, and there was disappointment that it did not prove possible until very recently for Bisham to be selected for the necessary capital expenditure. Permission was given for extensive work to start in 1974. In spite of hopes deferred and the limitations of its accommodation, the unique character, setting and beauty of Bisham Abbey have ensured that it has always been well used and given it a specially warm place in the affections of all who go there.

The appointment of a warden of this first Centre was obviously a key matter. He or she had to be single and to be willing to sleep in the only bedroom available for a warden's exclusive use, which contained a four-poster bed and which, together with the drawing-room, was among the Council's obligations under the lease to preserve as historic period pieces! Technical qualifications in physical education were not looked for as it was felt that the training could be given by the Council's own technical staff and the instructors supplied by the bodies using the Centre. What was wanted was someone keen on physical recreation, good at administration and staff relations, who could be trusted to exercise a sufficiently firm discipline over the resident students to satisfy the owner and her sister – both of whom lived near at hand and kept a close and somewhat apprehensive watch on everything that was going on – that the precious fabric of Bisham Abbey had been entrusted to safe hands.

Kathleen Murmann was a wise choice for the first Warden. She had been Bursar of a girls' boarding school. She knew the neighbourhood well, and was an experienced Officer in the Girl Guide Movement. Her influence did much to ensure that residence at the Abbey meant far more than training in physical activity alone. In her four years as Warden, she laid sound foundations for her successors, all of whom, helped by their wives, have made their own valuable and distinctive contributions. They were Malcolm Harris (1949–1953), Jim Lewis (1953–1963), John Taylor (1963–1967) and Brian Lee (1967–1972), the last-named having previously served as Deputy Warden at Lilleshall for six years.

Many served Bisham Abbey well, and the later Centres, too, as Domestic Bursars, Assistant Domestic Bursars and Secretaries, and the names of those with long service are given in an appendix, but mention must be made here of Jean Casselton's cheerful service as Bisham Abbey's Secretary since 1961.

The programme of the new Centre developed gradually. The facilities were not at first good enough for high-level coaching events – indeed at that stage in the development of the conception of a National Recreation Centre the emphasis lay on introducing people to physical recreation at all levels rather than on high standards of performance. The first events were some weekend courses, one-week courses in ballroom dancing and camp leadership, and a four-day senior staff conference. But the main event of the first summer was a series of eight one-week 'physical recreation training holidays'. They were so successful that they continued for many years. Coaching was given to young people of both sexes and aged between 16 and 25 in archery, ballroom dancing, basket ball, bicycle polo, canoeing, cricket, fencing, Association and Rugby Union football, women's hockey, judo, netball, rambling, rowing, lawn tennis and weight lifting. There was no difficulty in recruiting coaches of high quality to spend a week at Bisham or pay shorter visits there, and among them were Dan Maskell, Kay Menzies and Peggie Scriven (lawn tennis), Sydney Wooderson (athletics), John Dudderidge (canoeing), and George Smith (soccer). The *Times Educational Supplement*'s editorial comment in September 1946 was: "The CCPR is for ever putting good ideas into practice and that of 'physical recreation training holidays' should prove a winner."

A review in *Physical Recreation* of the first five years of 'training holidays' showed that 1,700 young people had attended. Lawn tennis, soccer, canoeing, and athletics were the most popular activities, with archery and fencing not far behind. Recruitment for women's team games had been disappointing. Those attending had all worked hard and made very good progress in what they had chosen to do, and some had already been acting as coaches. Those attending were largely drawn from school-leavers, office workers, students and teachers, and it was thought a matter for regret that so few had come from industry or the distributive trades.

Wartime experiences had made sleeping in dormitories less unwelcome than it has since seemed to become, and Bisham soon became popular for conferences – soccer referees and administrators, factory sports officers, industrial welfare workers, keep-fit leaders, youth leaders and organisers used it for this purpose.

As its facilities improved and its reputation spread, Bisham was used increasingly by the governing bodies of sport both for coaching courses and their own 'training holidays' – archery, athletics, fencing, canoeing, gymnastics, men's and women's hockey, rounders, Rugby League football, and weight lifting prominent among them. Many courses were held in ballroom dancing, national dancing and folk dancing.

A small Management Committee was set up in 1948 under the wise chairmanship of Lord Hampton. J. Eaton Griffith succeeded him in 1961 and remained chairman until 1972, devoting much time and thought to Bisham's many problems. In 1954 he had been responsible, as President of the International Lawn Tennis Federation, for arranging for competitors in the Wimbledon Lawn Tennis Championships to be invited to have lunch and tea at Bisham and enjoy its amenities on the middle Sunday in the Wimbledon fortnight, establishing a tradition which lasted many years. T. G. Bedwell also did much for Bisham, not only as a committee member for many years, but also as a close friend of the Centre and its staff. A House Committee arranged an Annual Ball to raise funds for Bisham, and from 1957 onwards grants from the Historic Buildings Council helped to relieve the CCPR of the heavy burden of maintaining the structure. The Abbey, its dovecote and two barns had been listed in 1955 as of special architectural or historic interest under Section 30 of the Town and Country Planning Act of 1947.

In the first fifteen years of Bisham Abbey's transition from a historic manor house into a National Recreation Centre, the CCPR enjoyed the professional advice and help of Arthur Llewellyn Smith, M.B.E., F.R.I.B.A., and since 1961, a similar position has been occupied by representatives of Knight, Frank and Rutley. The first statutory capital grant towards improving the residential facilities of Bisham Abbey was one of £2,500 from the Ministry of Education in 1949, but an even more welcome change in official policy came when, following the Wolfenden Committee's Report, the Ministry agreed to make annual grants towards the maintenance costs of Bisham Abbey and the other National Recreation Centres established by that date. After the deaths of Miss Vansittart Neale and her sister Mrs. Elizabeth Paget, a grant of £27,500 from the Ministry in 1962 enabled the Council to purchase Bisham Abbey and some additional land from the Abbey Estate. Further land was purchased at a later date.

As the Council did not own the Abbey for the first seventeen years of its use as a National Recreation Centre, an official opening could hardly take place, but in June 1956, Prince Philip, as the Council's President, paid an informal visit to the Centre. This was a source of great encouragement to the Committee and the staff who had worked so hard to make the Centre a success.

Lilleshall Hall

Early in 1947 the people of South Africa made a gift of over a million pounds to Great Britain as a tribute to this country's wartime achievements, and, in the light of the increasing demands made on Bisham Abbey, the Council felt justified in making an application to the committee set up by Mr. Attlee, then Prime Minister, to administer the South African gift, for a grant of £120,000 to enable a second National Recreation Centre to be established nearer centres of population in the North of England. Ellis Smith, Mayor of Durban, then in London in connection with the South African gift, paid a visit to Bisham, and must have been impressed with what he saw, because in January 1948, the CCPR were given a promise of the grant asked for.

The search for suitable premises took nearly two years. Any new construction was ruled out by statutory restrictions. Many were the likely and unlikely buildings looked at in the North of England by members of the staff. In the end, Basil MacNay was given a temporary appointment to concentrate on the search. His inquiries eventually led him to Lilleshall Hall, near Newport, Shropshire, which though not in the North was accessible to it. Apart from some doubts about the ease of getting there – the nearest main line railway station was Wellington, nine miles away, and cars were much less common in those days – Lilleshall seemed – and indeed proved – an admirable choice.

It was a former seat of the Duke of Sutherland, built in the early nineteenth century, in a rural, woodland countryside, which had been purchased shortly before the war by Herbert Ford as his own residence and for development as a tourist

centre in the West Midlands with an emphasis on its lovely
and extensive gardens. During the war, it had been used by
Cheltenham Ladies' College and later by Dr. Barnado's, and
its brief life as a resort and pleasure-garden had been forgotten.
Though substantial alterations would be required, it could be
made to accommodate the Council's target of 100 residents in
rooms for between two and six. The experience gained at
Bisham had shown that a comprehensive range of facilities
could only be put to full use if there were beds for an adequate
number of residents. It had a large ten-acre field which,
suitably treated, would make excellent playing fields, and there
was adequate space for building extensions. The former stable
yard had been roofed over and a maple floor laid, which made
it a fine indoor training area. There was also a nine-hole golf
course adjoining, which Centre residents could use, together
with the no less appreciated bar, as temporary members.

The place was bought and a satisfactory financial agreement
made with Mr. and Mrs. Ford, who continued to live there.
Llewellyn Smith supervised the conversion of the buildings,
and the technical staff at Headquarters, in close consultation
with the governing bodies of sport, planned the lay-out and en-
largement of the facilities. A training area with covered jumping pits for athletics, an asphalt court for basket ball
and net-ball, four hard and three grass lawn tennis courts,
and three outdoor artificial cricket wickets were the first new
facilities to be provided, to be followed shortly by a large
Redgra area for hockey and soccer practice, which is now
flood-lit.

Bought at the end of 1949, the Centre was ready for its new
use early in 1951, though in fact the first and triumphant test
of its comfort and convenience as a residence was made by the
CCPR's Annual Staff Conference, when the central heating
system proved able to withstand the peculiarly Arctic conditions
of December 1950, in happy contrast to some chilly remem-
brances of early days at Bisham!

Earlier in 1950, Jim Lane had been appointed Warden and
has held the post with unflagging energy and signal success
ever since. He had had a background of social and boys' club
work, experience of running a residential settlement and
wide interests in physical recreation. His knowledge of cricket
together with his membership of MCC enabled him to estab-

lish early and close contacts with the 'high-ups' in the cricket world, notably Harry Altham, then MCC's President. Many important cricket events figured in Lilleshall's subsequent programme, including the first coaching conference to be called by MCC which met for two days in December 1951, with many illustrious cricket names among those present. In an article written two years later for *Physical Recreation,* Harry Altham, describing the conference as "memorable", said that "it provided an indispensable and, thanks to the remarkable atmosphere which Jim and Win Lane create and sustain there, a recurring inspiration. It is here that MCC have staged their advanced courses for senior county coaches, from which these men have gone back to run courses for schoolmasters and youth leaders in their own areas."

Jim was a welcoming host, and he was even able to meet the exacting requirements of parties of professional footballers who frequently came to Lilleshall for a few days' training in a relaxed and peaceful atmosphere. The most outstandingly successful of these was the two weeks' stay of England's Soccer team before the World Cup in June 1966. For their historic triumph in the competition perhaps Lilleshall and Jim Lane might justly claim some credit, a view endorsed by Sir Alf Ramsey himself when he visited the Centre in 1967 to unveil a plaque commemorating the England team's stay. The event was the subject of a special appeal in Shropshire which raised £2,000 and enabled Lilleshall to acquire some special equipment, including a video tape apparatus.

In recent years, Jim Lane has had the assistance of a deputy: Brian Lee from 1961 to 1967, and Mike Greenwood from 1967 to 1972. His title, as that of the other Wardens, was changed to that of Director in 1969. He has been a Justice of the Peace since 1957. Many other staff have contributed greatly to the successful running of the Centre. Margery Sykes was its Secretary from 1950 to 1966, and Hattie Ellis was Domestic Bursar at Lilleshall from its opening in 1951, with a short break in the 'sixties, until her sudden death in July 1973

The official opening ceremony was performed by a most gracious Princess Elizabeth on 8th June 1951. In glorious sunshine she toured the grounds – the gardens ablaze with azaleas and rhododendrons – and saw a diversified display of activity: archery, athletics, fencing, judo, weightlifting, basket ball, soccer, netball and lawn tennis, followed by coaching in the indoor cricket school.

After an act of dedication by the Bishop of Lichfield, the Princess, from an open-air platform in full view of some 2,000 guests, declared the Centre open and expressed to the people of South Africa, represented by C. H. Torrance, the Deputy High Commissioner, and other guests, the emotions of gratitude felt by British sport for so welcome and timely a gift. Sir Stanley Rous presided over the ceremony and briefly outlined the Centre's future programme. A memorable afternoon ended with guests enjoying American Square Dancing with Kenneth Clark of the EFDSS as caller.

The main feature of Lilleshall's first summer was the Summer School from 21st July to 8th September, during which nineteen courses, each lasting a week, ten days or a fortnight, gave training in a wide variety of activities, many of them run by the governing bodies and concluding with an examination for a coaching award. Of the 400 places available, 380 were taken.

And so, Lilleshall, like Bisham five years earlier, started to build up its own programme. The events in its twenty-one years as a National Recreation Centre are too numerous even to give a representative selection. All that must be said here is that more and more of the governing bodies have come to look upon Lillehall as their own national or regional coaching 'home' – in particular those of cricket, Association Football, Rugby League and Rugby Union Football, lawn tennis (including squads for the Davis and Wightman Cup teams), badminton, hockey, lacrosse, netball and the Professional Golfers' Association, together with several movement and dance organisations. With rare exceptions Lilleshall has also been the scene of the CCPR's annual staff conferences – generally held in mid-Winter.

Major improvements to Lilleshall's facilities have been :
(1) A pavilion on the playing field built with a grant from a South African charitable trust and officially opened by Prince Philip in November 1954.
(2) The magnificent King George VI Sports Hall, a 120-foot square indoor hall with a specially designed non-glare double glass roof. This hall is large enough for two lawn tennis courts and can be used also for badminton, basketball and netball. Its construction was made possible by a grant of £56,000 from

King George VI Memorial Foundation, and it was opened in October 1955 by Lord Bridgeman, Lord Lieutenant for Shropshire and chairman of the Centre's Local Advisory Committee.

(3) Three new halls of residence, and a house for the Director, grant-aided by the Department of Education and Science. The halls, providing single and double rooms for students and replacing some dormitories and sub-standard bedrooms, brought the total bed accommodation to 120. The halls were commemorated with the names Eaton (1963), Colson, and Altham House respectively, the first as a tribute to J. Eaton Griffith, chairman of the Lilleshall Management Committee from 1952 to 1963.

(4) A fine new building – the Queen Elizabeth Hall – consisting of a large movement and dance studio, two lecture rooms (one of them with tiered seating for 130), three squash courts, and a students' refreshments bar. This was also provided through a capital grant from the Department, and was officially opened in April 1967 by Denis Howell, M.P., then Minister with special responsibility for sport.

The chairman of the Centre's Management Committee from 1963 until its transfer to the Sports Council was Alan Miller and its architect since 1954 Frank Roberts, F.R.I.B.A., of Raymond Hawkins and Roberts. Mr. Roberts gave signal service to Lilleshall over a long period, and later at Plas y Brenin. It is worth recording that, in order to supplement the statutory grant for the buildings, an appeal, suggested by Bronwen Lloyd Williams and launched by the Committee, for sponsors to furnish bedrooms in the hostels raised over £2,000 from sports bodies, schools and individuals – the names of the donors being commemorated by plaques in the rooms.

When free from residential courses the facilities at both Bisham and Lilleshall have had some purely local use, but in the case of Lilleshall this has been particularly extensive – the floodlit Redgra area, the indoor cricket school and the squash courts being in regular use by local clubs and the local college of further education for training and practice, and there is a far greater demand for the lawn tennis courts in the King's Hall from a wide area in the West Midlands than can be met.

Plas y Brenin

The successful establishment by the CCPR's Scottish Section of Glenmore Lodge in the Cairngorms in 1948 as the Scottish

Centre of Outdoor Training and the great surge of interest in adventurous activity referred to in the previous Chapter, served to emphasise that, though two National Recreation Centres had been established to promote the development of games and sports, no corresponding advance in the sphere of outdoor activities had been made by the CCPR in England and Wales.

When the King George VI Memorial Foundation was set up in 1952, the CCPR submitted a memorandum to the Foundation suggesting that no more appropriate memorial to his late Majesty could perpetuate his interest in physical recreation and the work of the CCPR than the establishment of more National Recreation Centres in the United Kingdom. In particular, the Council applied for grants to enable it to set up a centre with good sports facilities in Scotland, and one suitable for climbing and other outdoor activities in Wales, preferably in Snowdonia, and for the addition of a large indoor sports hall at Lilleshall.

General Sir Arthur Dowler, Secretary of the Foundation, visited Bisham and Lilleshall, and there were meetings with the CCPR's Officers. In March 1954, came the stupendous news that the Foundation were setting aside £400,000 for National Recreation Centres. Of this sum, £60,000 was the amount allocated for the Snowdonia Centre, and the Author was entrusted with the pleasant job of exploring the area and trying to find the right premises. Places were looked at on the Menai Straits which offered facilities for a wide range of water activities while being within reasonable reach of the mountains, but nothing seemed just right, and the arguments increasingly pointed to a Centre in the heart of the mountains themselves, even at the expense of foregoing the water.

After a few possible but unexciting properties had been viewed near Beddgelert and Llanberis, the Author heard privately that Eugene Brunning, owner of the three-star 150-years-old Royal Hotel at Capel Curig, a man with wide business interests, was so worried about his staffing difficulties at the Royal that he might be prepared to sell if a suitable buyer came along. The Author went at once to see him, and, while waiting on the hotel terrace with its incomparable view of the Snowdon horseshoe mirrored in the twin Mymbyr Lakes, as though an omen, he ran into Sir Ben Bowen Thomas, Permanent Secretary of the Welsh Department of the Ministry of Education, who was having his after-lunch coffee with Haydn Davies, H.M.I. He told them of his mission and their response was enthusiastic : "Wonderful, if you can get it !"

Mr. Brunning proved willing to negotiate, and a visit from Arthur Gem, J. B. Henderson, T. Glyn Davies and P.C.C. clinched the deal, and the hotel – furniture and all – was acquired at a price well within the grant, though the sacrifice of the licence, in accordance with opinions prevalent at that time, was a sad loss! Mr. Brunning advised us to take over Emrys Roberts, the manager, with the hotel. We did, and Emrys was the Centre's loyal and hard-working Bursar for its first thirteen years, as well as a most valuable contact with the neighbourhood. The name 'Plas y Brenin' (The King's House) found favour, even though Sir Ben initially feared a hostile reaction from Welsh Nationalists to any use of the word 'king', until he recalled that the name Coed y Brenin had been given to a forest not far away without arson or bomb explosion! The news of the Council's impending acquisition of the Royal was received with almost incredulous enthusiasm, not least in the mountaineering world.

The new Centre differed from Bisham and Lilleshall in that, in addition to an administrative and domestic staff, the hazards of the mountains as well as the nature of the skilled instruction to be given demanded that it should have its own full-time resident staff who were specialists in mountain activities.

Two wardens with excellent qualifications were successively appointed. The first withdrew his acceptance and the second died suddenly before he could start. But the committee had no doubts about appointing as Chief Instructor John Disley, as distinguished a performer on the mountains as he was on the athletics track as an Olympic steeplechaser, and, as his assistants, Tim Aron, B.A., and Roger Orgill. They started at Plas y Brenin early in 1955.

Major G. I. Milton, married with two small children, was appointed Warden and came into residence in July 1955. 'Gim', as he was always known, had been an Officer in the Regular Army, and Bursar of Kingham Hall Trust, Oxfordshire since 1951. He had done much work with the Brathay Exploration Group and led one of their expeditions. He shaped the early course of Plas y Brenin and directed its work with enthusiasm and devotion.

In the meantime, Cook and Arkwright, a firm of surveyors, supervised the many essential alterations to the premises, including the installation of the very necessary drying rooms and showers. The first 'try-out' event was a CCPR senior staff conference from June 6–8, followed by a month's Outward Bound course for girls. The drying rooms were not ready for the first few weeks of the Centre's use but, miraculously, the summer of 1955 was one of the driest ever recorded in the Welsh mountains. (Later, Llewellyn Smith and Frank Roberts were, successively architects to Plas y Brenin).

To run this Centre, it was essential to have a management committee composed, at least in part, of men who knew the mountains well. It was a moment of great pleasure when Sir John Hunt, having been sounded in London, paid the Centre a visit and agreed to accept the Chairmanship. The other first members were Dr. Charles Evans, Sir John's deputy on the 1953 Everest Expedition, now Sir Charles; Mansel Williams, Caernarvonshire's Director of Education; J. B. Henderson, Chairman of the Outdoor Activities Advisory Committee; and a representative of the CCPR's Welsh Committee. Haydn Davies, H.M.I., later joined the committee as observer representing the Department of Education and Science, to be followed, on his sad and sudden death, by Emrys Ll. Davies, H.M.I. A representative of the British Mountaineering Council was added soon afterwards and, more recently, a representative of the National Ski Federation of Great Britain.

Plas y Brenin had a busy and successful first summer, 350 attending its first series of mountain training holidays, receiving training in mountain walking, map and compass work, mobile camping, rock climbing and canoeing. Initially the number of students was limited to forty-five; later this became as many as sixty. Some time was to elapse before a full all-the-year-round programme was built up and the unrivalled facilities there put to full use. Much effort was spent in bringing them to the notice of local education authorities, youth organisations, colleges of education and physical education, and all the specialist outdoor activity bodies represented on the Council. Many experimental courses were run – for example for staffs of approved schools, and apprentices in industry. As one result, the Rainer Foundation (London Police Court Mission) and Tube

Investments Ltd. started their own centres in the neighbourhood.

A panel of competent and enthusiastic voluntary instructors was created, the number of full-time instructors slowly increased, and generally included a woman, and the programme of activities gradually enlarged to include field studies, winter mountaineering, local history and legend, and an occasional course in fly-fishing, at which the number of students invariably exceeded the number of fish caught! Gim Milton, who was a great lover of all animals, tried hard to get riding established as one of the Centre's activities and much time and money was spent on the purchase and stabling of horses and the necessary equipment, laying down a circular track for a 'riding school' and employing specialist riding instructors, including one brilliant but temperamental Hungarian riding master. Gim even tried to persuade the committee to purchase a neighbouring sheep farm to provide winter pasturage. But though the presence of horses added to the interest and variety of the place, Capel Curig was hardly suitable for riding courses, either in the form of pony trekking or more advanced equitation. After a couple of years, the expensive experiment was abandoned with some relief. But expansions in more promising directions were constantly being devised.

John Disley left in 1957 and his place as Chief Instructor and Deputy Warden was taken by John A. Jackson – married to a wife who shared his enthusiasm for the mountains – a schoolmaster with wide Himalayan and Alpine experience and author of a book on mountaineering, who brought with him a wealth of new ideas and great determination to put them into practice. The Annual Report for 1956–57 was able to record that the monthly average of 'day-persons' had nearly doubled the previous year's and that, in all, 1,238 men and boys and 599 women and girls had trained there during the year. In addition to courses open to all, direct bookings from schools, colleges, university departments and specialist bodies steadily increased. Of the youth organisations, the Boys' Brigade and the National Association of Youth Clubs used the Centre in its early years. Skiing was incorporated into the programme and, so that its practice would not depend upon climatic vagaries, not only was a machine for snow-making bought and a suitable ski slope rented but, later, an artificial nylon ski slope erected, which proved so useful a facility that, over the years, it was improved, considerably enlarged, flood-lit and provided with its ski tow.

To meet the growing needs of students and resident staff, improvements to the premises were continuous. An additional grant from the King George Foundation made possible the purchase of 'the Cottage', which was adapted to provide a house for the Deputy Warden and his family, a married instructor, and domestic staff as well as a fine field studies room and a camp equipment store. Better accommodation was provided in the main building for a lecture and demonstration room, staff and students' common rooms, and a domestic staff's dining room, and these were followed by the building of an extension for a students' lounge and bar, and some single bedrooms. Additions for staff accommodation included the lease of Bryn Engan, a detached property on the other side of the river Llugwy.

Plas y Brenin is different from Bisham and Lilleshall in having to rely for many of its training facilities not on those which are part of the Centre but on those provided by nature or owned by other people. The goodwill of farmers and landowners was therefore essential, and Plas y Brenin was at pains to see that all its students observe 'The Country Code', and show the farmers whose land they use that their courtesy is appreciated. As a mark of its gratitude for their cooperation, Plas y Brenin has organised an annual 'Farmers' Night' in the autumn, to which farmers and their wives are invited to dinner, followed by the traditional 'noson lawen', the nearest English equivalent to which is 'a night of fun', consisting of songs to the accompaniment of harp and piano, and recitations, sentimental or jocose, preceded and succeeded – if not on Chapel premises! – by appropriate liquid refreshment. A good time is indeed had by all, and many English students realise for the first time that, in Snowdonia at least, Welsh is very much a living language.

The wide developments in the movement for 'outdoor education' referred to in the previous Chapter found Plas y Brenin not only ready and willing to play its part, but also prepared to take the initiative in the work leading to the establishment, during the 'sixties, of the Mountain Leadership Certificate which was administered by a committee under the CCPR's auspices (consisting of representatives of the CCPR, the SCPR, the British Mountaineering Council and the Association of Scottish Climbing Clubs). The major responsibility for training and assessment under this scheme fell on Plas y Brenin, as also did the further move towards establishing a recognised professional qualification for the increasing number of men and women who were taking up paid posts as wardens or instructors at mountain centres of various types.

An important contribution towards mountain safety was the production by the staff of Plas y Brenin in 1961, at the suggestion of Sir John Hunt, of *Safety on Mountains,* a small handbook the sales of which in successive editions have reached many thousands.

As the field of Plas y Brenin's responsibilities extended, it became not only possible but necessary for it to concentrate on higher level events than the all-comers' 'mountain training holidays' with which its life started : leaders, instructors, teachers and serious students became its main concern. This required a larger instructional staff and an even greater care in selecting them. Very many men and women with two or three years' experience on the staff of Plas y Brenin have moved on to responsible posts in charge of other Centres or as lecturers at colleges of education. Though a recurrent personal loss to Plas y Brenin, the turn-over of staff there has greatly enriched the national development of outdoor education.

Gim Milton left Plas y Brenin in 1960 for the Bursarship of Oundle School. John Jackson was appointed to succeed him, and filled the post of Warden (now Director) with ability and originality. Among John's accomplishments is photography and he has made some admirable publicity and instructional films while at Plas y Brenin, including 'Climb when you're ready', in collaboration with British Ropes Ltd. His colour transparencies also supplement his rare skill as a lecturer on the mountains. Rooger Orgill deservedly succeeded John as Chief Instructor and Deputy Director. He had widened the field of his expertise while at Plas y Brenin, and to rock climbing and spelaeology were added canoeing, sailing and skiing, in the last of which he has gained a national reputation. He also found a Danish wife at the Centre – she had come to learn English (and perhaps Welsh too) there while doing a stint of domestic work, but remained to become a wife and mother.

Prince Philip visited the Centre in June 1956 and proved

himself thoroughly at home. Sir Stanley Rous, who had come to receive His Royal Highness, was offered to his surprise a lift on the Prince's helicopter and accompanied him on his visit to Bisham Abbey which was his next landing place. Many other distinguished visitors have paid official and unofficial visits to Plas y Brenin, including Sherpas Tenzing and Gompu, Dr. Hugh Dalton, Sir David Eccles and Edward Short (both when Minister of Education), Christopher Chataway, Sir Keith Joseph and Denis Howell, Minister for Sport, who was accompanied by several members of the Sports Council. Mr. Howell and his colleagues were so well impressed by their visit, (which came just at the right period in the financial year!) that Plas y Brenin's application for a grant for a heated pool for canoe training and 'drown-proofing' fell on receptive ears.

Many members of staff have contributed to the reputation and atmosphere of Plas y Brenin. There is no room to mention them individually except for the instructor David Humphreys who has now been there for eleven years, and for two of the women instructors, Jo Scarr and Barbara Spark. Jo was a Cambridge graduate in archaeology and had learnt her climbing while at Cambridge, Nea Morin describing her, in *A Woman's Reach,* as "probably the finest young woman climber in the British Isles". Barbara Spark was a student of physical education at I.M. Marsh College and had her first experience of the mountains at Plas y Brenin. She proved so adept a pupil that with Jo, she became a member of the women's historic expedition to the Himalaya led by Countess Gravina in 1961–62. Their joint talk about their experiences on the expedition at a CCPR's staff conference was a never-to-be-forgotten delight. Jo left Plas y Brenin to get married and live in Australia and Barbara also left, after a sad climbing accident while on holiday in the Lake District, from which, happily, she recovered sufficiently to become a lecturer in outdoor education at University College, Bangor.

In 1965, Sir John Hunt gave up his chairmanship of the Centre regretfully and was succeeded by Jack Longland, who had also by that time accepted the chairmanship of the Council's Outdoor Activities Advisory Committee and was becoming increasingly identified with the CCPR's work.

Just as the Wardens became Directors, so the Centres changed their names. In 1969 Bisham and Lilleshall became

'National Sports Centres', and Plas y Brenin, 'the National Mountaineering Centre'. Since 1965, it has been one of the Mountain Rescue Posts in the area, a function which is no sinecure, and its programme leaflet for 1972 showed that its widened curriculum included 'Search Survival', 'Mountain Structure and Life' and 'Expedition Photography' as well as courses for skiing instructors, organisers of 'orienteering' and introductory and assessment weeks for the mountain leadership certificate. The artificial ski slope and a cross-country ski training circuit has made it possible for the Centre to run courses for Senior Coaches and Artificial Slope Instructors for the Award of the National Ski Federation of Great Britain, as well as training weekends in personal performance. The Department of Education and Science has recently given official recognition, as a 'supplementary course for qualified teachers', to Plas y Brenin's one term's training in outdoor education.

Finances of the Centres
The fees received from students could never meet the costs of maintaining and running the first three National Recreation Centres, and the CCPR faced the continual problem of how high fees could be raised without taking them beyond the reasonable means of those capable of profiting most. The initial charge of between £4 and £5 a week has risen inevitably over the twenty-seven years since Bisham was first opened until it now ranges from about £18 to £22 a week, according to the Centre and the subject of the course, with a reduction in the case of young people. The amounts raised by the National Sports Development Fund proved insufficient to meet the constantly increasing deficits, and a great burden was lifted from the CCPR when the Department of Education and Science announced that, in line with a recommendation from the Wolfenden Committee of Sport, its grant to the Council for 1961/62 would include £20,000 towards meeting the maintenance costs of Bisham, Lilleshall and Plas y Brenin.

Another great relief to the Council was the announcement by the Department in 1963 that it was setting aside £400,000 over a four-year period to enable capital improvements to be made to the three Centres. This enabled the Centres' committees to plan ahead and made possible many of the extensions and improvements detailed in the foregoing pages.

Plas y Brenin was the last of the CCPR's National Recreation Centres to be established from voluntary resources, and the CCPR no longer assumed lightheartedly at the outset that it could shoulder the burden of maintenance deficits. The four later Centres whose story now follows were built by capital provided from statutory sources – local, national or a combination of the two – and, though the Council accepted the responsibility of administering them with careful regard to economy and efficiency, the cost of running them was removed in advance from the CCPR's shoulders. In other words their value had already been proved and the deficits on their work accepted as a statutory responsibility.

Crystal Palace

Sir Gerald Barry, the distinguished journalist, who was director-general of the 1951 Festival of Britain and whose creative imagination lay behind its chief features, was appointed in 1952 as the London County Council's consultant for the redevelopment of the destroyed Crystal Palace Exhibition Site, some six miles from the centre of London. He proposed that the site – in a sylvan setting on the Sydenham heights with a public park nearby – should be used for two main purposes, the upper park for a permanent National Exhibition Centre, and the lower for a National Youth and Sports Centre.

The Exhibition Centre proposal became stranded on financial shoals for some years and was eventually totally submerged. The Youth and Sports Centre, however, found favour and prompt support, though the name was later changed to National Recreation Centre, and is now Crystal Palace National Sports Centre. The LCC announced in November 1954 that they were prepared to build such a Centre at an estimated cost of £1,750,000, provided that the maintenance deficits, considered likely to be not less than £45,000 a year, could be met from some other source. They also expressed the hope that the CCPR would undertake to manage the Centre, and the CCPR agreed, provided they were safeguarded against financial loss.

The support given to the project by Sir Isaac Hayward, then leader of the LCC, was a crucial factor in its acceptance and the Minister of Education, Sir David Eccles, also showed an early interest in it, as providing a place for medium-scale indoor and outdoor spectator events, which could be televised if desired. He undertook that his Ministry would grant-aid the maintenance of the Centre by £10,000 a year, a promise which proved to be a valuable precedent a few years later when the CCPR were negotiating for grants to help to run the other National Recreation Centres. Soon afterwards, the City Parochial Foundation announced that they would give a similar annual sum for the Centre's first five years, on the strength of its expected contribution to the training of leaders and coaches for London's young people. In 1955, the King George VI Foundation stated that £100,000 was being earmarked from the National Recreation Centre allocation for building the proposed residential hostel. So the financial skies were lightening considerably.

The Government's severe restrictions on capital expenditure delayed a start on the Centre for some years, but the interval was made good use of, for careful planning and consultation between the various agencies concerned – the LCC's own planners and architects, the CCPR's technical staff, and the governing bodies of sport, especially the Amateur Swimming Association. In the summer of 1960, the LCC made a final decision to go ahead with the scheme. M. J. Gleeson's were given the building contract at an estimated cost of £2,185,000 and 1963 fixed as the provisional opening date. The facilities were planned to include: (1) a large, multi-purpose sports hall containing an indoor arena with provision for 1,300 spectators, and an eight-lane Olympic-size swimming pool, diving pool and shallow teaching pool, with permanent seating for 1,800 spectators, six squash courts, an indoor cricket school, three training halls, a lecture room and extensive changing accommodation; (2) a floodlit stadium with cinder running track encircling a central grass area, with stands, partly covered, for 12,000 spectators; (3) a floodlit covered athletic training area and floodlit indoor and outdoor Redgra pitches for soccer, hockey, netball etc.; (4) six hard lawn tennis courts (two floodlit); (5) restaurant and reception area; (6) an original and distinctive eleven-storey residential hostel for 140 students in single or double rooms, with dining, lecture and common rooms; and (7) houses for senior staff.

After the LCC had promised to meet £25,000 of the annual deficit, which meant that £45,000 of the running costs for the first five years was assured, the CCPR announced at its 1960 AGM that it had agreed to administer the Centre for the LCC and in November of that year, Prince Philip, as the Council's President, visited the site and drove in one of the building piles. A Joint Management Committee was set up on which both the LCC and the CCPR were represented, which included among its official members the Clerk to the LCC and the CCPR's General Secretary. One of its first actions was to appoint a Director for the Centre, and Emlyn Jones, one of the CCPR's technical advisers, was selected for the important new post, and started in it in October 1962. Shortly afterwards followed the appointments of a Deputy Director, Engineer, Admissions Manager, Sports Hall and Grounds Managers, Bursar and Secretary.

Crystal Palace, the first purpose-built Sports Centre in the country and on a scale far exceeding that of the others, was eventually ready for use by May 1964 – the final capital cost proving to be £2,900,000 – and it was officially opened by Prince Philip on 13th July 1964 in the presence of a large and distinguished gathering, including Lord Hailsham, Lord President of the Council, who had been appointed Minister with special responsibility for sport by the Conservative Government in December 1962, members and officials of the LCC, and representatives of other local authorities, the King George VI Foundation, The City Parochial Foundation, and the CCPR. After warm tributes had been paid at the opening ceremony to the LCC's vision of the Centre and their determination to secure its realisation in spite of many formidable obstacles, the touring party, led by Prince Philip, saw displays and demonstrations of swimming, diving, underwater swimming, lawn tennis, table tennis, badminton, basketball, netball, soccer training, athletics, keep-fit, judo, gymnastics, lacrosse, archery, squash and weight training, organised by the national governing bodies and several training colleges and schools.

From its opening day, the Centre has been well used and has always presented a sight of varied and vigorous activity. The co-operation between the LCC (the Greater London Council since 1965) and the CCPR in planning and running the Centre was admirably harmonious throughout, and it was a happy augury that Arthur Gem, Chairman of the Centre's Committee since 1961, was not only the CCPR's Deputy Chairman but had spent virtually the whole of his professional life as the LCC's Senior Inspector of Physical Education. Though many eminent people have served as the GLC's and the CCPR's representatives on the joint committee, it is right to single out for special mention P. B. (Laddie) Lucas, who held the very responsible chairmanship of the Centre's Finance Sub-Committee for its first seven years.

The Centre has had a threefold use : (1) the primary one of providing the best possible facilities for the residential training to the highest possible standard of coaches and leaders for very many governing bodies of men's and women's sport, (2) as the venue for national or regional competitive championships demanding accommodation for spectators as well as contestants, such as swimming, diving, water polo, athletics, basketball, gymnastics, badminton, netball, and fencing; and (3) to give opportunities to individuals, ranging from top-class performers to novices and school children, to improve their skills by intensive coaching, training and practice, or to participate in physical activity for pure enjoyment and recreation.

Under this third heading comes the Centre's scheme under which members of the general public can become 'authorised users' for a modest annual subscription, entitled to use many of the facilities for a small fee, when they are not needed for organised training courses or spectator events under the previous two headings. During 1971, it was calculated that 550,000 visits to the Centre were paid by 'authorised' and other non-residential users. The facilities for swimming, lawn tennis, and squash rackets are in particular demand by authorised users and, early in the Centre's life, an arrangement was made with the Inner London and Bromley Education Authorities under which about 3,000 school children a week use its facilities in term time. The broad and flexible services offered by the Centre could only have been achieved by the hard and imaginative work of the staff under Emlyn Jones – they achieved miracles of transformation to meet the constantly changing use to which the various facilities were put.

The splendid welcome given by the governing bodies and the general public to the opportunities offered them by Crystal Palace, combined with efficient and economical administration, ensured that the deficits on running the Centre were kept within acceptable limits. The Department of Education and Science increased its annual grant to equal that of the GLC and, later, an agreement was reached between the GLC and that Department (later the Department of the Environment) that the cost of running the Centre should be shared equally between them.

Experience of use showed that the Centre's basic plans were not only imaginative but sound – the only flaw of any consequence was the failure to prevent the noise made in the swimming bath from reaching the sports hall, and vice versa. Certain gaps in the original provision have since been filled, and the catering facilities substantially enlarged. The most important improvement to the facilities, however, was the laying down of a new 'Tartan' athletics track in the arena, the first in Europe. In addition to being usable in all weathers, it requires virtually no maintenance or preparation for competition. The capital cost of £67,400 was met in the ratio of 3 : 1 by the Government and the GLC, and the track, which has proved of very great value to British athletics, was officially opened in May 1968 by Denis Howell, M.P., who had become Minister for Sport and Chairman of the Sports Council in 1965. After an uncertain start, Crystal Palace has now been wholeheartedly accepted as the national headquarters for British athletics.

In the nine years of its life, Crystal Palace has been the scene of too many events of national and international importance to be listed here. And any attempt to mention the distinguished sporting 'personalities' who have used the Centre would sound like an international sporting 'Who's Who'! However, it got off to a quick start, and, appropriately enough, world records were soon set up, both in the swimming pool, and on the athletics track. In its second summer, an International Sports Festival and Exhibition for ten days in August 1965, initiated by a commercial company, with the Festival being held at the Centre and the Exhibition on the vacant site adjoining, though disastrous financially for both the company concerned and the CCPR, served not only to bring the facilities to the notice of a large public but also gave many members of the CCPR's staff valuable experience of organising displays and competitions of a very high standard in the sports hall, stadium and swimming bath. Many useful lessons were learned. The Centre has proved as well adapted for conferences as for practical activity, and an outstandingly successful international conference was held on 'Sport in Education and Recreation' there in July

1966 under Arthur Gem's Chairmanship. The CCPR arranged it with grant-aid from the Department of Education and Science, and Olive Newson, one of the Council's Principal Executive Officers, was the organiser. In May 1969, Her Majesty the Queen attended the Centenary Gala of the Amateur Swimming Association there.

World championships have been held in judo and fencing at the Centre and among the sports staged at international level have been lawn tennis, table tennis, badminton, basketball, volleyball, netball, boxing and karate.

Shortcomings in the original provision for the accommodation and comfort of spectators at stadium events had long been evident, and in 1970 the hard benches were replaced by tip-up seats and better provision made for press, radio and TV reporting. Another substantial improvement was the enclosing of the previously windswept, if covered, 110 metre training area for athletics and re-laying it as a 'Tartan' track. Four of the lawn tennis courts were converted to Tennisquick in 1971. A most useful additional facility is a floodlit artificial ski slope just outside the Centre's boundary, provided in 1965 by the LCC and administered by the CCPR.

Cowes National Sailing Centre

The marked growth of interest in sailing as a recreational activity in the 'fifties has already been referred to, and, within a period of ten years, the number of sailing clubs in membership with the Royal Yachting Association had increased from 600 to about 1,200. In this expansion of sailing the CCPR had played a considerable part, having since 1951 arranged many one-week courses for beginners, schoolmasters, coaches, boat builders and others at fifteen different centres, attended in all by 8,000 people. Many of its staff were skilled and enthusiastic sailors – notably, John Bradley at headquarters, and Fred Briscoe, Alix Cowie, Ralph Logan, Bill Park and Geoff Richards in the regions. In its growing programme of sailing courses, the staff had the advice of a sailing advisory group under the chairmanship of Jason Borthwick, a group which was also responsible for the production and publication in 1966 of a *Water Sports Code* with grant-aid from the Department.

In the school world there was also a growing interest in sailing, encouraged by the Department of Education and Science who had their own Sailing Panel, ran courses for teachers and produced instructional films. A number of enthusiastic organisers of physical education, backed by their authorities, came together to form a National Schools Sailing Association which did not, however, seek representation on the CCPR until 1968.

So it was natural that both the Department and the CCPR should be eager to develop sailing in a more professional and systematic way than was possible with the existing facilities in the country, even though many sailing clubs and places like Bisham Abbey made, and were to continue to make, valuable contributions to the activity. Private discussions with a number of interested parties eventually led to a proposal to the CCPR from the Department in 1964 that the CCPR should be grant-aided to take over and develop as a National Sailing Centre a site at Cowes, which had formerly been a boat builder's yard and had been in use for a short time by the Ocean Youth Club. The site had many advantages – it was on the West bank of the river Medina with a wide stretch of sheltered water, but also with direct access to the incomparable Solent, on which training could be given in a wide range of coastal and tidal sailing. Moreover the County Authority of the Isle of Wight were in warm support of the project.

The proposal was carefully examined. The buildings available for the Centre's use were, to put it mildly, unprepossessing, being in the main wartime buildings designed to resist bombs rather than grace the waterside; the scenic outlook was unattractive; and there was opposition on the part of a section of the RYA's membership to having a new sailing centre at Cowes at all. The 'pros' and 'con's' were weighed at some length but, in the end, after a special representative meeting called by the Department, the doubters were convinced, the RYA withdrew their opposition and the CCPR accepted the Department's offer.

The national economic situation made the financial negotiations very difficult, and the CCPR had to accept substantial modifications to the plans proposed, which meant a reduction in the scale and capacity of the Centre. But the happiest factor in the whole situation was the skill and imagination with which the county architect, F. H. Booth, A.R.I.B.A., planned and supervised the creation of an attractive residence for some fifty sailors out of such unpromising material. The sea wall was repaired and strengthened, and a new concrete slipway constructed.

Bert Keeble, a schoolmaster with an expert's knowledge of sailing and a book on the subject to his credit, was appointed Warden. He started at Cowes in April 1965, but the financial moratorium imposed just afterwards meant that all building operations had to be suspended and Bert had to spend a spell in a teaching post arranged by the cooperative local education authority. Money was so tight that the CCPR launched a special appeal to help to equip the Centre and supplement the statutory grant. No help was forthcoming from the charitable trusts approached, but in 1966 and 1967, over £2,000 was raised by the CCPR from well-wishers. The Whitbread Sports Fund generously provided a 'William Whitbread Chart Room'. The total cost of establishing Cowes in the end was £127,000.

It was ready for use in June 1968, and was officially opened on 2nd May 1969 – in inclement weather, but by a characteristically cheerful Prince Philip, the Council's President, who arrived by the Royal Barge from the *Britannia*. Sir Stanley Rous presided over a somewhat curtailed outdoor ceremony, followed for the many visitors by an inspection of the Centre's premises and by unusually welcome refreshments.

A management committee for the Centre had been set up at the end of 1967 with Jason Borthwick as chairman – his experience and personal connections with the sailing world were of great value. The committee included representatives of the Royal Yachting Association, the National Schools Sailing Association and the local education authority (through Bill Barrett, its Chief Officer) and an observer from the Department. With only four years gone, the Centre was still in the 'building up' stage when it was transferred to the Sports Council in 1972, but it had proved its efficiency and usefulness. A Chief Instructor and assistant instructors had been appointed, and they were assisted by many volunteers. Its summer courses are in 'dinghy sailing' and 'dinghy racing' (elementary and advanced), 'tidal experience for inland sailors', 'coastal cruising', safety boat handling' and training and examinations for the RYA and NSSA certificates. Arranging a programme to use the Centre's resources and staff fully during the winter months has presented many problems, but courses have been held in 'sea angling', 'navigation and pilotage', 'wet suit making', 'rope and canvas

work' and 'environmental studies'. Among the important conferences held at Cowes have been two on 'Water Safety' attended by representatives of all water sports. During the Cowes
Regatta, residential accommodation is made available at the
Centre for racing crews.

The Centre is well equipped with escort vessels and a variety
of appropriate craft, including a Jollyboat, the gift of Mr.
Borthwick. Prince Philip has made to the Centre the permanent
loan of *Fairey Fox*, a 24-foot, high-speed centre-board boat
previously held at Dartmouth.

National Sports Centre for Wales

The various Centres established by the CCPR were designed for
students from Wales as much as for those from any other part
of the country – in fact, all of them were more accessible to
Wales than to the Northern parts of England. In practice,
Welsh men and women and Welsh governing bodies of sport
and Welsh branches of United Kingdom governing bodies have
made regular use of them, particularly Lilleshall, at which the
Welsh Committee and its Games and Sports Committee have
each held meetings.

But it was natural that Wales should nourish the hope that
some day it might have its own National Centre, not only as a
legitimate expression of national aspirations, but on the basis
of proved demand and need. In 1960 the CCPR's Welsh Committee called attention to the need for a multi-purpose Sports
Centre in Wales, which could be used for training and for the
staging of international events, and in May 1963, Lord Aberdare in the debate on sport in the House of Lords said that a
Sports Centre was required in Cardiff, "something in the nature
of the Crystal Palace National Recreation Centre." The survey
of sports facilities carried out by the CCPR's staff in Wales
and published in 1964 led to the appointment of a joint committee of the CCPR and the Welsh Joint Education Committee
to take action to remedy the deficiencies revealed by the survey, among which was a residential sports centre. The formulation of plans for a National Centre was greatly expedited by
the offer by Cardiff City Corporation of an $8\frac{1}{2}$-acre site for
the Centre in Sophia Gardens, in the heart of the Welsh capital.
An application to the Department of Education and Science
for a grant for a Centre in Cardiff which would also provide

accommodation for the CCPR's Welsh Office was made by the CCPR in December 1964.

Denis Howell, M.P., when Minister for Sport, met members of the committee and expressed general sympathy with the idea. The headquarters and Welsh staff of the CCPR then drew up detailed proposals for the Centre, and these were submitted to the Department in April 1966, together with an estimate of £459,000. The national 'moratorium' prevented any immediate consideration of the proposals.

The next move was in November 1967 when Denis Howell had a private meeting with representatives of the CCPR, the Sports Council for Wales (set up in 1965) and Cardiff and Glamorgan local authorities. The Minister told the meeting that the Government was prepared to grant the whole of the capital cost – by then estimated as £600,000, but later proving to be £670,000 – provided Welsh local authorities were willing to undertake to meet fifty per cent of the deficit on running the Centre, in which case he was ready to make an early public announcement. Cardiff and Glamorgan then each agreed to contribute twenty-five per cent of the deficit subject to a maximum of £10,000 a year each, and suggested that other local authorities in Wales should be approached for contributions.

The Minister's announcement was delayed by the effects of devaluation of the pound, but at length it was possible for him to announce that a capital grant of £640,000 was to be given to the CCPR for building the Centre and that a start could be made on 1st June 1969. Ingenious and economical methods of construction had been worked out by the Williamson Partnership, a firm of architects and consultant engineers, and the building contract was awarded to F. G. Minter (South Wales) Ltd. T. Glyn Davies was appointed Chairman of the Centre's Management Committee in 1969. Denis Howell had the satisfaction of cutting the first sod on 13th November 1969 and the Centre was ready for use by October 1971. David Thomas, B.A., former schoolmaster and Warden of Bingham Sports Centre, Notts., was appointed to direct the new Centre and started with the CCPR in July 1970.

The Cardiff Centre was officially opened by Princess Anne on 12th June 1972, but the bilingual invitations to the ceremony had to be sent out in the name of the Sports Council for

Wales, not the CCPR, as the CCPR Welsh Section had been officially absorbed by that Council at the end of March 1972. CCPR's debt to Eric Edwards, Acting Deputy Secretary from of a National Sports Centre for Wales and for bringing it to fruition.

At this stage, it is fitting that this history should record the CCPR's debt to Eric Edwards, acting Deputy Secretary from 1965–67 and Principal Administrative Officer from 1967–72, for the immense load of highly-skilled technical and administrative work borne by him. The sudden death of a colleague meant that all the planning for Cowes was suddenly added to all the other Centres he was administratively responsible for, including the close preparation for the official scrutiny by the Department of the plans and estimates for the Cardiff Centre. His modesty would not easily reveal how tirelessly he worked for the smooth running of the Centres, including Crystal Palace.

The facilities at Cardiff include two halls, size 120 ft × 120 ft. and 120 ft. × 50 ft. (the latter being divisible into two as necessary), a gymnasium 60 ft. × 45 ft, a 24 m. swimming training pool (the Centre's proximity to the Empire Pool built for the Commonwealth Games of 1958 made a larger pool unnecessary), a fitness training annexe, a rifle range, four squash courts, two lecture rooms, social and refreshment rooms, together with residential accommodation for 60 students and staff and offices for the Sports Council and a number of Welsh governing bodies of sport. Outside is a grass pitch, a floodlit hard porous area and an area scheduled for floodlit lawn tennis courts.

In its first year, the Centre was used by 240,000 persons, and by over 180,000 in the following six months. Events held there have included a Festival of Movement and Dance, a Health and Beauty Rally, and national or international championships in netball, basketball, trampoline, men's and women's gymnastics, table tennis, volleyball, fencing, weightlifting, archery, judo and indoor hockey. For some types of events the main hall can accommodate as many as 2,000 spectators.

Holme Pierrepont National Water Sports Centre

The last of the National Recreation Centres with whose establishment and management the CCPR was concerned was designed to meet a need in the national sports provision which had long been evident. No suitable course existed in the country adequate for competitive rowing or canoeing by international standards and the facilities for certain other water sports were also very limited. Henley, used for the 1948 Olympic Games, could no longer provide what was needed, and the use of a mountain lake in Snowdonia for the aquatic events in the Commonwealth Games of 1958, though picturesque and imaginative, entailed severe drawbacks.

The construction of a National Water Sports Centre at Holme Pierrepont, three miles south-east of Nottingham, and lying alongside the River Trent, was made a practicable reality by the cooperation between the Nottinghamshire County Council and the Department of the Environment (on the recommendation of the Sports Council and the Countryside Commission), both of which gave grant-aid to raise the £1,500,000 required, with some assistance from private sponsors. Official approval to the project was given in 1969, and the CCPR, whose technical staff had a good deal to do with the initiation and working out of the detailed plans, in close cooperation with offices of the County Planning Department, was asked to administer the new Centre. G. S. Dibley, a member of the Council's staff since 1955, was appointed to be its Director in 1971, and the water facilities were in use by the end of that year. The Centre was soon playing an important role in the national training and competitive programmes of the Amateur Rowing Association, the British Canoe Union and the British Water Ski Federation, each of which is represented on the Centre's Management Committee, the Chairman of which is Ernest Major.

By the progress of events to be described later, the responsibility for administering the Centre was transferred from the CCPR to the Sports Council in 1972, and it was officially opened by Edward Heath, then Prime Minister, on a perfect July afternoon in 1973, in the presence of a large and distinguished gathering, including the Chairmen of the Nottinghshire County Council, the Countryside Commission, the Sports Council and the new CCPR.

The Centre, which grew from an idea conceived by the Nottinghamshire County Council, was created and moulded out of the waste excavation material from a derelict 270-acre area of worked-out gravel pits, and consists of a unique combination of facilities – a central 2215 m. by 135 m. stretch of water providing a 2,000 m. regatta course with six rowing or nine canoeing lanes, to be used for both training and competition, as well as for sailing, water-skiing, hydroplaning, long-distance and underwater swimming on a programmed basis. There are separate lagoons for angling and water skiing practice, and the whole centre is set within a 'country park', made from spoil and attractively landscaped with trees, picnic spots and play areas, which it is intended to extend for horse riding and other activities.

Adjoining the regatta course is a hostel for seventy residents in single and double rooms, dining room, lounge and refreshment bars overlooking the water course, conference and lecture rooms, alongside which are boat houses and trailer park, a judging tower, commentators' box and a stand for spectators. Across the water from the hostel are sloping, grassy banks from which many thousands more spectators can watch the water activities. A feature of the scene is a large electronic 'information board' for results, times and announcements. It is later hoped to add an artificial canoe-slalom course with water piped from the Trent. The Centre is well situated geographically, with excellent trunk routes from most parts of the country.

In 1972, the Centre received the Conservation Award of the Royal Institute of Chartered Surveyors and *The Times,* a 'special commendation' from the British Tourist Authority, and the 'Restored Gravel Workings Award' of the Sand and Gravel Association. It is playing an important part in national and regional training and competition for water sports, but also gives the local community an attractive centre for unorganised recreation. In its first full season of operation, the Centre was the scene of world championship events in rowing and hydroplaning, international regattas in rowing and canoeing, and national championships in rowing, water ski racing and canoeing.

CHAPTER EIGHT

The CCPR in Wales, Scotland, and Northern Ireland

The objects of the CCPR in Wales, Scotland and Northern Ireland, its methods of working, and the qualifications required from members of the staff were very much the same as they were in England, although there were some inevitable differences in the problems encountered and the nature of the success achieved. As an organisation, the CCPR was a single whole, incorporated under the same Memorandum and Articles of Association. The four countries within it had the same Patron, the same President, the same General Secretary. The national bodies concerned with physical recreation in any of the four countries were equally represented on the same Council. The policy of the organisation was laid down by the Council in Annual General Meeting and administered by the Executive Committee appointed by that Council on which all members served in a personal not a representative capacity and on which, also, members from any part of the United Kingdom could be nominated to serve. The technical and administrative staff were the staff of a single national, United Kingdom body, who met together at least once a year for staff conferences, and the headquarters technical advisers 'advised' the staff in all four countries of the United Kingdom equally.

These reflections are made to remove any misconceptions that the CCPR was in any sense a federation of separate and autonomous bodies. From the outset the Council worked throughout England and Wales and it was the Council that was invited to extend its activities to Scotland and Northern Ireland successively, on the strength of its reputation as an efficient and successful body with an exceedingly able person as its chief administrative officer. It was not a case of bodies on similar lines to the CCPR being established in Scotland or Northern Ireland, though the CCPR was wise enough to set up committees to take responsibility for guiding its work in those countries and in Wales, to each of which was deputed a wide measure of freedom of action, subject to general conformity with the Council's policy and the acceptance of the principle that the staff was a unity.

This Chapter, therefore, does not purport to give the history of the CCPR in Wales, Scotland and Northern Ireland. It merely calls attention to certain special characteristics of the work in those countries, and would be misleading unless read in conjunction with the rest of the book as a whole. Many of the distinctive elements in the story of the CCPR in the four countries consist of obstacles and difficulties which did not exist elsewhere. In some cases these were formidable and persistent, but, in singling them out for attention, as a fair record must, it is to be hoped that they will not give a false impression of the whole position.

Wales

Wales figured in the CCRPT's programme from its formation in 1935 and its first Annual Report mentions Bangor, Llandudno and Wrexham as among the places visited by the Organising Secretary or one of the Representatives. Women's Institutes in Cardiganshire, Merioneth and Pembroke asked for help, and the Welsh Council of Social Service showed every desire to cooperate. The Urdd Gobaith Cymru (the Welsh League of Youth) and Sir Percy Watkins were among its first members, and the former was represented on its first Technical Advisory Committee. In the second Annual Report, work in six Welsh counties was recorded, including three fortnight's visits from members of the very small technical staff. Subsequent reports give details of expanding work in Wales, from 1937 in cooperation with the Welsh Area Fitness Committee. As has been noted, Lowther College, near Abergele, was the scene of the Council's main Summer Schools for many years.

By the outbreak of war, three full-time Representatives were working in Wales, and because of the special wartime problems in the South, attention was turned to work with adults, especially in industry. The first step in setting up a committee in Wales to guide the staff was the formation, at the suggestion of the Ministry of Labour, of a Welsh Advisory Committee in June 1941, with Sir William Jenkins, M.P., as chairman and B. B. Thomas (later Sir Ben) as deputy, and with representation from the Ministry of Labour and the Welsh Department of the Board of Education. The illness and subsequent death of Sir William and the transfer of B. B. Thomas to another post led to the disbandment of the Advisory Committee. At the same time, the Welsh Youth Committee had set up a sub-committee to concern itself with the work of the CCRPT for young people. Members of this sub-committee held a meeting with the Council's General Purposes Committee in London under Lord Hampden's chairmanship in September 1942 to discuss the setting up of a Welsh Committee for the CCRPT, but negotiations broke down on the issue of the relative responsibilities of the CCRPT and the Welsh Youth Committee for the appointment and direction of the staff.

The next move was a meeting between Sir Wynn Wheldon, Permanent Secretary, and other representatives of the Welsh Department of the Board of Education and the CCRPT in London, when it was agreed that a Welsh Committee for the Council should be set up in May 1944 under the temporary chairmanship of Mrs Hopkin Morris. This committee appointed Mrs. Martha Mostyn as part-time administrative officer for the Council in Wales for the duration of the war, starting in September 1944. In December 1944, T. Glyn Davies, then Director of Education for Montgomeryshire, succeeded Mrs. Hopkin Morris as chairman, an office which he retained until the CCPR in Wales came to an end in March 1972. After 1949, the chairman of the Welsh Committee was 'ex officio' a member of the CCPR's Executive Committee and, in later years, of its General Purposes and Finance Committee as well, and regular reports on Welsh affairs were given to the Executive by Mr. Davies or a member of the staff. The Executive Committee also had an official representative on the Welsh Committee, and the Author acted in this capacity for some twenty years.

There were certain special problems attaching to the CCPR's work in Wales. One was the geographical factor. Apart from the counties of Glamorgan and Monmouth in the South and parts of Flintshire and Denbighshire in the North, the country is predominantly rural and mountainous in character, with difficult communications, especially in war-time, and it was hard to get people together for the sort of propaganda, training and coaching events which the CCRPT ran successfully elsewhere, a difficulty encountered equally, of course, by the youth organisations and sports bodies.

But an even more fundamental problem was the attitude to the CCRPT and the CCPR of local education authorities in Wales. In general, these were far less well-disposed to cooperatting with voluntary bodies than their counterparts in England, and did not give the Representatives the warm welcome they received in most English areas. In 1941, a factual report submitted to the Welsh Advisory Committee by Ivor Thomas, Regional Welfare Officer of the Ministry of Labour for Wales, of his interviews, and attempts at interviews, with local education authorities in South Wales revealed an uncooperative attitude to the work the CCRPT were trying to do.

The composition of the Welsh Committee set up in 1944 could only include representation of local education authorities on it by inviting any of them which wished to make use of the CCPR's services to appoint a representative. Only five accepted the invitation, three being counties in North Wales, and of these, one or two cooperated in name but not in fact. The attitude of the physical education organisers employed by those authorities was an important and often unfriendly factor in the situation. After some private negotiations, the Welsh Joint Education Committee appointed in 1950 an 'Assessor' to serve on the Welsh Committee and in 1960 the WJEC agreed to appoint four nominees on the Welsh Committee and became represented on the main CCPR Council. Though Plas y Brenin had been established in North Wales in 1955, it was reported to the Welsh General Purposes Committee of the CCPR in 1963, that the majority of education authorities in South Wales had not even accepted invitations to visit the Centre. The facts have been quoted to show that, whatever advantages the CCPR's staff enjoyed in Wales, cooperation with many local authorities was not a reality until fairly late in its history.

The next major difficulty was that of staffing. Except during the war, the CCPR normally had an equal staffing ratio of men Representatives in its first twenty years or so, but this was never true of Wales. Indeed, for many years the CCPR lacked even a single woman Representative in any part of Wales. Many explanations can be offered for this fact, but fact it was, and it imposed a handicap on the development of work for girls' and women's organisations. Though the men's staff in Wales averaged between four and five, there was never at any time since the war more than one woman Representative.

The other principal staffing difficulty was that of covering the whole area of Wales in such a way that members of the staff were not lonely outposts, out of touch with the rest of the team. For most of the CCPR's lifetime, one man Representative worked in North Wales and one in West Wales, working from their homes or a small office. It is a great credit to those who worked so much on their own that they achieved as much as they did, and retained the resilience and cheerfulness which a CCPR Representative needed if he or she was to be successful in the work.

A bright feature of the Welsh situation had always been the real interest and friendship shown to the Representatives in their work by H.M. Inspectors of Schools, men and women alike. They not only attended regularly and most helpfully at all CCPR Welsh committees but were at pains to do all they could to give the staff their personal advice and encouragement, and help them in their contacts. They would not expect their names to be recorded here but they can be assured of the lasting gratitude of the CCPR's staff whom they helped so much.

In response to representations from the staff, the Welsh Committee in May 1946 wisely rescinded its decision to transfer the Welsh office from Cardiff to Newtown, Montgomeryshire. E. H. Prater, a physical educationist and also a graduate in French of the University of Wales, was appointed full-time secretary of the CCPR in Wales in June 1946. During some very difficult years, Ted Prater worked hard to promote and extend the Council's services to many organisations, covering a wide field of activities, including new and untried ones such as pony trekking. He had good organising ability and in 1947 led the group of fifty British leaders who attended the course in Strasbourg referred to in Chapter Five. As Honorary Secretary of the British Empire and Commonwealth Games Council for Wales, he acted as manager for the Welsh team that competed at the Commonwealth Games in Vancouver in 1954 and played a leading part in the negotiations that led to the Commonwealth Games' being held in Cardiff in 1958. He left the CCPR in 1959 and became Welsh Secretary of the Duke of Edinburgh Award.

Harold Oakes, an Englishman from St. Helens who had won his spurs as a Representative of the CCPR in the Yorkshire Region, was appointed to succeed Ted Prater. He has a fine record of achievement in Wales. He got on well with the Welsh, and built up a notably fine team spirit among his colleagues. He was given the status of Regional Officer in 1962, and Cadfan Davies moved down from North Wales to become Senior Representative. Harold Oakes had the satisfaction of seeing his dream of a National Sports Centre for Wales in Cardiff come true, and he has become the first director of the autonomous Sports Council for Wales.

Apart from giving the staff a sense of support and encouragement in their difficult and sometimes lonely jobs, the various committees and sub-committees of the CCPR in Wales served a useful purpose in bringing together representatives of governing bodies of sport and voluntary youth organisations with each other and with representatives of statutory bodies. One committee that was often talked about but never set up was an outdoor activities advisory committee. The obstacle was that, though Wales is pre-eminently a country where non-competitive outdoor activities thrive most gloriously (when the weather permits!), the national voluntary bodies organising those activities and working hard to see that the facilities which make them possible shall not be diminished in almost every case have their headquarters in England. The development of those activities in Wales as in England was always a concern of the CCPR's Outdoor Activities Sub-committee, which sat in London.

Many men and women gave great service to the CCPR's Welsh Committees, some over a long period. For nearly all his very long tenure of office, Glyn Davies enjoyed the warm support of Lt-Col. Ralph Hawkins as his deputy, and Colonel Hawkins was also chairman for most of its life of the Welsh Games and Sports Committee, which was set up in March 1950, and grew from small beginnings – it lapsed in 1957 and was revived in 1960 – to be an important and influential body. Other committee chairmen giving valuable service were Roy Evans, Arthur Rees and the late Geoffrey Gadd, the last two as successive chairmen of the committee for North Wales.

Reference was made in Chapter Six to the important International Physical Education Conference held at Barry Training College from 11th to 17th July 1958 as a curtain-raiser to the Commonwealth Games. Attended by 186 men and women from twenty-five Commonwealth countries, it was organised by the UK Committee for International Conferences on Physical

Education, of which P.C.C. was the honorary secretary, with the help of a Welsh Advisory Committee, of which the chairman was Professor Arthur Watkins and the honorary secretary Dr. Emlyn Stephens, Director of Education for Glamorgan.

Apart from the very many local training events it ran in various localities, the CCPR organised its own annual residential courses using the splendid facilities of University College of Wales, Aberystwyth, and these continued successfully each summer without a break from 1961 to 1972.

An appointment of particular interest in Wales was that of Ray Williams to be the Welsh Rugby Union's first national coaching organiser in 1967. Ray had served on the CCPR's staff as a Representative and Senior Representative in the West Midlands since 1956.

After the publication of the Wolfenden Committee's Report (to be referred to in the next chapter), Sir John Wolfenden addressed a crowded conference convened by the WJEC and the CCPR jointly in the Cardiff City Hall in July 1961. This led to the staff's being commissioned to make a survey of indoor facilities for physical recreation in Wales. The survey was published by the CCPR in 1964 under the title of *Sports Facilities in Wales* and had considerable impact, not least in emphasising the strength of opinion in favour of a National Sports Centre for Wales.

In pursuance of the Government's policy of setting up Regional Sports Councils throughout the country, a Sports Council for Wales was inaugurated in April 1965, and Harold Oakes appointed its secretary. The work of this Council led to a drastic change of emphasis in the activities of the staff, which became more administrative and as much concerned with facilities and grants as with training events. Nevertheless, so far as staff resources permitted, the Council's normal services continued. But from 1965, the CCPR's history in Wales becomes more a history of the Sports Council for Wales which it is not within the scope of this volume to cover.

The final meeting of the CCPR's Welsh Committee was held on 24th March 1972 and brought to an end the existence of the CCPR in Wales with words of appreciation to the chairman, the deputy chairman and the staff.

*   *   *

Scotland

From its earliest days, it had been the CCPR's hope and intention to work in Scotland as well as in England and Wales, and some Scots were among its first individual members. Early Annual Reports and committee papers make many references to those hopes and to a few exploratory visits to Scotland. In 1937, an application was made to the Scottish Advisory Fitness Council for a grant to enable the CCRPT to appoint a man and a woman Representative for work in Scotland. This was unsuccessful. Similar overtures during the war to the Scottish Youth Committee were turned down on grounds of expense. As none of its statutory grant could be used for work outside England and Wales, nothing could be done in Scotland until the end of 1944 when, as briefly mentioned in Chapter Four, the CCPR was officially invited by the Scottish Education Department to extend its field of work to Scotland.

The Committee had no hesitation in appointing May Brown as its Scottish Secretary, an appointment she held with cheerful and sagacious efficiency until her retirement in 1968, her services to Scotland being recognised by the M.B.E. in 1963. She was already well known in Scotland, not least for her wartime broadcasts of early morning fitness exercises, and she quickly recruited a staff of Representatives – Doris Robertson and Audrey Bell, who were the first, closely followed by 'Jock' Kerr-Hunter on his release from the Navy, Catherine Loader and Winnie Taylor.

Scottish accents, Scottish Country Dancing, and colour transparencies of activity in the Scottish Highlands soon became a feature of the CCPR's periodic staff conferences, which listened gladly to the success stories of all that was happening within the territory of this new addition to its strength.

A Scottish Section had been formed in 1945 with a strong Schottish Committee under the chairmanship of W. J. Stuart, who was succeeded in 1949 by Dr. Stewart Mackintosh, Director of Education for Glasgow. Kay Evans and George MacPartlin, the Council's Senior Advisers, helped the new body to develop on right lines technically and enjoyed their frequent visits to Scotland, and May Brown would be the first to recognise how much the sound administrative pattern owed to the example and advice provided by P.C.C.

Summer Schools were held at St. Andrew's University, which

drew many people from south of the border, and many large-scale propaganda sporting events were staged in various towns and cities, for example, the Youth and Recreation Exhibition at Kelvin Hall, Glasgow, for over a fortnight in September 1947, and the Festival of Sport at Waverley Market, Edinburgh, for ten days in February 1951, which attracted 80,000 spectators. In 1949, the Section was grant-aided by the Department to appoint H. A. L. Chapman as the first full-time Athletics Coach for Scotland.

But a most exciting development was the offer to the Scottish Section by the Scottish Education Department of Glenmore Lodge, a Forestry Commission's property in the Cairngorms, to serve for three years as an experimental centre for the development of outdoor activities, the Department agreeing to meet any maintenance deficits. The offer was eagerly accepted in 1947, and the new Centre was officially opened in September 1948 by the Secretary of State for Scotland, with Robert Clark as its first Warden.

Glenmore Lodge, called 'the Scottish Centre of Outdoor Training', soon attracted students by the beauty of its surroundings and the wide variety of activities – it could serve as a base for mountain walking, rock climbing, camping, sailing, canoeing, and field studies – and by the quality of the instruction provided. Stewart Mackintosh became chairman of its management committee, and his interest in it led to its extensive and regular use for part of the year by successive parties of boys and girls from Glasgow schools, a use that was its financial salvation and, after some years, imitated by Edinburgh and Lanarkshire Education Authorities. After the initial example set by Anstey College of Physical Education, it was used each year to provide training in outdoor activities for students from universities and other colleges of physical education as well as for members of the general public.

Charles Cromar, already a CCPR Representative in Scotland, became Warden of Glenmore in 1949, and the Centre's success led the Department to extend the lease. After a few more years, a grant was made to enable a new purpose-built Glenmore Lodge to be built not far from the old in 1969, a Centre which has made under its successive wardens an outstanding contribution to the development of mountain leadership training in the United Kingdom. Relations between Glenmore Lodge and

Plas y Brenin were always those of friends and partners in a pioneering enterprise.

But this later development of Glenmore Lodge lies outside the history of the CCPR for, as early as 1951, it was made known to the Council's Honorary Officers and General Secretary that the current of national opinion in Scotland as well as the Scottish Committee's growing self-confidence and desire to handle its own affairs without any reference to London, dictated that the Section should seek constitutional separation from the CCPR and become the fully autonomous Scottish Council of Physical Recreation. Arguments were put forward by the CCPR's General Purposes and Finance Committee as to the advantages of preserving a single body to speak for physical recreation in the whole of the U.K. and of maintaining a united staff, cooperating with and learning from each other. P.C.C., in a private (and prophetic) letter written to Dr. Mackintosh in November 1951, expressed her deep inner personal conviction that the proposal for autonomy was a retrogressive one "Now that the peak of CCPR unity has been reached with the accession of Northern Ireland," she wrote, "the Council is competent to speak with one voice on really big matters affecting physical recreation national policy, to bring to bear the full potential of every part of the United Kingdom and to pursue any decision reached with singleness of purpose. Split it into parts (two to begin with and, without doubt, four later on) and you at once dissipate its force, destroy its *assured* singleness of purpose and open the door for unilateral action – in short, you lessen the strength of the whole and of each of its component parts." At the same time, she added, if Scotland, after considering her arguments, still felt that separation was the right policy, she would advise the Executive as General Secretary that they should agree.

The 'winds of change' were blowing too strongly. To the Scottish Committee the case for autonomy transcended all other arguments, and the Scottish Council of Physical Recreation was incorporated as an independent body in June 1953. Many personal links were preserved and cooperation in some spheres continued, but the organic unity of the CCPR as a United Kingdom body was broken, never to be restored.

In the years that have followed, the Scottish Council played a big part in developing physical recreation in Scotland. It worked in cooperation with the Scottish Education Department, the Scottish Tourist Board, local education authorities and all its member-organisations, earning their continued respect and confidence. In 1958, Inverclyde was established near Largs as a Scottish National Recreation Centre with a grant of £125,000 from the King George Memorial Foundation, and was officially opened by H.M. The Queen. May Brown became Secretary of the Advisory Scottish Sports Council when it was formed in 1965, and she was succeeded in that office by Ken Hutchison, C.A., when he followed her as General Secretary of the SCPR in 1968. When the Scottish Sports Council became an autonomous, executive body, with its own Royal Charter, the SCPR's staff and assets were transferred to that body, Ken Hutchison became the chief executive officer, and after nineteen years of separate existence the Scottish Council of Physical Recreation's formal life came to an end on the 15th November 1972.

Northern Ireland

In October 1947, the Ministry of Education for Northern Ireland followed the example of Scotland and invited the CCPR to send two officials to Belfast to discuss the possibility of the CCPR's extending its work to Northern Ireland. The invitation was gladly accepted and plans submitted as to how this might be done. P.C.C. suggested that a staff consisting of a Secretary with technical knowledge and administrative ability, and two Technical Representatives should be appointed at an estimated annual budget of £4,210. This was more than the Ministry were prepared to spend and, after somewhat protracted negotiations, agreement was reached in November 1948 that the staff should consist of a man and a woman Representative, at an annual cost of £2,630.

The first CCPR Representative appointed to take charge of the Council's work in the Province early in 1949 was Ford Spence, a devoted Scot who was never known to appear in public not wearing the kilt. He was given a warm welcome and made a vigorous start from a small office in Belfast. Later that year, Joan Clayton joined him as a woman colleague, but her health failed and she was succeeded by Joyce Robinson the following year, by the November of which the Ministry were so pleased with the work being done that they agreed to the appointment of an additional man Representative, the annual budget being increased to about £4,500.

Requests for help were received from all parts of the Province and contacts gradually enlarged, the staff being received with warm appreciation. Shortage of playing fields and other facilities was acute, the organisation of most sports was weak, and among the special difficulties met was that few events could be arranged on Sundays because of the general attitude to Sunday observance. But progress was steady. Summer Schools were held at Portrush and, later at Stranmillis College, at which new sports such as judo, fencing and basketball were introduced. Close contact was also made with the Ulster College of Physical Education when it was established in 1955, the Principal of which, Miss O. M. Pim, was a firm ally of the Council and served on its Northern Ireland Committee.

The Ministry's officials were always most friendly and helpful, though negotiations about grants from year to year were no easier there than elsewhere! J. M. Benn was the Ministry's liaison officer with the CCPR until 1963, when he was appointed the Ministry's Permanent Secretary. Later, Mr. Benn became Commissioner for Complaints and Ombudsman for Northern Ireland. As liaison officer, he was followed by L. Arndell. Both liaison officers and their recent successor, J. Finney, showed great support for the CCPR and attended its Executive Committee and Annual General Meetings in London whenever possible. They were well backed up by L. B. Dickinson and Rhona Jackson, the Ministry's Inspectors of Physical Education, and the CCPR's staff in Northern Ireland never lacked friends at high level.

To establish some form of democratic foundation for the Council's work, an Advisory Panel was set up in 1952 under the chairmanship of W. H. Smyth, who had initiated the original invitation to the CCPR when he was at the Ministry and had now retired. In 1954, Ford Spence left the CCPR to enter the hotel business in Scotland and was succeeded by Eric Edwards, who had been a Representative in London and South-East Region for the previous three years. His first job was to establish a CCPR Section in Northern Ireland, on similar lines to the earlier Scottish Section, electing its own committees and holding annual general meetings. The inaugural meeting of the Section in October 1955 was presided over by Lord Wakehurst, the Governor of Northern Ireland, who agreed to become President. Sir Stanley Rous and P.C.C. attended the meeting to wish the new Section well.

Its strength increased until it represented sixty-five Northern Ireland organisations and had nineteen individual members.

Lord Wakehurst retained office as President until he retired from the position of Governor, and his successors in that high office, Lord Erskine of Rerrick and Lord Grey of Naunton both accepted the presidency of the Section. In 1954, Philip Smiles had succeeded W. H. Smyth as chairman of the Northern Ireland Panel and became chairman of the Northern Ireland Committee when the Section was formed. He was followed by Captain T. D. Morrison in 1961, who handed over to Roy Hunter, Director of Education for County Londonderry, in 1962. Mr. Hunter served until the Section became the Northern Ireland Council of Physical Recreation in 1972, representing Northern Ireland on the main Executive and General Purposes and Finance Committees.

The work in Northern Ireland followed the normal CCPR pattern of giving advisory and practical services to all bodies trying to promote physical recreation – local authorities, sports and outdoor activity bodies, and youth organisations. The value of contacts with England and Wales was repeatedly emphasised by the people of Northern Ireland, and many students from there – some helped by Whitbread bursaries – attended courses at National Recreation Centres. Relations with Plas y Brenin in the development of outdoor activities were particularly close. John Disley visited the Province and members of the Northern Ireland staff got valuable training and experience at Plas y Brenin. The technical advisers spent time in Northern Ireland whenever possible. George Hickling, the CCPR's specialist in weight lifting and handling paid a visit. So too did most of the National Coaches of English governing bodies, including Walter Winterbottom, then the Football Association's Director of Coaching. He spoke at a weekend conference of Northern Ireland governing bodies in 1957, designed to spread the gospel of coaching, though the effect of his message is said to have been somewhat diluted by the fact that earlier in the day the un-rated Irish League team had beaten his own team of English League 'stars' in Belfast!

The development of outdoor activities – including mountaineering, camping and canoeing – featured strongly in the programme. In 1954, Ballagh Cottage, a small property in the Mourne Mountains which could accommodate a maximum of seventeen people at a time, was rented and converted as a base for mountain activities and proved a most valuable acquisition. It was in great demand, especially at weekends, and was useful evidence as to the need for a residential centre on a larger scale. A grant from the Ministry of about £20,000 enabled a start to be made on establishing the Tollymore Mountain Centre. The Pilgrim Trust added a welcome £500 and the NSDF helped with the purchase of equipment. Lord Hunt paid a visit to Northern Ireland to 'cut the first sod' in October 1966. Financial restrictions caused a delay, but the very attractive log-built Centre, with sleeping accommodation for twenty-four, was ready for use by 1968, and was officially opened by Captain W. J. Long, Minister of Education, in May 1970. Edward Hawkins was appointed as Warden/Instructor in 1970 and the Centre has been well used. It has an advisory committee under the chairmanship of Alistair McDonald, Director of Physical Education at Queen's University. A Mountain Leadership Training Board has been set up for Northern Ireland, with L. B. Dickinson now retired from his position as Inspector, as chairman.

Games and sports were not neglected, and a great deal of administrative and secretarial help has been given to the sports bodies as well as technical advice in the development of their coaching schemes. The CCPR was constantly pressing the Government and local authorities for more and better sports facilities; both indoor and outdoor, and particularly for purpose-built multi-sports centres. In 1960, the Belfast Corporation agreed to convert the large 80 ft. by 40 ft. gymnasium in the old Victoria Barracks in that City for use as a Recreation Centre suitable for a variety of indoor sports, the CCPR agreeing to administer its use. The CCPR ran many courses there, used it as a fitness training centre, and leased it to many different sports bodies for regular use by rota. But as it stood in an area of the City highly vulnerable to sectarian violence, its use as a Recreation Centre had reluctantly to be brought to an end in 1969.

The need for Indoor Sports Centres has now been recognised in Northern Ireland and plans for a number of new Centres have been agreed, the first at Antrim being completed. Many swimming pools have been recently opened and, in spite of the turbulent political situation, many extensive new sports facilities should be in use soon.

The special recommendation of the Wolfenden Committee on Sport in 1960 that the grant to the CCPR in Northern Ireland should be increased so that it could offer greater administrative and secretarial help to the governing bodies of sport was promptly accepted by the Ministry. This led to a feeling of closer partnership between the sports bodies and the CCPR's staff.

Meanwhile the CCPR's staff was expanding. Eric Edwards left for an administrative post at CCPR Headquarters in 1958, having accomplished much constructive work, and he was welcomed in Northern Ireland soon afterwards as P.C.C.'s successor as the Executive's representative on their committee. He was succeeded as Secretary of the Northern Ireland Section by John Wheatley, a Representative in the London and South-East Region, who led the Section to new fields of achievement until he was appointed Regional Officer in the South-West in 1969, leaving behind a fine record of service to Northern Ireland in his years there. He had strong interests in athletics and mountaineering and was deputy leader of the Ulster Expedition to the Taurus Mountains for a month in 1964. This consisted of twenty-eight adult mountaineers, botanists, ornithologists, surveyors and photographers, accompanied by twelve young holders of the Duke of Edinburgh's Award.

John Wheatley was followed as Northern Ireland's Secretary by George Glasgow, who had been a Representative in Northern Ireland since 1955, and later a Senior Representative. There was particular satisfaction in Northern Ireland that one of its own sons had proved himself worthy of that position.

The relations between the CCPR and its Northern Ireland Section were outstandingly warm and friendly, and the Northern Ireland Committee were at pains to emphasise their appreciation of the relationship. This was expressed most eloquently by Lord Grey, Governor of Northern Ireland and President of the Section, when proposing a vote of thanks to Prince Philip at the CCPR's Annual General Meeting in 1971, a speech which all who heard it will long remember for its dignified yet moving references to the crisis through which his country was passing at that moment. In his address at the Section's Annual General Meeting in December 1971, the Minister of Education Capt. The Rt. Hon. W. J. Long, M.P., said: 'We have always valued especially having a body which operated here under day-to-day local control but which at the same time drew strength and knowledge from the national organisation.'

As we shall see, the events which led to the setting up of an independent Sports Council for Northern Ireland inevitably involved the weakening of the constitutional and personal links which had bound the Northern Ireland to the CCPR since 1948. A Northern Ireland Council of Physical Recreation is continuing as the voice of sport and 'a consultative body on relevant matters'. Early in 1974, the appointment of a Northern Ireland Sports Council was announced under the chairmanship of Colonel E. D. R. Shearer, C.B.E., T.D., D.L., who has had long and close connections with the CCPR's work.

Though much still remains to be done, the achievements of the CCPR in its twenty-four years of work in Northern Ireland were substantial and a cause for justifiable pride on the part of all who contributed to them, especially for the staff – administrative, technical and secretarial – whose cheerful efficiency remained unimpaired in spite of so many adverse conditions. Seen in perspective, what they have done will bear much fruit in terms of human well-being and happiness.

CHAPTER NINE

The Wolfenden Committee on Sport:
1957 - 1960

The circumstances leading to the setting up of the Wolfenden Committee on Sport have been explained briefly in Chapter Six. It was given the following terms of reference : "To examine the factors affecting the development of games, sports and outdoor activities in the United Kingdom and to make recommendations to the Central Council of Physical Recreation as to any practical measures which should be taken by statutory or voluntary bodies in order that these activities may play their full part in promoting the general welfare of the community".

Sir John Wolfenden agreed to accept the Chairmanship as soon as he could be free from the immediate aftermath of the Report of the Home Office Departmental Committee on Homosexual Offences and Prostitution, bearing his name, and was published in 1957. Sir John was then Vice-Chancellor of Reading University and had an exceptionally wide knowledge of the whole field of education and the social services. His experience of sport included that of having been a hockey 'blue' at Oxford and Headmaster of two Public Schools.

The other members who agreed to serve on the Committee were Mrs. Mabel Allen, a physical educationist and former H.M.I.; Dr. Gerald Ellison, then Bishop of Chester and now Bishop of London, who had been a rowing 'blue' and umpire of a long series of University boat races; Miss Betty Clark, Headmistress of Benenden School; Sir Godfrey Ince, former Permanent Secretary of the Ministry of Labour and National Service and then Chairman of Cable and Wireless, Ltd., who had close connections with cricket and soccer; Jack Longland, Director of Education for Derbyshire and, among other things, a former Cambridge athletics 'blue' and Everest climber; David Munrow, Director of the Physical Education Department of Birmingham University; Tony Pawson, an industrial welfare officer and part-time sports journalist, who had had an outstanding career as Association footballer and cricketer, with an Oxford 'blue' at both; and Sir Arthur Porritt, the distinguished surgeon, famous Oxford and Olympic sprinter, and member of the International Olympic Committee, who later became Governor-General of New Zealand and is now Lord Porritt.

Between them the members of the Committee were able to bring to their inquiry a wide range of relevant knowledge and experience. None was a member of the CCPR's Executive – indeed only two were members of the Council – and they could approach their task with complete independence. The Author was appointed Secretary to the Committee – being relieved of some of his CCPR duties for the purpose – and Shirley Brewer (now Mrs. Cockerill), an Oxford graduate with secretarial training, became his Assistant, having been sent by Heaven in answer to an advertisement.

After the terms of reference and composition of the Committee were settled, its early work was accompanied by some slight controversy. The British Olympic Association, the British Empire and Commonwealth Games Council and the National Playing Fields Association each made representations that they had not been given their "rightful place" in setting up the Committee, possibly fearing that the CCPR might attempt to use it to increase its own power and influence at the expense of other bodies. Sir Frederick Browning, who held office on all three of the bodies as well as being a member of the CCPR's Executive, asked that it should be recorded in the Executive's Minutes that he greatly regretted the complaints received from the three bodies, which he regarded as unjustified, a judgement which subsequent events may be considered to have confirmed. Lord Exeter and Lord Luke, chairmen of the BOA and NPFA respectively, were among the first to be invited, with their colleagues, to give oral evidence to the Committee, and suspicions were, it is hoped, removed.

Then the Scottish Council of Physical Recreation, having agreed to the suggestion that the inquiry should cover the whole of the United Kingdom, together with the Welsh Committee of the CCPR, wrote separately to Sir John Wolfenden claiming direct representation on the Committee from Scotland and Wales so that special consideration should be given to the position in those countries. Scotland added a demand that the Committee should present its report to the SCPR as well as to the CCPR. Sir John replied that the Committee had decided against having any geographical basis for its membership, and that the straightforward constitutional position was that a Committee of that kind reported to the body that had set it up. To ensure that no special factors in Scotland, Wales or Northern Ireland should be overlooked, however, the Committee invited the SCPR and the Welsh and Northern Ireland Committees of the CCPR each to appoint up to three 'advisers' or 'assessors', who would be given the opportunity of sitting with the Committee to discuss their own special problems. This course was followed, though it was found on further examination that, apart from certain minor differences arising from geography or tradition, the main "factors affecting the development of games, sports and outdoor activities" were very much the same in all parts of the United Kingdom.

After Sir John had paid a special visit to the CCPR's staff conference to learn from them what issues they would like the Committee to include in its discussions, the Committee held its first meeting at the CCPR's headquarters in Bedford Square in January 1958. During the next two years, the Committee were given written and oral evidence from a vast number of organisations and individuals, all of which was received on the understanding that it would be kept confidential to the Committee. Its Report was presented to the CCPR in September 1960 and was published at once under the title *Sport and the Community*. By February 1961, the first edition of 10,000 was exhausted and a further 5,000 printed.

As some copies of this report are still available for purchase from any office of the Sports Council, it is not proposed in this Chapter to do more than call attention to some of the Committee's recommendations particularly affecting the CCPR, and to throw certain light on the evidence received by the Committee which is not contained in the Report itself.

In the course of its work, the Committee had many contacts with members of both Houses of Parliament. Among those who gave early oral evidence was Philip Noel-Baker, M.P., both as an individual and as Chairman of the Parliamentary Sports Committee. The latter was an informal all-Party group of Members of both Houses interested in sport, which had originally been formed to stimulate fund-raising for the British Olympic Association, but had later expanded its activities to include the discussion of various legislative matters affecting sport such as rating, entertainments duty, income tax, purchase tax and the subject of finance for sport generally. In addition to the BOA, representatives from the CCPR and the NFFA attended its meetings and helped in the preparation of evidence to be used in making representations to various Ministers in the Government.

Sir John accepted an invitation from Mr. Noel-Baker to address a meeting of this committee in December 1958. As one result, he agreed to send a personal letter to each member of the House of Commons and to a number from the House of Lords inviting them to submit, for the benefit of the Wolfenden Committee, their opinions on such matters as the extent, if any, to which sport should be financed from public funds, what Government Department was the most appropriate to be concerned with the encouragement of sport; how strongly it was felt that national prestige was really at stake in international sporting events, and the allied question of how far Britain's traditional attitude to sport could be, or should be, maintained.

Nearly a hundred replies were received to Sir John's letter, and, of those who wrote, Elaine Burton, Philip Goodhart, P. B. Lucas, and Ian Mikardo from the Commons, and Lords Bridgeman, Cottesloe and Weeks from the Lords, subsequently gave oral evidence to the Committee.

As mentioned in Chapter Six, a Departmental Committee under the Chairmanship of Lady Albemarle was set up by the Ministry of Education in November 1958, and its Report, *The Youth Service in England and Wales,* was published in February 1960. A private discussion between Lady Albemarle and Sir John Wolfenden as to the respective functions of the two Committees made it clear that no overlapping between the two was likely, and that both could carry on their work independently. Sir John, however, arranged a social meeting between Lady Albemarle and members of his Committee, at which Lady Albemarle told the latter about the likely conclusions of her Committee. A paper prepared for the Wolfenden Committee by its Secretary on *The Relation between Youth Work and Sport,* was also circulated to members of the Albemarle Committee at Lady Albermarle's request.

The CCPR gave its own written and oral evidence to the Albemarle Committee in 1959 and one of the CCPR's main proposals was that governing bodies of sport and outdoor activity associations should be regarded as integral parts of the youth service and should, where necessary, be given grant, both nationally and locally, in respect of their work with young people between 15 and 20.

The Albemarle Report laid great stress on the value of physical recreation within the youth service and devoted many paragraphs to various aspects of it. In particular, it urged that those concerned with sports clubs and specialist groups in the area should be associated with the youth service through representation on local youth advisory committees. It paid high tribute to the contribution made by the CCPR to the youth service and recommended that a special additional grant should be made by the Ministry to enable the CCPR to develop its experimental and pioneering work, especially in the field of coaching courses.

Though the Government announced its general acceptance of the Albemarle Report on its publication, the particular recommendations contained in it about physical recreation do not appear to have been given much attention.

Whether or not the national voluntary youth organisations were concentrating their hopes exclusively on the work of the Albemarle Committee, the Wolfenden Committee were disappointed with the replies received from some of them to the questionnaire which the Committee had sent to them, as to all other organisations represented on the Council of the CCPR. Some of the replies seemed to suggest that the Committee's inquiry was not regarded as applicable to their activities. One youth organisation stated that its views on the questionnaire would be of little value, as it used physical activities for character-training rather than for producing athletes. The Secretary was instructed to reply that the Committee were themselves not primarily concerned with sport as a means of producing athletes!

At its meetings, the Wolfenden Committee received oral evidence from many individual witnesses and a wide range of organisations. Among the latter were governing bodies of sport, youth service organisations, the Ministry of Education, the British Association of Organisers and Lecturers in Physical Education, the Physical Education Association, the County Councils Association, the Association of Education Committees, the Association of Head Mistresses, the English Folk Dance and Song Society, the National Association of Groundsmen, and the Sports Turf Research Institute. Among the individuals were five National Coaches of governing bodies of sport – Harry Crabreee, Geoff Dyson, Dan Maskell, Eileen Taylor and Walter Winterbottom – Sir John Hunt of the Duke of Edinburgh's Award, and Sir William Emrys Williams of the Arts Council.

To discuss the influence of the Press upon sport, the Committee saw a panel of sports editors, and a group of sports journalists. On the question of amateurism and professionalism, they held separate and highly confidential sessions with representatives of six of the major sports bodies, and two groups of men and women who had distinguished themselves in international competition. Sir Adolphe Abrahams, Dr. Roger Bannister and Dr. Otto Edholm came to help the Committee to decide whether there was any conclusive evidence as to a causal relationship between physical exercise and health.

The CCPR itself gave written evidence to the Committee, and, in addition, oral evidence was given by Sir Stanley Rous and P.C.C., and, at another session, by four of the Council's most experienced regional Representatives – Perry Alderslade, Kay Latto, Harry Littlewood and Geoffrey Richards. Towards the end of the Committee's work, P.C.C. was invited to attend a special meeting of the Committee at which she argued with skill and cogency but without success against what she understood to be the Committee's intention of recommending that grant aid for sport should no longer be administered through the Ministry of Education.

P.C.C.'s arguments might have had more effect had the Ministry chosen to give oral evidence at a higher administrative level than they did. But no-one could be found to speak to the Committee with any real authority about the Ministry's policy. Though the Assistant Secretary concerned with the administration of grants for sports bodies and the two Staff Inspectors of Physical Education showed no lack of conviction about the importance of physical recreation, their evidence could not conceal the fact that they had to work within severe financial restrictions and that the development of sport was not high among the Ministry's priorities.

The vast volume of written and oral evidence which the Committee read and listened to convinced them that there was an overwhelming case for making more statutory finance available for sport. As to the machinery though which this should be given – in spite of the warnings that had come from many witnesses against repeating the errors of the National Fitness Council, the Committee's own strong resistance to the establishment of anything that could be called a Ministry of Sport and a reluctance to introduce an administrative separation between sport and the youth service – the Committee decided unanimously that there was no hope of sport's getting the 'new deal' they felt was required unless a new body, independent of the Ministry of Education, was set up, which would receive finance from the Government and disburse it in the most appropriate directions.

So they recommended the establishment of a Sports Development Council so that "more and more people may be enabled to enjoy the recreative benefits of sport, games and outdoor activities." This was to be "a small body of six to ten persons of varied experience who have a general knowledge of the field and such personal standing as will give them accepted authority and influence." The Council was to be directly responsible to the Lord President of the Council or directly appointed by the Chancellor of the Exchequer. It would have under its control an annual expenditure of the order of £5,000,000 to be distributed in cash, either by way of non-recurrent grants or in assistance towards the recurrent expenditure of the composite bodies and the individual governing bodies of the various sports. There would also be, the Committee recommended, an annual allocation of a similar additional sum to be sanctioned for capital expenditure by statutory bodies.

The establishment of a Sports Development Council was the Committee's main recommendation. There were over fifty other recommendations on various aspects of sports development, all important but less fundamental, and the Committee were unanimous on all points except what was the ultimate solution to the admittedly difficult situation about amateurism. Though of great interest in themselves, the full recommendations of the Report are not germane to this history of the CCPR.

Of the CCPR itself, the Wolfenden Committee wrote : 'It is beyond dispute that this body has made an outstanding contribution to the development of physical recreation since its formation and that the statutory grants it has received have been money well spent. Its affairs seem to us to have been conducted with wisdom and it has in increasing measure gained the confidence of its constituent organisations, including the governing bodies of sport ... We have no hesitation in declaring our conviction that an organisation constituted and staffed as is the CCPR has a vital part to play in the development of sport in this country."

Recommendations about the CCPR were that :

(1) The technical and administrative resources of the CCPR in the regions and of the SCPR should be strengthened to enable them to meet future demands.

(2) Statutory financial support should be available towards the maintenance costs of National Recreation Centres.

(3) Financial aid should be given to the CCPR in Northern Ireland to enable it to give greater administrative help to sports bodies.

(4) The appropriate statutory bodies in Wales and Northern Ireland should continue to give encouragement and financial assistance to residents there who wished to attend leadership courses at the National Recreation Centres situated in England and Scotland.

This mainly factual Chapter about the work of the Wolfenden Committee cannot end without an expression of the deep debt owed not only by the CCPR but by the whole community to the Chairman and each member of the Committee for the time and thought they devoted to the problems they were presented with. With one exception, they all held full-time and responsible positions in other work, yet for over two and a half years they spent what must have seemed endless hours absorbing immense piles of circulated evidence and attending meetings on 58 days. They were led by Sir John Wolfenden with unvarying good humour and unequalled skill both as chairman of a meeting and as a master of lucid exposition and argument. With the exception of Sir Godfrey Ince all are still alive to know how great a part their Report has played in the development of sport in the fourteen years that have passed since its publication.

This Chapter might perhaps be concluded on a light, somewhat personal note. On the Saturday of the week in which the Wolfenden Report was published, the Author happened to be attending an 'old members' dinner' at University College, Oxford. In his reply to the toast of "The College", the Master, Professor Arthur Goodhart, referred to the Report and said that those present would be glad to know that 'a Univ. man' had acted as secretary to the Committee. He noted that the Preface to the Report had credited him with "unrivalled knowledge of fact" in that field. With some apprehension, he said, he had taken down from his shelves the previous Wolfenden Report and was relieved to find that no similar claim had been made for the Secretary of *that* Committee!

CHAPTER TEN

First 'Post-Wolfenden' Years:
1960 - 1965

The long-term consequences of the Wolfenden Committee's Report provide interesting sidelights on the mutability of political judgements. This Chapter will be concerned with the early reception given to the Report, as well as the main events in the history of the CCPR from 1960 until early in 1965, when the Labour Government set up an Advisory Sports Council and invited the CCPR's new General Secretary to leave his job to direct it.

After copies of the Report, as an act of courtesy, were presented informally to representatives of the Ministry of Education, the British Olympic Association, the National Playing Fields Association, and the Scottish Council of Physical Recreation, its contents were made known to the world at a Press conference taken by Sir John Wolfenden at the Waldorf Hotel on 28th September 1960.

The reception given to the Report by the national and provincial Press was very wide and for the most part enthusiastic. There was much editorial comment as well as analysis in the news and sports pages, and it was the subject of many amusing cartoons, some based upon the inevitable comparison between the subject matters of the two Wolfenden Reports! A memorandum compiled at the time for the Executive Committee's information quoted comments from no fewer than sixty-three newspapers and other periodicals – even *The Economist* devoted two pages to it. For a Report by a Committee set up by a voluntary body this was a very rare amount of attention, which no Government could ignore.

The Report was circulated immediately by the CCPR to all organisations and individual members on the Council, as well as to Ministers of the Crown and Members of Parliament, and comments invited. It was submitted to all the Council's committees and sub-committees for their consideration, and many national and local bodies called conferences to discuss it, including the Standing Conference of National Voluntary Youth

Organisations. Sir John addressed the Council's A.G.M. in November 1960 and a well-attended meeting of Members of Parliament arranged by the Parliamentary Sports Committee the following month. Later, that Committee sent an all-Party deputation to urge on the Chancellor of the Exchequer the case for accepting the Report.

Early in January 1961, the CCPR submitted to the Government and circulated widely an eagerly-awaited printed statement of its own views on the Report's recommendations. In this context, it is necessary to distinguish between the views of the Council as an association of over 200 national organisations and those of its Executive Committee. The overwhelming majority of the former, as the Statement declared, supported the establishment of a Sports Development Council as recommended by the Wolfenden Committee. So, too, did the SCPR and the CCPR's Welsh Committee, although they wanted separate Sports Councils for Scotland and Wales. But, as it was apparent from the outset that the Executive Committee would not be unanimous on the subject, it was decided by the Honorary Officers that the wisest course was not to press the matter to a vote (to the disappointment of some members) and so to advertise the disagreement, but to include in the Statement a note to the effect that though there was unanimity in the Council that more money should be made available for sport, there were some within it who advocated, first, that the Ministry of Education should continue to have responsibility for distributing grants for sport, possibly with the help of a small but strong Sports Committee to advise it, and, secondly, that the Government should set up an International Sports Committee with powers to grant-aid bodies concerned with international competition and festivals. The Statement added that the CCPR would neither welcome nor feel appropriate the suggestion that had been made (though not in the Wolfenden Report) that the CCPR itself might be entrusted with allocating any additional funds made available.

Though the staff at their annual conference in January 1961 had a valuable discussion on the Report's recommendations, they, too, were discouraged from expressing any corporate view about a Sports Development Council.

Before the General Election of 1959, which confirmed a Conservative Government in power, the Conservative Political

Centre had published a Conservative Committee's report, *The Challenge of Leisure,* which advocated the setting up by the Chancellor of the Exchequer of an independent Sports Council with an income of £5,000,000 a year, and the Labour Party had published an official booklet entitled *Leisure for Living,* which declared it to be the Party's policy to form a Sports Council within the Ministry of Education, with a similar sum to spend. The Conservative booklet, however, was not a specific election pledge; the latter had not gone beyond a promise to provide more playing fields and facilities for sport.

The Wolfenden Report was first discussed in Parliament in a somewhat inconclusive Debate initiated in the House of Lords by Lord Aberdare on 15th February 1961, in which the Bishop of Chester made an impressive maiden speech. Replying to the Debate, Lord Kilmuir, the Lord Chancellor, said that the Government were considering the Report in the light of the CCPR's comments. As a start, provision had been made in the 1961/2 Estimates for grants towards the maintenance of the three National Recreation Centres and the SCPR's Centre at Largs, and for additional grants towards national voluntary bodies' coaching schemes. The CCPR naturally welcomed the prompt additional grant for the Centres, and also the extra grant from the Northern Ireland Ministry which the Wolfenden Committee had asked for.

The House of Commons debated the Report on 28th April 1961 and many complimentary things were said about it, both by Denis Howell for the Opposition and by Kenneth Thompson, Parliamentary Secretary to the Ministry of Education. The latter, however, expressed reservations about a Sports Development Council and said the Government wanted longer to devise the best kind of machinery "for achieving the end desired".

What was said by the Government in both Houses produced a chill of disappointment – typical Press headlines were : "Nix for the Boys", "Kilmuir smashes Wolfenden for Six", "M.P.'s. impatient in both parties", and "Still tied with a shoestring".

In his 'Little Budget' in July 1961, Selwyn Lloyd, Chancellor of the Exchequer, said that, as part of the restrictions being imposed on public expenditure, action to implement the Wolfenden Report would have to wait, but, on 8th May 1962, following his Budget speech, he announced that he proposed to start in a modest way to make good some of the deficiencies pointed out by that Report. An extra £1,000,000 would be added to the capital investment programme in the current year, and the Ministry of Education would be authorised to spend an additional £200,000 under the Physical Training and Recreation Act – £100,000 on capital grants for voluntary projects, and £100,000 on grants to help with the coaching and administration of sport. A Sports Council was still being considered.

Addressing the CCPR's A.G.M. in November 1961, Sir David Eccles, Minister of Education, was non-committal about the Wolfenden Report, but thought that young people should be expected to pay a realistic amount for their leisure-time activities, a sentiment from which no one dissented. Helpful information about what was being done in other countries came from *Central Government Aid to Sport and Physical Recreation in countries of Western Europe*, a pamphlet by Denis Molyneux of Birmingham University, in September 1962.

The next official move was the appointment by the Government of Lord Hailsham, Lord President of the Council and Minister for Science, as 'Minister with special responsibility for Sport', in addition to his other duties. In announcing his appointment in the Lords, Lord Hailsham said that the Government, while agreeing with the diagnosis of the Wolfenden Report, did not agree with the remedy it proposed of establishing a Sports Development Council. In January 1963, Lord Hailsham appointed Sir Patrick Renison, former Governor of Kenya, as his Principal Adviser on Sport, an office in which he was succeeded in January 1964 by Sir John Lang, former Secretary of the Admiralty.

The appointment of Lord Hailsham at least gave an assurance that the needs of sport would be considered at a high level. Official contacts between him and the CCPR soon took place, and in February 1963 Lord Hailsham saw representatives of the CCPR, the British Olympic Association, the National Playing Fields Association and their Scottish counterparts. Subsequently, he and his Adviser received various memoranda from P.C.C. and Walter Winterbottom (who was about to succeed her). As a result of his own thinking and the advice he received from various sources on the subject, Lord Hailsham decided against setting up either a Sports Development Council or an advisory committee and to work through 'the composite bodies'.

The appointment of Lord Hailsham did in fact produce a marked increase in Government spending on sport, both on grants to the governing bodies for coaching and administration and in capital grants for facilities to local sports clubs. The restriction preventing single-activity clubs from qualifying for grant was removed. A coordinating committee of officials of Government departments was set up under the chairmanship of Sir Patrick Renison, and, later, Sir John Lang, one of the results of which was the issue of a Joint Circular in August 1964 by the Ministry of Education and the Ministry of Housing and Local Government, urging local authorities and local education authorities to plan together – helped by voluntary organisations and industrial interests – to extend the provision of facilities for sport and outdoor activities and also to review the use of existing facilities. The Ministry of Housing and Local Government asked local rating authorities to look sympathetically on applications from sports clubs for discretionary rating relief under the terms of the Rating and Valuation Act of 1961.

Though he resisted all the arguments put forward for setting up a Sports Development Council by many of those who took part in the excellent Debate in the House of Lords on 22nd May 1963, initiated by Lady Burton (as Elaine Burton had become in 1962). Lord Hailsham at the Council's A.G.M. in October 1963 praised the CCPR's initiative in setting up the Wolfenden Committee, whose Report he described as "the catalyst that had brought about a change in public opinion, in Parliament as elsewhere". He thought that the Government had made a start on all the main aspects of the problem without waiting for new legislation and without suggesting any interference or control. In the following month the Government announced that it was prepared "in suitable cases" to help British amateur teams to take part in international sporting events abroad – a new and important concession. The CCPR was represented by Walter Winterbottom on the committee set up to consider applications.

In March 1964, the CCPR arranged a meeting at Shell House at which Lord Hailsham, accompanied by Sir John Lang and representatives of the Ministry of Education and the Ministry of Housing and Local Government, spoke on the Government's policy on sport to about 250 representatives of governing bodies of sport and outdoor activity associations, and dealt with questions. He claimed that £14.6 m. would be spent in 1964/5 on sports facilities outside educational institutions, compared with £6 m. in 1961/2. The CCPR's own financial position was also more satisfactory as its grant from the Ministry had risen from £140,000 in 1960/61 to £337,000 in 1964/5, though some of the increase was explained by the move to new offices in 1964.

Parliamentary pressure for a Sports Development Council, however, continued. In a Debate in the House of Lords on 13th May 1964, again initiated by Lady Burton – which the Bishop of Chester, with true Christian charity but perhaps over-generously, described as "a feast of oratory lasting over six and a half hours"! – at least five Peers asked the Government to re-consider its decision about it.

On the 23rd June 1964, Quintin Hogg (as Lord Hailsham had by then become on renouncing his Peerage) again resisted pressure for a Sports Development Council in replying to a Debate initiated in the House of Commons by J. P. W. Mallalieu. He gave this account of his position: "To begin with, I was always attracted to the Sports Development Council. I had experience as Lord President with other bodies like the University Grants Committee and the research councils which are administered in the kind of way that the Wolfenden Com-mittee originally suggested for such a council. But a great deal of water has flowed under the bridge since that suggestion was originally made, and I think that if Honorable Members opposite pursue the matter they will find, for instance, that the CCPR which originally sponsored the suggestion has, like myself, been rather steadily moving away from it, after having been initially attracted by it ... Originally I intended to create an advisory council, advising me in my coordinating functions, which would have been in substance a sports development council without some of the objections raised against it. But when I came to try to appoint such a body I was faced with the following dilemma. In order to carry out the work which one has to carry out ... one must have access to the composite bodies, the CCPR, the NPFA, the SCPR and the British Olympic Association. Either a sports development council is the same as those bodies, in which case it is really superfluous, or else it is different from those bodies, in which case it is really objectionable. Once cannot divorce oneself from direct access to the bodies whose cooperation one really needs. There are no fewer than 300 governing bodies of sport in this country, and the sports development council would have to be representative of them. But how could it be representative of them unless it were to supersede the CCPR and the Scottish equivalent?"

Mr. Hogg's curiously inexact statement of the attitude about a Sports Development Council adopted by the CCPR provoked Lady Burton – who, as a member of the CCPR's Executive and General Purposes and Finance Committee has good grounds for knowing the truth of the matter – to write to *The Times* protesting that the Minister had no authority for his statement about the CCPR's view. Receiving no public withdrawal from Mr. Hogg, she raised the subject somewhat forcefully in the House of Lords, which raised the piquant question whether a Noble Lord was entitled to doubt the accuracy of a statement made by a Minister 'in another place'. However, the official reply was given that Mr. Hogg had been stating an opinion, not making an official pronouncement.

Attention must now turn from the atmosphere of controversy and speculation that followed the publication of *Sport and the Community* to more specifically CCPR affairs. During these years the national and regional technical staff were playing an increasing part in advising local authorities and other bodies about facilities. They were active in promoting the formation of local sports advisory councils, consisting of representatives of local authorities, sports bodies, the NPFA and the CCPR. In 1963 and 1964, they took the initiative, applauded by Lord Hailsham, of calling a number of regional conferences on facilities. The setting up of the Northern Advisory Council for Sport and Recreation under the Chairmanship of Geoffrey Petter, H.M.I., as the result of a conference called by the North-East Development Council in conjunction with the CCPR and NPFA, proved a prototype for the Regional Sports Councils to be established by the Labour Government in 1965. In 1964, the CCPR joined with the NPFA to publish *Community Sports Halls* by G. A. Perrin, the Research Fellow appointed by the Regent Street Polytechnic and the NPFA.

Two special services to governing bodies in 1962 should be recorded. A special meeting of the Games and Sports Committee under Lady Burton's chairmanship met Peter Dimmock of the BBC and John MacMillan of ITV to talk about sport on television, a topic of burning interest to all sports. The plea of the smaller governing bodies for more time on the medium was heard with sympathy, although the difficulties were not overlooked. In December representatives of thirty-three sports bodies met the staff at their annual conference at Lilleshall to discuss a paper by George McPartlin, and it was agreed that: (1) governing bodies should combine at regional and local levels to take joint action in representing the need for facilities to local authorities, and, (2) a small team under Peter McIntosh's chairmanship should conduct an inquiry into coaching awards. This inquiry produced valuable recommendations about titles and grades of award, as well as a survey of the use made by different agencies of the coaches trained under various schemes.

A staff conference discussion on the Wolfenden Committee's recommendation about the recreational use of reservoirs and other waters led to the Executive's calling a small conference in 1961 with Jack Longland in the chair and attended by representatives of the Nature Conservancy, the British Canoe Union, Amateur Rowing Association, Royal Yachting Association, British Water Ski Federation, and National Federation of Anglers. This was followed by productive contacts between the CCPR and the British Waterworks Association and the Institution of Water Engineers, and an agreement with the Birmingham University Department of Physical Education to undertake a sample survey of the use of inland waters in the West Midlands. The resulting survey, *Inland Waters and Recreation,* published by the CCPR in 1964, played an extremely valuable part in persuading many water authorities to take a less restrictive attitude about the use of their waters for recreation. One suggestion appended to the survey was that the CCPR should draw up in conjunction with appropriate bodies a code of behaviour for water users. This was done and the *Water Sport Code* was published by the CCPR in 1966, financed by the Department of Education. The cost of publishing the survey was borne by the Whitbread Sports Fund.

In this period the CCPR submitted evidence to the Newsom Committee on the education "of pupils of average or below average ability", to the Crathorne Committee on Sunday Observance and to the Pilkington Committee on Broadcasting. P.C.C. was appointed a member of the Youth Service Development Council set up by the Minister of Education after the

Albemarle Committee's Report in 1960. Accompanied by Ruth Keeble, she represented the CCPR at the Fourth Congress of the International Association of Physical Education and Sport for Women and Girls in Washington in 1961. The following year A. L. Colbeck made a seven weeks' tour of East and West Pakistan to advise the Government there on the development of physical recreation, and in 1965, Ken Gill spent six weeks on a similar mission to Hong Kong. The attendance of the Queen and Prince Philip at a special performance of Bertram Mills Circus in 1960 produced £4,831 for the Council's funds, and a profit of £2,830 was made by two performances of a Festival of Movement and Dance at the Empire Pool, Wembley, in 1963 – the chief guests were Princess Alice in the afternoon and Sir Patrick and Lady Renison in the evening.

Sir Clarence Sadd was the Council's Honorary Treasurer for fifteen years and had never ceased to astonish and delight his audience with his 'tour de force' of presenting the financial accounts in considerable detail completely from memory at successive Annual General Meetings. He died in 1962, and was succeeded by Robin Brook (now Sir Robin) who had been Deputy Honorary Treasurer since 1960. By profession a banker, Mr. Brook was a former sabre Champion who had represented his country at the Olympic Games of 1936 and 1948. During the war he gave distinguished service in Special Operations Executive. The same year also saw the death of Lord Hampton, a member of the Executive since 1935 and Chairman of the Bisham Abbey Committee, one of the Council's oldest and firmest friends.

Meanwhile a great change was taking place in the CCPR's regional staffing structure. A single administrative officer was in charge of the Council's work both in Wales and Northern Ireland but in the nine English regions the establishment consisted of two Senior Representatives of equal status, a man and a woman, supported by a varying number of men and women Representatives. Though this duality of control had parallels elsewhere in the physical education profession, for instance in the case of men and women organisers employed by local education authorities, its unsuitability for the CCPR's changing circumstances was increasingly apparent, and strong arguments pointed to the need for a single person in each region to be in administrative charge. But to see the need for it was one thing; to achieve it in practice quite another. For it meant either the introduction of new staff from outside to occupy senior posts or the demotion of some members of the existing staff who would have to occupy subordinate positions vis-à-vis colleagues with whom they had previously been equal. Either course presented difficulties.

Nevertheless P.C.C. felt that the needs of the organisation must have precedence over personal feelings. The General Purposes and Finance Committee agreed in 1959 that the Ministry should be asked to approve – and that meant accepting the financial implications – a proposal that the future regional establishment should include a Regional Officer and two equal Senior Representatives. The Ministry agreed that the new establishment might be tried out on an experimental basis in 1961 in four regions – the East, the North Midlands, the North-West, and the South-West. The new posts of Regional Officer were publicly advertised at a substantially higher scale than that of a Senior Representative. It had been hoped, and indeed represented to the Ministry as part of the plan, that the new posts might attract outside candidates with suitable administrative and educational qualifications. This did not happen, and of the four new posts, only one went to someone from outside the organisation; three existing Senior Representatives, two men and one woman, got the others. But after a year's trial, the Ministry agreed to the extension of the scheme, and of the five new Regional Officers, the best candidates in the view of the Staff Appointments Committee were three men Senior Representatives, one previous Senior Representative who was attracted back to the CCPR, and one from outside, who had to be replaced before long, also by an 'outsider' who proved a better choice. Hardly any women on the staff applied, so the CCPR senior staff became much more masculine than it had been.

But there were some unfortunate repercussions. Two men Senior Representatives with long service who had not been selected for appointment as Regional Officers showed themselves so unwilling to cooperate with their new chiefs that their departure from the CCPR's service became inevitable. It was an unsettling time, and although the majority of the staff accepted the new arrangement loyally, some wounds were slow to heal. But though the operation was a painful one which had to be carried out without any anaesthetic, the later experience of the CCPR vindicated it abundantly.

But an even more momentous event in the CCPR's history was the decision of P.C.C. to resign from the General Secretaryship – a decision which she made known to the Officers in April 1962. She agreed to remain until her successor was appointed and fully initiated into the work, but hoped that this would be not later than March 1963. Attempts to make her change her mind were fruitless, but the prospect of losing her leadership and unique abilities caused surprise and dismay throughout the organisation. She was well below retiring age and though through all her time with the CCPR she had suffered much pain and physical disability through chronic diabetes and rheumatoid arthritis, her condition had not been noticeably deteriorating. Nor had there been any decline in her clarity of thought, powers of organisation and strength of will, nor in the understanding of people that had always characterised her.

She gave the main address at the A.G.M. in November 1962, and in it she said no more about her reasons for resigning than, "Everywhere there is a fresh surge of change. That is why I felt that now was the time to hand over to a *man* with qualities and abilities additional to my own". On another occasion she said that she did not approve of "founder-secretaries" who clung to their jobs too long, adding that she couldn't afford to retire, but wanted to do something different before she was too old. Many of those who knew her well have speculated as to why she resigned when she did. No-one knows for certain, but some who knew her best feel that, apart from the continuing strains of the work itself and some personal dissensions which worried her a lot, she was far-sighted enough to see that the future of the CCPR which she had built up would be bound up with certain tendencies in the world of sport which were inimical to some of the ideals to which she had devoted her life.

In the next Chapter an attempt will be made to give a picture of the sort of woman she was and the way in which she worked, which may help those who did not know her to understand her part in the CCPR's story more fully. An Appendix contains some of the public tributes made to her on her retirement in 1963, and on her death in 1972.

She left the CCPR in good shape. Its new regional establish-

ment was virtually complete, it had strong and stable committees, and a competent and for the most part long-serving staff;
its relations with the Ministry of Education and its constituent bodies were better than they had ever been, the
harassing problem of National Recreation Centre deficits seemed
at an end, and its general financial position was strong.

The post of General Secretary was advertised, and Walter
Winterbottom's appointment to it created a greater public sensa-
tion than the news of P.C.C.'s resignation. For W.W. (as we
shall hereafter call him) had been the Football Association's
Director of Coaching, which then carried with it the 'hot seat' of
being England's team manager, since 1946. For his services to
football he was made O.B.E. on leaving the FA.

W.W. had received a teacher's training at Chester College
in the 'thirties and, after four years' teaching, had taken the
physical education course at Carnegie College, after which he
served as a lecturer on Carnegie's staff until the outbreak of
war. He was with the RAF during the war, the last two years
as Wing Commander in the Air Ministry's Physical Training
Branch, with responsibility for organising training and advising
on matters of establishment facilities and equipment.

W.W. started with the CCPR in January 1963 and over-
lapped with P.C.C. until she left at the end of March. The
transfer of power from P.C.C. to W.W. as secretary to the
Council's major committees was accomplished smoothly – the
latter had the advantage of having worked extremely closely
with his new Chairman and former chief, Sir Stanley Rous.
Moreover, he already knew personally many of the CCPR's staff.
He soon showed that he had no intention of conceiving the post
of General Secretary of the CCPR as P.C.C. had conceived it,
and there were many consequent changes in attitudes, relationships and methods of work. W.W. shared with P.C.C. the
capacity for unremitting hard work, and his unrivalled contacts
in the world of international and professional sport as well as
on the men's side of physical education were valuable assets.

W.W. brought with him to the CCPR his personal secretary,
Sheila Hughes, who gave him the kind of devoted personal
service that P.C.C. had enjoyed from Beryl Heathfield. Later,
Sheila shared W.W.'s secondment to the service of the Sports
Council.

The CCPR had long outgrown its attractive Georgian Headquarters at 6, Bedford Square, home of the original Duke of Bedford, and no further extension could be built or other device found for adding a single desk in them. With the help of the Ministry of Works and grant from the Ministry of Education, new offices were found at 26, Park Crescent, near Regent's Park tube station, premises which had just been reconstructed after war damage. The CCPR headquarters and London and South-East regional offices moved there in September 1964, Beryl Heathfield, who had served both the CCPR and P.C.C. personally so cheerfully and efficiently for fifteen years, postponed her retirement from her post with the CCPR to organise the operation.

The Ministry's greater generosity to sport made it possible for the new offices to be large enough for the CCPR to offer office tenancies, secretarial and tea-room facilities, and the use of committee rooms to governing bodies of sport who had either no office at all or a very unsatisfactory one. The offer was eagerly accepted, and among the bodies who had their offices alongside the CCPR at Park Crescent were the Amateur Athletic Association, the British Canoe Union, the British Cycling Federation, the British Amateur Gymnastic Association, the Hockey Association, the Squash Rackets Association, the English Table Tennis Association, the All-England Netball Association, the All-England Women's Lacrosse Association, the Amateur Rowing Association, the British Mountaineering Council and The Keep Fit Association. The arrangement of having the CCPR's offices in such close proximity to the offices of many of the governing bodies proved in practice to have more advantages than had been hoped for, especially in terms of personal relations. Later developments made it necessary to acquire more office space, (In 1973, the Sports Council, the new CCPR and many governing bodies moved to 70 Brompton Rd, S.W.3.)

Other developments at this time were: (1) the establishment of the Mountain Leadership Certificate in 1964, administered by a Joint Board of the CCPR and the British Mountaineering Council, under the chairmanship of Jack Longland who had accepted the chairmanship of the Council's Outdoor Activities Advisory Committee in 1962 and had also been chairman of a special working party set up to examine the whole question of how to provide training for leadership in mountain activities;

and (2) the agreement in 1964 by the Ministry that the CCPR should be grant-aided to appoint its first Research Officer – the post went to John Birch.

The CCPR was represented at the important 'Countryside in 1970' Conference organised primarily by the Nature Conservancy, in London in November 1963, and at its successor in 1965, and played a part in its study-groups.

At the 1964 A.G.M., the Chairman announced with great regret the resignation from the Executive of B. L. Pearson, who had been one of the Council's earliest friends at the Board of Education in 1936, and paid tribute to the value of his services. Since his retirement from the Civil Service, Mr. Pearson had served on the Executive, General Purposes and Staff Committees. T. G. Bedwell, who had also been a valued member of those three Committees, as well as of the Bisham Abbey Committee for many years, resigned his membership in 1963.

At the General Election in October 1964, a Labour Government pledged to create a Sports Council was returned to power, and Denis Howell, Joint Under-Secretary of State for Education and Science, succeeded Quintin Hogg as Minister with special responsibility for Sport. In January 1965 a special meeting of the CCPR's General Purposes and Finance Committee was called to consider a request from Mr. Howell that W.W. should be released from the CCPR on secondment for a maximum of two years to take up the post of Director of the Sports Council which the Government proposed to set up. The Committee felt they must accede to the Minister's request and W.W. left the CCPR for his new post the following month. The Author became Acting General Secretary, George McPartlin was made Technical Director and Eric Edwards Acting Deputy Secretary.

On 3rd February 1965 the Government announced in both Houses of Parliament that they had decided to establish a Sports Council to advise them on matters relating to the development of amateur sport and physical recreation services, and to foster cooperation among the statutory authorities and voluntary organisations concerned. Mr. Howell as the Minister responsible would be its chairman and members would serve in a personal capacity. Two members of the CCPR's Executive were appointed members of the new Sports Council – Lady Burton and A. D. Munrow. The latter, feeling that his new responsibility was incompatible with continued membership of the Executive resigned from the Executive.

The Government made it known that they had decided to set up an advisory Sports Council rather than the executive body that had been promised, in order to achieve quick action without the need for special legislation. That it was intended to be an active and effective body was evident from the facts that its chairman was the Minister and that W.W. had been given the title of 'Director', which might have seemed incongruous in a purely advisory body. Sir John Lang was made Deputy Chairman and Denis Molyneux, seconded from the staff of Birmingham University, became Deputy Director.

CHAPTER ELEVEN

Phyllis Colson—Founder and Master Builder

Many who read this history will have known P.C.C. personally, will retain their own mental picture of her, and will have made their own assessment of her personality and abilities. The part she played in the conception, creation, development and day-to-day functioning of the CCPR until 1963 was so crucial that some aspects of its history can only be fully understood in the light of her own characteristics. The aim of this Chapter, therefore, is to attempt to convey to those who did not know her some impression of the sort of person she was, her methods of working, and of the qualities which enabled her to persuade so many men and women not only to share her vision and sense of purpose but, in the case of civil servants, to give her the practical support of their Ministry, and, in the case of honorary officers, committee members and many others, to devote many hours of their leisure to working with her and for her, in some instances over many years.

Though a history may try to be factual and objective, this Chapter must inevitably be somewhat personal and subjective, for there can be no such thing as an objective assessment of a personality or a relationship. But though reactions to P.C.C.'s personality differed, there was universal agreement among all who came into close contact with her that she was a remarkable woman with very rare gifts. My picture of her will be based upon my knowledge of her for thirty-five years, during twenty of which I was her assistant, seldom spending less than an hour in her company every day the office was open, and seeing her at work in the most varied circumstances. She was an inveterate letter writer, and I have a fat collection of the letters she wrote me, not only when I was on holiday or ill, but often written in the evenings at her home when she wanted to clarify her mind (or mine) on points we had been discussing together during the day. I wish I had had the benefit of studying her personal correspondence with other people, but none has been volunteered, except a significant Christmas card message to a very old colleague in 1971.

The main facts of her career have been given in Chapter Two, but some extracts from her early testimonials reveal better than anything else could, some of the qualities that characterised her throughout her life.

Miss S. G. Anthony, Headmistress of Liverpool College for Girls wrote of her in February 1926 : "Miss Phyllis Colson was a boarder in this school from April 1915 to December 1922, and she ended her school career as a school prefect and as Head of the School and of her House. She was also captain of games, a most efficient Guide Lieutenant and an active member of the school societies. She was thoughtful and reliable in these positions of responsibility and showed a distinct gift of leadership and power of understanding girls of varying age and disposition. She had good general ability and many intellectual interests; she could have read for an Honours Degree at the University had she not wished to specialise in physical work. I have pleasure in recommending her as an assistant mistress as I believe she will be a loyal, public spirited and efficient member of a staff. I think she will grip her classes well and inspire them with her own enthusiasm. She will always be ready to give help and will never spare herself where the good of the girls or the school is concerned."

Margaret Stansfeld, Principal of Bedford Physical Training College, wrote the same year : "Miss Phyllis Colson finished her three years' training in the Bedford Physical Training College in July 1926, when she gained the full College diploma. Miss Colson is one of the very few students whose teaching has been marked 'excellent'. She is also a very good disciplinarian, maintaining her discipline in an easy friendly manner which never arouses antagonism. All her games are good, hockey and netball being her best games. She can teach National, Ballroom and Country dancing – the latter being particularly good – and as she has passed the 'conjoint' examination of the Chartered Society of Massage and Medical Gymnastics, she can undertake cases needing special remedial treatment. I can very warmly recommend Miss Colson as a mistress who will be very valuable in any school – she brings enthusiasm, interest and marked ability into her work."

For her teaching in schools, she gained the following tributes :

"She was in no way daunted by difficulties ... The standard of work rose rapidly. For the very young children, Miss Colson invented many charming singing games, and the results in prompt obedience, increased self-confidence and alertness were most delightful to watch. No heavy or dull child could resist for long the fascination of those games ... She is gifted with unusual grace and charm. She has strong views about her work of which she fully realises the importance, but she has the power of urging her wishes with gentleness and restraint." And : "She holds the girls' attention, making them eager to reach and keep a very high standard, and there is always evidence that they not only enjoy but derive real moral and physical benefit from her influence and instruction. Miss Colson's work is known for its freshness and variety. She is brisk and prompt, at the same time showing unfailing patience and kindliness. She has great powers of organisation, and would be quite equal to planning the physical education of a town or district on the most modern lines. Miss Colson is of attractive appearance and is bright and courteous in manner. She is a lady by birth and upbringing, and has the highest sense of duty."

A doctor in the West End who was a family friend wrote : "I have known Miss Phyllis Colson from the age of one. I know her to be a girl of sterling character and ability, with ambition and the concentration necessary for success in her calling .. I have known her father, Mr. Charles Colson, C.B.E., late Civil Engineer to the Admiralty, and mother for twenty-five years and esteem them as among my best friends." For her work with the National Council of Girls' Clubs she earned this commendation : "... is very able, an exceptionally good teacher and has real gifts as an organiser ... Addressed meetings successfully, undertook a considerable amount of office work and interviewing ... possesses the essentials of reliability, conscientiousness, and intelligence, together with a considerable experience of procedure ... won the respect and affection of all with whom she worked."

So it was all there from the start. Leadership, reliability, powers of organisation, efficiency, determination, understanding of people, sense of duty, intelligence, teaching gifts, unusual grace and charm, excellent personal relations, never arousing antagonism, "Will never spare herself" and, perhaps above all else, "inspiring with her own enthusiasm". Not a word quoted needs to be unsaid. Never have testimonials been more accurate and far-sighted.

The state of her health determined the direction of her career early in her life. Arthritis, of increasing severity, made itself evident soon after she left college, and made her realise that she had no long future as an active teacher. Her sister tells of an article P.C.C. wrote on arthritis, in which she recalls that a doctor had warned her that she would be in a bath chair by the time she was thirty. She made a private vow that it would be full-time work and no bath chair for her, and that inward resolve sustained her throughout her life, in face of a disability to which anyone with less courage would have surrendered. She turned to a post in girls' club work which involved both teaching and organising, and gave an outlet to her inborn desire to do some good in the world. In 1934, a coma led to the diagnosis that she was also a severe diabetic and would have to be on insulin for the rest of her life. She was forced to give up the girls' club job and, when she had recovered sufficiently, set to work to improve her qualifications for an administrative career by taking a short course in secretarial work in a good London college. The lessons she learned there about office management, business methods, lay-out of memoranda and so on were evident in all her future work and in the training she gave her staff, both secretarial and technical.

Her arthritis developed into rheumatoid arthritis, and that, together with diabetes, meant that many normal avenues of enjoyment and activity became closed to her. As she could no longer enjoy physical recreation herself, she concentrated her immense intellectual energies exclusively on trying to see that more opportunities were provided for other people to enjoy it. All her life she worked very long hours. She required only a few hours' sleep and survived on a minimal diet, of which the staple items appeared to be an apple, a biscuit and a piece of cheese. She gave up cigarettes in the 'fifties and never drank more than an occasional glass of dry sherry or wine.

She moved between her flat in the Edgware Road and the office, generally by taxi or in a friend's car, bearing a heavy bag full of the work she had done or was going to do. In the morning, she usually arrived at the office well before anyone else, and, when she had no committees, she liked to leave for home soon after four to start her real work on papers. She took her frugal lunch at her desk, except when she had a lunch-time engagement, which was something she avoided so far as possible. On most mornings she would arrive at the office with drafts of letters or memoranda for her colleagues' scrutiny, to see if they could suggest improvements, which was not often. Her first job was to go through the incoming post, which she marked out to the appropriate department or person, and then she would dictate to her two secretaries until about 11 o'clock. She would normally spend the rest of the day in interviews with colleagues or visitors. Because she did so much work at home in the evenings and at weekends, she managed to have time to see a surprising number of people in the day. Each day she would have on her desk a large sheet of white paper on which had been jotted down in her neat handwriting the initials of the people she wanted to see and the points she wished to see them about.

My turn generally came at the end of the morning, perhaps 12.30 or 12.45, and I could never be sure whether I would be free to go out for lunch before 2.0 p.m.! By the time we met, she had normally dealt with her most pressing business and was fairly relaxed and ready to enjoy discussing the day's business or 'letting off steam' about one or other of her colleagues or committee members who hadn't been behaving exactly as she would have liked them to! I had a useful safety-valve function when she was exasperated about something. She was always accessible to every member of the staff even the most junior clerk and most senior staff at HQ had regular sessions with her. One of the secrets of her influence over her colleagues and one cause of their devotion to her was the personal interest she took in them and members of their families as individuals. She would never forget to start an interview with an inquiry about the progress of someone who was ill or of a son or daughter who was starting a new job. She was always a sympathetic listener to anyone who wanted to confide in her about a personal problem, and she gave much shrewd counsel.

She was liable to diabetic comas in the office, but her personal secretary or other woman colleague was quicker to recognise the symptoms than she was herself, and to take appropriate measures. One of her surviving notes to me reads: "I gather you got let in for the beginning of a diabetic attack this morning. I *am* sorry and do apologise most profusely. It always makes me so terribly ashamed – particularly the type which seems to knock one out straight away. All I can remember is saying that I was glad Hailsham had written so welcomingly – nothing then until nearly 2 p.m.!"

In spite of the constant pain in which she lived, she was seldom anything but cheerful: a little weary perhaps but never miserable or sorry for herself. Sometimes she would talk about some aspect of her health, but that was infrequent. When she seemed obviously unwell, she would reply to inquiries with a rather abrupt "Oh, I'm all right". Apart from the occasional outburst, she kept her troubles to herself, whether personal or in connection with CCPR affairs.

In my first summer with the CCPR in 1944, when the time came to take some sort of wartime holiday with my family, I felt rather guilty, as P.C.C. was working very hard and showing no signs of taking a break. I broached the subject with her, and she sent me a letter which is worth quoting at length because it reveals so much about her attitude to her work, her colleagues, and to life in general. "I *hate* your thinking of holidays as you are doing", she wrote, "there is honestly no need to. For the life of me I cannot *really* see why the fact that I choose one form of life should make you feel uneasy or 'guilty' at choosing another. After all, you are not only convinced that your attitude is right but you know by now that I also think it is right *for you*. I quite realise that my attitude may seem peculiar but how I reason is thus: (a) There is a great deal of work to be done; if I take more time off, less work will be achieved, and, at the moment, I don't think that would be right. (b) If there was any evidence at all to show that my work would be better if I had normal leave, things would be different. (c) Although I frequently curse it, I *like* work and, funnily enough, get quite a lot of my enjoyment and re-creation from it! (d) I have extremely quick powers of recuperation, thank goodness, and can get from a few hours' real *fun* (in my own way) quite as much as I often get from a longer leave. (e) At the moment, apart from wanting time off to cope with the flat, etc., there is nowhere I specially want to go – you wait until we can travel abroad again! – and I *hate* holidays for holidays' sake, as it were. (f) I have not got the home ties that you have and am, therefore, much more free to please myself. If I had a husband and children, my relaxation and pleasure would be gained with them. Incidentally, living alone leaves me with more time to read, etc., than you probably have.

"I hate comparisons of any sort. We are all different and it seems to me that there's no reason why we should not be content to be different in our need and desire for a conventional type of leisure just as much as in other things. If you, or anyone else, continue to feel 'guilty' because you take your rights and wants, I shall be driven to do what I *don't* want, just for the sake of appearances. I'm afraid that would seem to me dishonest and unfair to the CC who would be paying my salary. Actually it's all rather amusing, as I *have* been trying v.hard to seize a few days lately, and shall probably do so before long.

'I must end this epistle by saying that I *do* understand your feelings, and would prob. feel likewise in the circs.! Although in doing so, I don't think I'd really be right. However, I'll be good!

Yours P.C.C.

P.S. I enjoyed our talk. By the way, surely you've gathered that I feel hols. *are* v. important, specially for people leading the rackety life of Reps.?"

She not only knew and cared about the personal circumstances of the staff — and this extended to the office cleaners, because she arrived before they had finished their work and always chatted with them — but she was intensely interested in whether people were happy in the work they were doing. If not, she tried to do something about it; there was no 'like it or lump it' attitude about P.C.C. She responded quickly and sensitively to anyone's difficulties. She made such high demands on herself that though we knew we couldn't reach her standards, we would have felt ashamed not to try to imitate her so far as we could. As she herself admitted, she was always obsessed by the need for speed and, if she gave you a particular job to do, you knew you would have no peace until you did it, so you learned to put everything else aside or take it to do at home! But the demands she made were never unreasonable. She had that quality so essential in a good administrator but so sadly lacking in many enthusiasts or 'ideas men' of seeing the practical implications in terms of work, of any new scheme or line of action proposed.

She achieved results much more by example than by *telling* people. She was a born teacher, whether of a group of leaders or a personal secretary. She produced 'guides' galore – *Headquarters Office Guide, Regional Office Guide, National Recreation Centre Guide* – all containing detailed and carefully indexed instructions on procedure and finance, all periodically revised. Nothing was too insignificant – what information should be given on training course leaflets, how petty cash and other financial records should be kept, literary conventions to be observed about e.g. the use of capitals for Region and Headquarters when used as nouns and of 'smalls' for regional and headquarters when used adjectivally, how to complete all the periodical reports and statements required by Headquarters. The practical advantages of these guides in ease of working and uniformity of organisation were immense, particularly for new Representatives who joined the staff with little experience of administration.

Her own powers of organisation were impressive – every contingency was provided for and responsibilities allocated with precision. In any event for which she was responsible – annual general meetings, conferences and committees – things were so well planned in advance that she always had time to talk to individual people who wanted to see her, and never appeared harassed or distracted. She had a beautifully clear mind – a quality evident in everything she wrote or said and she seized on the point of any argument with great rapidity. Though not easily diverted from any course of action her instinct or 'hunch' told her was the right one, she would always listen to contrary points of view with courtesy and attention. She was very skilful at 'letting other people have her way' and making it appear that the suggestion for a course of action she favoured had come from the other person. She never made the mistake of arousing antagonism by being over-forceful, though she seldom accepted and did not like accepting defeat. She had a quiet persistence which won respect, as did the way she marshalled her facts and arguments. It was always clear that the cause she was fighting for was the CCPR, not herself. She sought no personal publicity – no photograph of her ever appeared in any Annual Report – and disliked it when, as sometimes happened, her colleagues did not follow her example. Their function was to be 'back-room boys' and she was uneasy when any of them seemed disposed to want to step out on to the balcony.

Her emotions were under complete control and it was seldom easy to know what she was really thinking, in public or in private. She was essentially feminine and no-one ever suggested she was anything else, in spite of her abilities. She took a woman's interest in her dress and appearance and had a woman's knowledge of male psychology. She knew how to appeal to male protectiveness and how to flatter men, and she acted with consummate skill the rôle of the helpless and ignorant female who wanted male help in traditionally masculine fields of finance, commerce or negotiation with lawyers. She knew that most men didn't like women who got the better of them, and in one letter she sent to me while I was on holiday she referred to the 'very trying talks' she had been having about the Ministry's annual grant to the CCPR with one of the few successive Assistant Secretaries at the Ministry of Education whom she found uncongenial and unresponsive. "I won't trouble you with details now", she wrote, "as you will be able to read my reports on your return, but by Thursday afternoon I really thought that I had got to the point where I couldn't stand any more. In the end I 'scored' several points, but I knew that to do so was tactically bad : Y. is the last person to take kindly to being 'scored over' by a woman and unfortunately it seems quite impossible to coax *him* to have the ideas!"

She preferred to do important negotiations on her own without being accompanied by an Officer or a deputy, as this gave her freer range for her tactical skill. And she was generally more successful in her dealings with people at the top, such as Ministers and higher civil servants, probably because they were quicker at seeing her virtues than lesser mortals! Two of the tributes to her printed in Appendix A speak of her as being 'ruthless'. This was a quality I never saw in her. Determined, she certainly was, and pertinacious, but ruthlessness was a quality I think she lacked. She had not got the capacity to ignore other people's feelings, which the ruthless person has. She went through agonies before she could be persuaded by her senior colleagues that someone should be 'sacked', and there were several members of the staff she felt ought to be 'sacked' without being able to bring herself to the point of action. When she did 'sack' somebody – never without the most convincing justification – she always succeeded in doing so without making a personal enemy of the man or woman. However much she wanted to get rid of some 'useless' committee member – a contingency by no means rare – she could never do so if the person concerned wanted to continue. She would even get a nomination for him or her, if asked to do so.

Once she wrote to me: "One of my many weaknesses is that I LOATHE rows". And she had no weapons in her armoury for dealing with bullies. She just collapsed weakly in face of rudeness, on the rare instances when it occurred. She knew that people's temperaments and methods of working differed and allowed for it, but she resented it when a challenge to her authority was represented as 'a personal clash'. She wrote: "It may be old age, but I for one have got to the point (ashamed as I am to admit it) where I'd rather have a little less expansion, if need be, and more cooperation and feeling of colleagueship". On another occasion, she wrote to me: "I am a bit upset because I have reason to believe that X" (a senior colleague) "told me a deliberate lie yesterday – a quite unimportant matter. Nasty feeling. We all, I suppose, tell minor lies – but not, I hope, deliberate and quite unnecessary ones."

Naturally there were some conflicts within the office about the way the CCPR should be run, not least about the devolution of responsibilities to various members of the staff and whether the administrative and technical sides of the organisation should, or could, be divorced. Quite clearly, the CCPR could only be run as it was because the principal executive officer was able and prepared to get through such an enormous amount of detailed work. Though she saw the need in theory, P.C.C. never found it easy to divest herself of final responsibility for everything that took place within the CCPR. And this was particularly true about relations with the staff. She was present at all new appointments interviews, and liked to keep in touch with each new member of the staff individually – direct rather than through a third party. She visited the Regions, Scotland, Wales and Northern Ireland as well as the Centres whenever she could. At national staff conferences, she not only gave the opening and final addresses and took the chair for all discussion sessions, but found time for personal 'chats' with virtually every single one of the sixty or more people present, often from before breakfast until after midnight. And she would similarly see any member of the regional staff or Centre Warden who visited Headquarters on any occasion. Only in this way she felt, could she keep her finger on the pulse of the organisation in the way she thought necessary.

It was a method of working open to obvious objections, of which she was well aware. But she knew no other way of working, and, with one or two exceptions, the staff accepted it gladly. They liked the interest she took in their work individually and her accessibility. And she certainly knew what was going on. With an ear close to the ground, she knew where there were personal dissensions or where the relations between the sexes were not good. She was the recipient of confidences and of grumbles, too, and some in senior positions were afraid that she knew too much and that her methods encouraged 'tale-bearing'. There were constant pleas for 'a chain of command', a phrase she detested, perhaps wrongly.

Though she would not have admitted it, even to herself, there was more than a suspicion of 'divide et impera' about her methods. She liked all the staff to have good personal relations with her and cultivated them assiduously, but seemed uneasy and surprised, if she heard that her colleagues, even senior ones, had been discussing some policy matter among themselves. Perhaps she might have done more to promote good relations among the staff themselves. If she knew that two were at 'loggerheads' – say a man and a woman Senior Representative in a particular Region – she would see them separately but never bring them together in her company to thrash things out, and perhaps 'knock their heads together'! And she was apt to treat the Honorary Officers and committee members with exaggerated respect, as though they were a different order of beings from the staff, and to be very possessive about them.

Fundamentally, the only one she trusted was herself, and perhaps her methods did not encourage all the staff – particularly those at Headquarters – to reach their full potential. Some accepted the situation; others were irked by it and made no secret of their views. She always disclaimed any suggestion that 'she *was* the CCPR'. She was no dictator and never desired the title 'Director', as she disliked the implications of the word. No one bore that title in the CCPR while she was there. But she was 'facile princeps' not 'primus inter pares' – 'the obvious chief' not just 'first among equals' – and it would be false to pretend otherwise. But she never talked in a proprietary way about the CCPR and never said 'my staff', or even thought it.

She was content to work behind the scenes, and did so most effectively. She never expressed in public, and very seldom in committee, her own view on any controversial matter, however strongly she felt – for example about the establishment of a Sports Development Council, the desire of the Scottish Section for autonomy, or the CCPR's title. In this way she kept friends with everybody, avoided head-on collisions, tacitly discouraged the airing of contentious topics at committees and conferences, while preserving her own freedom to exercise influence quietly.

She never thought of herself as an important figure in the world of sport. When invited to big sporting events such as the Cup Final, Soccer Internationals or Wimbledon, she went more for public relations than for pleasure, though she did admit to a partiality for matches in which Stanley Matthews was playing! While not indifferent to Britain's success in international sport, her real aim in life was to provide physical recreation for ordinary people, and it took some time before her colleagues were able to persuade her that National Recreation Centres should work at the highest possible level of performance if they were to justify their cost and make their maximum contribution.

She was essentially forward-looking, so much so that retrospection or reminiscence was positively distasteful to her. In 1956, she wrote very truly: "So far as the CCPR goes, I do not find it easy to think of the past – perhaps because the future has always seemed more important." Even in her retirement she never wanted to talk about the CCPR of the past – her concern and anxiety was with the CCPR of the present. Even 'post mortems' on events that had just taken place didn't interest her. As soon as one hurdle was overcome, no opportunity was given to relax and recover – the next hurdle had to be tackled at once. Her bent was practical rather than reflective, and though she tried to conceal it, she never had much time for debates, which she thought were rather pointless intellectual exercises, not worth spending time on. Though she organised and took part in several international conferences, she valued them for the opportunities they gave for personal contacts rather than for any hope of concrete results. And she seldom warmed to a suggestion of having an outside speaker for the CCPR's A.G.M., always preferring a practical display of the CCPR's work through visual aids. And it is perhaps significant that in her time the CCPR never organised an annual conference in a way common with so many other national voluntary organisations.

An insight into both her preoccupations and her methods is given in this extract from a letter she wrote me while I was on holiday during her last summer with the CCPR: "I don't quite know what makes you say 'August ought to be quiet' at HQ! These are just a few of the things I have been wrestling with or ought to have tackled and haven't: Annual Report proofs – real crisis about accounts; all A.G.M. papers – barely touched; National Sailing Trust; Crystal Palace estimates – not started; Regional Officers' applications – a real 'issue' with the Reps.; Executive elections – I've muffed it; W.W. – meeting next week; UK Asscn. memo – not started; Memo re duties – not finished; regional expenditure memo – just started; Staff Conference programme; staff group preparation – not started; and Appreciation of H.A.C. – not started. I think I could go on for ever! I am not trying to lam it on but your remark struck me as *so* funny: Actually I'm feeling quite desperate as I can see no hope of getting through even the essentials by Thursday ..." She then proceeded to write in some detail about her health and a new treatment she was having, and ended by "I don't know why I've mentioned all this – perhaps because my usual buddies are away!"

She genuinely didn't enjoy making public speeches, but whenever she did so, she was most effective. Some of her most inspired addresses were those delivered at the beginning of staff conferences when she set the tone for the whole subsequent proceedings, and those at the end, when she sent us all away in a mood of unity and high ideals. She had the gift of making speeches sound spontaneous which had in fact been prepared verbatim very carefully beforehand.

The news of P.C.C.'s decision to retire evoked an outburst of loyalty and affection on the part of staff and committees alike. It was impossible to imagine what the CCPR would be like without her, and few were happy at the prospect. At her last A.G.M. in November 1962, Prince Philip, in his presidential remarks, said that the tremendous admiration and gratitude of all members of the CCPR for her work from the time of the Council's conception to the present day should be put on record. A great many others had also worked very hard indeed for the CCPR from the beginning but he was sure they would forgive him for saying that she was really responsible for all its success and for its present standing. There was no doubt, he said, that the CCPR had achieved a very important position in the country. One had only to look at the list of bodies represented on the Council to see how many different organisations there were who saw the value of a common meeting ground.

P.C.C. made it clear to the Executive that it was not retirement in the normal sense. She would want to work for both interest and financial reasons. As the CCPR had filled her life for twenty-eight years, it was time she tried to widen her horizons. The staff gave a farewell party to her one evening in December 1962, when she was presented with a nest of inlaid mahogany tables, a travelling alarm clock in a pigskin case, and a filigree brooch set with her favourite blue tinted moonstones. Typically, she sent a 'thank-you' letter to all who had contributed, saying "I am delighted with them all and still feel utterly amazed by the £200 cheque." After her last Executive, she was presented on behalf of the Council by Sir Stanley with a piece of antique silver and a cheque, and the April 1963 issue of *Sport and Recreation* contained a number of tributes, which appear in the Appendix.

She left on 31st March 1963, having, by agreement with the Ministry, been given a part-time paid post as Consultant to the CCPR. She was seldom in fact, 'consulted' and this hurt her as she felt that she was getting money by false pretences. A very few days after her retirement, she wrote to me, "Everyone's lurid assurances that it would be well-nigh impossible for me to wrench myself away from the CC seem to have been quite inapplicable. I appear to have slid out of the saddle without any difficulty whatever, though I don't pretend that I have yet hitched to any particular future star! Thank you very much for both perorations in *Sport and Recreation* – it was good of you to be so generous. Among my many shortcomings is one that few people realise – complete and genuine inability to feel satisfaction, gratification, pride or anything of that kind, when I hear or read tributes to my work. Anna Broman always used to say it was a tremendous lack on my part and I certainly think she was right. Nevertheless, though it all leaves me as detached as ever, I can still feel wonder, even gratitude, to those who bother to speak or write." (Dr. Broman had been one of her closest and oldest friends, a niece of the famous Madame Osterberg who founded Dartford College, and whose assistant Miss Stanfeld had been).

She had always suffered so much pain, that it was a surprise to those who knew her that she did not completely collapse when the anodyne of looking after the CCPR was removed from her life. But she found plenty of other anodynes. The Duke of Edinburgh's Award made her a General Consultant in 1963, and the following year she was employed by the Award Office to carry out "a constructive examination of the operation and effectiveness of the Scheme". Her report was presented in the Trustees of the Award in 1965. Its contents were confidential, but its recommendations were regarded so highly that she was made one of the Award's Trustees in 1965. She did much personal work for some charities which had long had her support and allegiance, and she remembered them in her Will. For many years she spent part of the short periods of holiday she allowed herself, helping at one of the Rudolf Steiner Schools for Handicapped Children in this country, and she did clerical work for the London Samaritans. She also took to painting in oils in her retirement and showed surprising talent in that field.

Many of her former colleagues in the CCPR and in her profession kept in touch with her. Indeed, their devoted personal service helped her to live as long as she did. Her interest in the world of physical recreation was undiminished, though, not surprisingly, she was not happy about everything that was happening. She continued to attend meetings of the Youth Service Development Council. She was created C.B.E. in 1964, and was made the CCPR's first Honorary Life Vice-President the same year. Both nationally and internationally, she had many honours from her profession, including the Presidency and Honorary Membership of the Physical Education Association and the Titre Honorifique de la Fédération d'Education Physique. From 1962, she was a governor of Dartford College of Physical Education. Truly, in her were exemplified the finest traditions of women's physical education in this country – per-

sonal discipline, aesthetic sensibility, the concept of physical education as a means to social and moral ends, and a sense of
proportion about athletic prowess and success in team
games.

In the first couple of years after her retirement from the
CCPR I saw little of her. Our talk would inevitably have been
of 'shop' and I knew that she was sore at her neglect. It seemed
wiser to pursue our separate courses. After I became Acting
General Secretary, we saw more of each other. As always,
she would dictate the subjects of conversation and, as always,
it was of the present and future, not of the past. She did not
conceal her uneasiness about the setting up of a Sports Council
and its probable ultimate effect upon the CCPR. She could not
grasp that, in any case, the CCPR could not survive the removal
of her own all-pervading influence without great changes. It was
sad to feel her disenchantment.

She came to most A.G.M.'s and the Executive lunches that
followed them. After my last A.G.M. in November 1967, she
wrote, "The A.G.M. gave me personally a most peculiar feeling
– one which I hadn't anticipated and which wasn't a very
happy one. The nearest I can get to putting it into words is
to say that it was as if my own connection with the CC was
being finally severed. Stupid and untrue, I know. Throughout
these $4\frac{1}{2}$ years, I have felt both detached and objective, but as
long as you were there, I knew that at least my interest was
welcomed. It certainly won't be *truly* so from now on. I don't
mind but it's just an odd feeling."

Her later letters became more communicative about her
health. "I go into King's College Hospital for about a
fortnight for an op. on my right eye", she wrote. "I am despic-
ably terrified. Unfortunately I have got to cope with not only
the fear and distaste which most people feel but with a deep-
seated pathological – and therefore wholly irrational – terror of
hospitals and operations, even of doctors. It makes me feel
very ashamed, but it is *very,* very real". In March 1968:
"Things haven't been very easy during the last few weeks –
the usual insides trouble and a severe setback with eyes. Oh!
for some PEACE. That's all I want". The following year she
was again suffering "extreme eye trouble ... practically no
sight, and pain which nearly sent me berserk I am ashamed
to say ... I now have to insert artificial tears almost hourly –

what a life! Still, I'm back to the contact lens, and can, therefore see again, thank goodness."

In July 1970, after Eldon Griffiths had succeeded Denis Howell as Minister, she wrote, "I wonder how Walter will get on with his new boss and vice versa!". By August 1971, she had learned of the plans for the merger of the CCPR with the Sports Council and revoked the bequest of £1,000 she had made to it in her will. To her 1971 Christmas card to one of her very old colleagues, she added the note, "I often wonder how you are. Well, I hope. No doubt you know that the poor old C.C. is being killed off – sacrilege! I might have been able to 'take it' if I thought the new set-up would be progressive. I don't. Too political. Bang goes a 'life's work' to which *you* made a most valuable contribution."

The end of her life came in hospital on 26th June 1972. A Memorial Service was held at the Church of St. Martin-in-the-Fields on 12th October, arranged by June Mack, one of her former secretaries. Phyllis Spafford read the lesson and Sir John Wolfenden gave an eloquent address of deep insight, which is reproduced in Appendix A.

The immense congregation which assembled from all parts of the country to salute her memory proved that – far from 'going bang' – her life's work lived on in the hearts of all who had worked with and for her. Apart from the perpetuation of her name in Colson House at Lilleshall and in the Colson Memorial Fund established by the CCPR, the "vision splendid" that inspired her had been communicated to countless others and lives on "not on tablets of brass but woven into the stuff of other men's lives".

CHAPTER TWELVE

Committees, Staff and Finance

Many incidental references have been made in earlier Chapters to the CCPR's committee structure, staffing and finances but, to complete the picture, some more general and synoptic comments are called for. As the drawing up of the CCPR's initial constitution, on which all its administration was based, was P.C.C.'s work, it seems appropriate that these comments should follow the Chapter about her.

The Council itself consisted of two types of members – individual members, men and women elected by virtue of their services, actual or potential, to the CCPR or to physical recreation in general; and representative members, one appointed by each national body concerned with physical recreation directly or indirectly, which had applied for such representation. The total final membership of the Council was about 300, of whom 80 were individual members and the remainder representative members. The Council met once a year at an A.G.M., its principal business being to elect the President, Honorary Treasurer and the members of the Executive Committee, and to receive and approve the Annual Report and financial accounts.

At the 1944 A.G.M., a motion proposed by H. G. H. Chandler of the Amateur Boxing Association, and seconded by E. J. Holt of the Amateur Athletic Association that individual members should be honorary members and have no votes, was heavily defeated.

In all, the Council met thirty-seven times, at the YWCA's Queen Mary Hall twelve times and at International Students' House nine times. Presiding were Lord Astor, five times, Lord Hampden, ten times, Prince Philip, thirteen times, and Sir Stanley Rous, nine times. Special speakers who addressed the Council, at or after the A.G.M., were Sir Wilson Jameson (chief medical officer of the Board of Education), Sir John Wolfenden (twice), Sir David Eccles (Minister of Education), Philip Noel-Baker, M.P., the Marquess of Exeter, P.C.C., Lord

Hailsham, Lord Rupert Nevill, Sir Harry Pilkington, Denis Howell, M.P. (twice) and Eldon Griffiths, M.P.

The Executive Committee, consisting of about thirty members, met not less than three times a year. It appointed its own chairman and deputy chairman, and its own sub-committees, of which the most influential was the General Purposes and Finance Committee, consisting of the Honorary Officers and about ten other members of the Executive. This had two important standing sub-committees – the Staff Committee and the Staff Appointments Committee. The other main sub-committees of the Executive were the Welsh and N. Ireland Committees, the Management Committees of the National Recreation Centres, the Games and Sports Committee, the Outdoor Activities Committee, and a third committee with a somewhat fluctuating life, title and function, called originally Recreative Gymnastics and Dancing, then Indoor Physical Recreation and General Technical Committee, but revived in 1969 as the Movement and Dance Committee.

One of the remarkable features of the CCPR was the permanence and stability of its composition – there were, of course, 'birds of passage', but, generally speaking, Honorary Officers, committee members and staff, once appointed, stayed for life. In its thirty-seven years, it had three Presidents – Lord Astor (ten years), Lord Hampden (six years) and Prince Philip (twenty-one years) – five Honorary Treasurers – Lord Hampden (two years), Sir Percival Sharp (seven years), Sir John Catlow (three years), Sir Clarence Sadd (fifteen years) and Robin Brook (ten years) – two Chairmen of the Executive – Lord Hampden (ten years) and Sir Stanley Rous (27 years) – and two Deputy-Chairmen of the Executive – Sir Stanley Rous (nine years) and Arthur Gem (twenty-seven years). Similarly, the chairmen of most of the other committees, especially the Centre Committees were long-serving, as can be seen from Appendix B. The average length of service of members of the Executive was considerable. Of the thirty members in 1972, fifteen had been members in 1962 and six in 1952.

The fact that Officers, chairmen and committee members served on an average for so long meant that all committee meetings took place against a background of extensive knowledge of the CCPR's aims and work, and of considerable knowledge by the members of each other, which tended to save time and to lead to smooth despatch of business – some might say too smooth! It would be true to say that within the CCPR, the Council trusted the Executive, the Executive trusted the General Purposes and Finance Committee, the General Purposes and Finance Committee trusted the Honorary Officers and the Honorary Officers trusted the General Secretary. This happy situation carried with it the risk of the development of either a dictatorship or an oligarchical form of government, but to a large extent the dangers were avoided.

One of the great strengths of the Executive Committee was that, with the exception of the Chairmen of the Welsh and Northern Ireland Committees, its members served in a personal capacity and not as the representatives of any particular body or interest. Though membership of the Executive was open to any member of the Council, whether individual or representative, who cared to stand, in practice the number of individual members on the Executive always far exceeded the number of representative members. For example in the 1962 Executive, there were twenty-three individual and nine representative members; in the 1972 Executive, the ratio was much the same – twenty-one to nine. Moreover, there was little competition from members to get elected to the Executive – not a very healthy sign. Very rarely indeed did the number of nominations exceed the places available, and so there was seldom any election.

So it could not be fairly claimed that the Executive was 'the voice of sport' in any representative sense. The lack of competition for seats on the Executive must be taken as implying that many of the bodies represented on the Council did not attach any particular importance to membership of it – either they regarded the Executive as a body concerned exclusively with the domestic affairs of the Council and not with wider issues or, in the Author's view more probably, they were so preoccupied with the business of their own particular bodies that they had no time or energy to spare to take an active part in the life of what they may have looked on as a professional servicing body. Indeed, the evidence does support the view that has been expressed by some that the largest and most influential sports bodies in the country, though ready to give general support to the work of the CCPR and derive what benefit they could from the services it offered, did not look upon it in any sense as their own creation or responsibility. Except in its very early years, active hostility to the CCPR on the part of any of the sports bodies was rare, though perhaps there was a fear in the minds of some that any strengthening of the power of the CCPR would be at the expense of their own freedom and autonomy.

Some further analysis of the Executive's composition in the sample years 1952, 1962, and 1972 may be of interest in showing the types of experience represented:

EXECUTIVE COMMITTEE MEMBERSHIP

Individual Members – elected
as members of the Council
for achievement in the
following spheres:

	1952	1962	1972
Sport	6	7	10
Outdoor Activity	1	5	4
Physical education	3	6	5
General education	2	3	2
Youth work	–	1	0
Miscellaneous	5	1	0
	17	23	21
Representative Members – drawn from:			
Sports Bodies	3	5	5
Outdoor Activity Bodies	1	3	1
Physical education	1	0	1
Youth work	4	1	0
Education	3	0	1
General	2	0	1
	14	9	9
Total	31	32	30

One striking feature is the declining part played by youth service bodies in the counsels of the CCPR, and the statistics confirm the comments made in Chapter Six. In its earliest days youth organisations provided about 20 per cent of the Executive's membership and were strongly represented on its Technical Advisory Committee. No fewer than thirteen physical recreation organisers were appointed by youth organisations in National Fitness Council days with grants from the NFC. Yet though the Council's membership throughout its life included nearly forty youth service bodies and the Council worked closely with many of them, nominations to serve on the Executive were seldom received from any of them during the Council's post-war life. Repeated attempts to form a sub-committee to concern itself with physical recreation in the youth service broke down through failure to find sufficient common ground, though about six of the national voluntary youth organisations were represented on the Outdoor Activities Committee and played a useful part on it. Similarly in Wales, it was never found possible to form a youth organisations sub-committee, though several of them were represented on the main CCPR Welsh Committee.

As the CCPR's individual members had been elected from men and women who had given many years' service to physical recreation and physical education one result was to make the Executive Committee a body able to bring to bear on any question a wealth of disinterested wisdom and experience. Its views could not be lightly disregarded. There was, however, an important direction in which it differed from most committees running voluntary organisations. Such committees are generally composed of men and women whose work, particularly in the direction of fund-raising, makes the continued existence of their organisation possible. Whereas, in the case of the CCPR, after 1937 its continuance depended on the success of P.C.C., supported on occasions by the Honorary Officers, in persuading the Ministry of Education (and during the war, the Ministry of Labour) to finance its activities. Even in the years of the National Sports Development Fund when additional funds were badly needed, neither the members of the Executive nor of the Council as a whole, though subjected at successive A.G.M.'s to what Prince Philip described as "the sad story" told by Sir Clarence Sadd, the Honorary Treasurer, took any collective responsibility for raising money. A few individual members and organisations gave donations, of which, as explained in Chapter Five, the most outstanding was the Football Association. But, in the main, it was left to the Council's professional staff, none of whom had been engaged or trained for the purpose, to arrange

money-making events and promote collections at National Recreation Centres. They showed their loyalty to the organisation
by working hard in this as in other ways. But providing finance
for the Council's work was not looked upon by the members
of the Council as their responsibility, and there is, in fact, no
record of any legacy being left to the CCPR by any of its few
wealthy members.

No-one can read through the volumes recording the proceedings of the CCPR's numerous committees without feelings
of profound respect and admiration for the value of the voluntary service given by their members, in terms of guidance, support and influence outside the committee room, as well as in
the personal encouragement they gave to the members of the
staff at all levels. This was the real secret of the CCPR's essential spirit – a devoted and hard-working staff, sustained in their
difficult work by the knowledge that they had the committees'
backing, interest and, often, personal friendship. In any voluntary organisation, this relationship between the voluntary committee members and the paid staff, delicately balanced so that
neither must usurp the function of the other, is a precious and
irreplaceable element. Apart from any other justification, the
fact that the staff had constantly to report on their work to the
committees kept them 'on their toes', as it were, and prevented
the organisation from being bureaucratic as otherwise it might
easily have become.

Agenda and Minutes for the Council's committees were prepared with great care, and a special 'Chairman's Agenda' always got ready for reference beforehand. Most meetings were
conducted with strict regard for the value of the members' time
– indeed, it sometimes seemed more important to finish a meeting at the time expected than to thrash out some controversial
issue to a conclusion. It was a rare thing for a vote to be taken
at a CCPR committee, and some members were known to
complain that in the prevailing atmosphere of geniality and
expedition, they were genuinely afraid of saying anything that
might seem to strike a discordant note or delay the proceedings.
Indeed, the fact that the Executive were not permitted to reach
an agreed conclusion – even by a majority vote – on the main
recommendation of the Wolfenden Committee led to a good
deal of dissatisfaction on the part of some members, who felt
that the Executive should have given clearer instructions to the

Honorary Officers and General Secretary who were to be its spokesmen at meetings with the Ministry of Education and with the Minister with special responsibility for sport. It would have been difficult to predict that an Executive which in 1961 did not come to any fixed expression of its views about a Sports Council should, ten years later, have reached a position where it had no real option but to agree to a merger with the Sports Council, as will be described later.

But controversy was rare and the normal meetings of the Executive, as of the General Purposes and Finance Committee, were pleasant and friendly occasions, presided over with easy bonhomie by Sir Stanley. Most deputies are seldom called upon, but Sir Stanley's football peregrinations and preoccupations meant that he had to miss many meetings, but Arthur Gem was always available to deputise, often at short notice, and did so as a chairman of practised skill.

Though attention has been paid to the Council's other committees in earlier Chapters, some further reference must be made here to the Games and Sports Committee, one of the Council's potentially most influential committees. The preparation of the Agenda for this committee caused the staff many headaches. Set up in 1943 at the suggestion of eight governing bodies "in order to remove misunderstandings between governing bodies and the CCPR", membership was open to representatives of all governing bodies of competitive sports represented on the Council. From an initial fifteen the membership steadily increased and some early suspicions of the Council were removed. The committee's title and terms of reference were changed from time to time, but a persistent problem was to give its proceedings real punch and vitality, and to persuade the larger governing bodies that its work was, or could be, sufficiently important to warrant their sending their 'top' men there. The difficulty was to produce an Agenda which would provide sufficient matters of interest and importance to give the meetings a real value, without encroaching on topics which some of the bodies would regard as impinging on their own spheres of sovereignty.

The possibility of forming regional sports councils was discussed as early as 1943 and 1945, though with suggested functions very different from those of the Regional Councils set up in 1965. Fitness badge schemes were considered several times, but no great enthusiasm for them emerged. Legislative matters, such as clothing coupons, entertainment duty, railway fares, purchase tax, income tax, rating of sports grounds, frequently appeared on the agenda, and the governing bodies clearly valued the help the CCPR was trying to give them in these fields. Reports of the staff's work in the development of games and sports were presented as attractively and comprehensively as possible and received with apparent satisfaction, and many useful meetings were held with the Council's technical staff working in Wales and the Regions, whose services in developing and often administering the governing bodies' coaching schemes were increasingly welcomed. The ability of the CCPR to offer office accommodation and secretarial facilities in 1964 was a great move forward.

In 1971, W.W. felt able to inform the Games and Sports Committee at one of its meetings that it had now become a real forum for sport, and that it could become as active and powerful as its constituent bodies wanted it to be. Under its successive chairmen the committee did valuable work – it brought the governing bodies not only into touch with the CCPR but also into closer personal relations with one another. When a merger of the CCPR with the Sports Council was first mooted, the committee's reaction was a lively one and showed how much the governing bodies had come to appreciate the opportunity to meet together under the auspices of the CCPR. Robin Struthers of the Hockey Association, the committee's chairman, played a vital part in the negotiations to secure that the bodies would continue to meet in conference as a group independent of the Sports Council.

During her General Secretaryship, P.C.C. served as secretary of all the CCPR's committees herself, with the exception of the Centres' committees, of responsibility for which she gradually divested herself. Soon after her retirement, a deliberate policy was adopted of spreading the committee secretaryships among different members of headquarters staff, both administrative and technical.

We now turn to consider the place of the CCPR's staff. When the material assets of the CCPR were transferred to the statutory Sports Council in June 1972, their capital value represented a very considerable financial sum. It is arguable that, in taking over the CCPR's staff, the Sports Council acquired an additional asset of even greater value.

Apart from the secretarial, clerical, domestic and maintenance staff in its offices and Centres, the CCPR in 1972 employed
a technical and senior administrative staff of about 110, of
whom 88 were qualified and experienced teachers, the great
majority having full professional qualifications in physical education. In addition to their technical and professional training, a
large proportion of them had had long and wide experience of
service with the CCPR. As one example, when the nine
Regional Officers of the CCPR and the Welsh Secretary became
Secretaries of the Regional Sports Councils and the Sports
Council for Wales in 1965, they brought with them an average
of nearly seventeen years' experience each of regional CCPR
work – a very valuable asset indeed. Similar length of experience
of CCPR work had been gained by htose employed at Headquarters and at the Centres.

The main unifying element in the men and women technical
staff was their professional qualification as physical educationists : this was a cohesive influence of great strength. Nearly
all of them had had some years' teaching in schools. They
joined the CCPR because they wanted promotion or wider
experience, or a change from school teaching, but the main
attraction was undoubtedly that the CCPR offered work that
was adventurous, varied, stimulating and utterly devoid of rou-
tine. It entailed hard work and irregular hours – a fact of
which everyone interviewed for appointment was left in no
doubt. The financial inducements were small – for new en-
trants, a teachers' Burnham salary plus a modest responsibility
allowance, with no opportunity for earning more through evening classes or vacation work. Salary scales were negotiated in
later years which bore more analogy with the Soulbury scales
for organisers employed by local education authorities. Holidays
were six weeks – shorter than a teacher's. Work at weekends,
over long evenings, extensive travelling and frequent absences
from home were accepted cheerfully as part of the job. There
was no such thing as 'overtime' or 'time off in lieu'. Promotion
prospects in the service were reasonable, without being dazzling.

By its nature the work attracted men and women of originality, ability, self-confidence and adaptability, and when they
joined the CCPR they found themselves welcomed into a close
and warm fellowship. Newcomers learned the job from their
seniors with some help from the Technical Advisers, but much

of the training given came through attendance at the annual five-days' staff conferences, to which P.C.C. had attached great importance from the Council's earliest days. They had an intensely serious purpose and a crowded timetable, even though the first staff conferences went under the disarming title of 'staff reunions'!

In the first ten years or so, much attention was given at staff conferences to practical work. For instance, a keen organiser of the Bicycle Polo Association which had lately joined the Council wanted the Representatives to help to develop bicycle polo, so a training session was arranged for the staff to try their hands – or more correctly, their seats – on such unusual mounts! Members of the staff with special skills were persuaded to take training sessions for their colleagues. Examples that come to mind are Bill Park with soccer training, Ray Williams with rugger training, Charlie Cromar with 'wide games', Barbara Dummett with ballroom dancing, Eve Clarkson and Janie Withers with square dancing, and George McPartlin, trying in vain to take the subject seriously, in stick work! But such pleasant and often hilarious occasions became a thing of the past, and attention was turned to discussions and lectures on more serious and theoretical if less sociable subjects.

These staff conferences served a number of extremely useful purposes. They kept the whole staff in touch with each other as a national staff – and this was especially important in the case of those working at Centres, who tended to be rather isolated from the rest – and they kept the staff well informed and up-to-date about national developments through talks by P.C.C., the Technical Advisers or special visitors. They enabled the staff to meet, and to discuss the Council's services with particular groups of the Council's membership – governing bodies, youth organisations and so on. The Ministry's liaison officers and other officials of the Ministry such as B. L. Pearson and John Swindale were welcome visitors at many conferences, and fruitful sessions about the CCPR's functions were held with them. Speakers came from outside bodies such as the National Parks Commission, the Central Council for Health Education, & H.M. Prison Commission. Sessions were held with the BAOLPE, the PEA and the National Association of Youth Service Officers to discuss cooperation. Denis Howell, when Minister for Sport, came more than once, accompanied by Sir John Lang. So did Eldon

Griffiths. Other staff conference speakers included Roger Bannister, Tom Bedwell, Dr. Wilfred Burns, Christopher Chataway M.P., H. C. Dent, Michael Dower, R. J. S. Hookway, Sir John Hunt, Arthur Ling, Jack Longland, A. D. Munrow, Sir Arthur Porritt, Tom Pritchard, Sir Ben Bowen Thomas, W. Tuxworth, R. E. Williams and Gerald Williamson. The main purpose was always to widen the staff's horizons and to foster good relations with the bodies they served. A pleasant tradition grew up of ending the conference with a final dinner at which the staff were hosts to guests they wanted to entertain, including the Honorary Officers and officials of the Ministry.

The work of the Council itself was naturally the major topic for discussion, and P.C.C. made it clear to the staff that it was not their function to decide policy. But the views of the staff as expressed, if not formally recorded, at their successive conferences did in fact have a marked effect upon the Council's work. It has already been noted that it was a staff conference discussion that led to the setting up of the Wolfenden Committee. In the view of A. L. Colbeck, a very long-serving, senior member of the staff : "it was the staff, from P.C.C. downwards, rather than the Executive which did most of the thinking and most of the initiating, especially in the exciting decade from 1951–1960." He writes of : "the annual heart-searching and painful reappraisals that characterised everything we did at staff conferences and, subsequently, in regions and at HQ. It was this constant questioning of our aims and methods which more than anything else in my view gave impetus and direction to the machine, and it was to P.C.C.'s eternal credit that she was able to keep us all with our noses in the same direction."

As will have been gathered from the previous Chapter, P.C.C. was not very democratically-minded, and she always tended to resist any move on the part of the technical staff to set up a form of machinery through which they could be officially consulted either about matters of CCPR policy or about their salaries and conditions of service. There was little 'trade union spirit' within the staff, though the question of salaries was of great concern, especially to the men. But such was the general confidence in P.C.C.'s negotiating skill and her devotion to the staff's interests, that 'leave it to P.C.C.' was accepted as the most rewarding course to follow.

On the matter of the CCPR's policy, there was more discontent about the lack of consultation, especially after the Sports Council was formed. At the staff conference in December 1966 the staff formally asked that the Honorary Officers and the Executive Committee should be informed of "their wish to be consulted about any moves affecting the future of the CCPR as an organisation." The Chairman expressed surprise at this resolution, and considered that it raised the question as to whether it was the committee or the staff who decided the CCPR's policy. He and the Deputy Chairman, however, sent a confidential letter to the Regional Officers assuring them that nothing was being contemplated which would in any way weaken the fabric of the CCPR or adversely affect the status and conditions of service of those employed by the CCPR. Some account of the part played by the 'staff group' in the final negotiations before the transfer is given in Chapter Fourteen.

Some attention must now be paid to the relations between the technical members of the staff and their fellow members of the physical education profession. These were far from uniformly good. With many prominent members of the profession, the CCPR's relations were excellent – many heads of men's and women's colleges of physical education and some organisers of physical education served on its committees and supported the work of the Council in various ways.

Though in its early years the CCPR's notepaper carried under its title the words "Initiated by the Ling Physical Education Association and the National Association of Organisers of Physical Education", P.C.C. admitted on several private occasions that for strategic reasons she had exaggerated the part played by the those two bodies in the formation of the CCPR. In a memorandum written by hand shortly before her death she said, "In 1935, as a member of the Committee of the Ling Physical Education Association, I had the direct entrée to their officers and committees . . . Without that intimate link, I should imagine that it would have taken far longer to get the CC floated, particularly under the umbrella of the profession . . . Temperamentally and because of the obvious advantage of making the two associations and all their members feel committed, I kept myself as an individual more and more in the background."

As has been noted, P.C.C. was elected to high personal office in the PEA. But cooperation between the CCPR and the

PEA was not always as close or effective as it might have been. No doubt, some envy of the CCPR's growing power and success may have played its part. It is perhaps a matter for regret that more members of the CCPR's staff did not show their support for the PEA by becoming subscribing members of their own profession's association and playing an active part in its activities. Some, it must be emphasised did.

Between the British Association of Organisers and Lecturers in Physical Education and the CCPR, relations at an official level were, bluntly, not good, and a historian must record that fact. But there was personal cooperation and friendliness between many members of both bodies – some of them had been to college together, some organisers had served for periods on the staff of the CCPR and some members of the CCPR's staff, including the man Technical Adviser, had been organisers.

As usual in such situations, the causes of the lack of cordial relations between the two bodies were complex and partly personal. One particularly strong-minded woman organiser who had great influence within the BAOLPE was personally antagonistic to P.C.C. And quite a number of others were jealous of P.C.C.'s ability and success. They felt that the CCPR got all the limelight, whereas they got none. But there were other and less discreditable reasons. In 1935, when the CCPR started work, less than one third of the local education authorities employed their own organisers, and there was not only a need but a welcome given for the stimulation provided by the CCPR's Representatives – through demonstrations, classes and propaganda. But with the growth of the number of organisers and the inclusion in the 1944 Education Act of post-school physical recreation as well as school work within the sphere of responsibilities of local education authorities and their organisers, ill-feeling grew. The CCPR was accused of 'moving in', creating interest and demand, and then withdrawing, leaving a void with no means of filling it. This was said in spite of the fact that the staff's instructions were never to work within the area of local education authorities without the latter's agreement, except in response to a particular request for service from a voluntary organisation. And there were even cases where education officers wanted the CCPR's help when their organisers did not! Some organisers said there was no need for the CCPR to work in their areas as they were doing all that was necessary. Others said, perhaps more candidly, that if the CCPR did successful work in their areas, it demonstrated that they themselves were not doing all that they should be doing, which was naturally unacceptable. The organisers of Birmingham (where the CCPR had its regional office!) would not cooperate with the CCPR in any work whatever.

But the picture was by no means uniform, and many local authorities continued broadmindedly to make the fullest possible use of the CCPR and to express publicly their thanks for its services – in these areas, both personal and professional relations between the Representatives and the local organisers were excellent, and both sides benefited from the cooperation.

The position of Her Majesty's Physical Training Inspectorate in relation to the CCPR was not always easy. On the one hand, the CCPR was heavily grant-aided by their own Ministry and it was public policy for its services to be fully used. On the other, they could not be expected to take sides or use more than gentle influence with local authorities or organisers who did not want to use the CCPR. Here again, the picture was uneven and, as individuals, some members of the Inspectorate were better disposed to the CCPR than others. Several of the latter changed their minds as the years went by and became firm personal supporters of the CCPR. In general, in their relations with the Inspectorate in England as in Wales, the CCPR had little cause for anything but gratitude.

Such attempts as were made periodically to get the BAOLPE and the PEA round the table with the CCPR for frank and constructive talks had disappointing results, and though no doubt the reasons will continue to be a matter for debate, the persistence of bad relations with the BAOLPE must be looked upon as one of the CCPR's failures. The situation was slightly improved with the appointment of the Regional Officers to service the Regional Sports Councils. This gave the CCPR closer official contacts with various departments of local authorities. Many organisers of physical education worked happily alongside the CCPR in developing facilities promoted by Regional Sports Councils and two organisers served on each Council as observers.

One example of good cooperation between the PEA, the BAOLPE and the CCPR was in the work of the United Kingdom Committee for International Conferences on Physical

Education, on which all three were represented and of which P.C.C. was the Honorary Secretary for a good many years, being succeeded by Peter McIntosh on her retirement. This body was concerned with the International Congress on Physical Education and Sports for Women and Girls in London in 1957, and the international conferences in Barry in 1958 and at Crystal Palace in 1966 mentioned in earlier Chapters; it also arranged for United Kingdom representation at conferences overseas.

The introduction of 'equal pay for equal work' into the civil service and the teaching profession in 1955 naturally had its repercussions within the CCPR. The committee decided that the policy must be followed by the CCPR and the Ministry showed no hestitation about increasing the CCPR's grant for the purpose. But what *was* 'equal work'? Though there was a good deal of overlap, by and large the men Representatives looked after work with men and boys, and the women with women and girls. And there was no escaping the fact that the demands of the former were in volume greater than the latter. Moreover, the worlds of educational administration and of specialist games, sports and outdoor activities were still very much male-dominated. Though nominally the responsibilities of the two seniors in charge of the CCPR's work in the Regions were equal, in practice the heavier administrative load was being borne by the men. The men accepted this situation quite happily so long as there was some salary differentiation. But when that differentiation was being eroded over a period of seven years, the men grew restive. The CCPR women staff had never themselves agitated for equal pay, and P.C.C. did not in fact believe in it, but equal pay was national policy and the CCPR had no option but to conform. Happily, the tensions created by equal pay were removed, at least in part, by the creation of the posts of Regional Officer in 1961 and the following two years, as described in Chapter Ten.

In the CCPR's latest years, the normal technical establishment in each Region was of six Representatives, with rather more in London and the South-East and in Wales. It became increasingly difficult to recruit suitably qualified women to the staff – perhaps because of the changing emphasis in the Council's work – and by 1972 the number of women on the technical and senior administrative staff was only 20 out of 110, a remarkable drop compared with earlier years. The facts of the situation led the Staff Sub-Committee to decide in 1969 that all future posts in the CCPR should be open to men and women equally.

The pioneering spirit of the early staff was well maintained throughout the CCPR's life and there is no doubt that the implanting of that spirit was one of P.C.C.'s major creative achievements. As Jim Lane, Director of Lilleshall, wrote to the Author recently : "I remember being very amused on joining the CCPR by P.C.C.'s attitude towards Reps' husbands and wives. She tended to regard them in much the same manner as a famous headmistress we knew regarded parents, as necessary (and she wasn't quite certain about this) evils. She seriously expected all the staff to be as dedicated and single-minded as she was. The astonishing thing was, I remember thinking, that within reasonable limits a high percentage of them were.'

There were great and original personalities among the staff and, naturally, there were 'difficult' ones. But the underlying feeling of unity was such that the death of one was felt as a personal blow to all. Madge Docking, one of the earliest Reps, with a personality all her own, died in 1957. George Cormack died while on a course at Lilleshall in 1962; John Bradley died equally suddenly in 1966; and Eve Clarkson and George Hickling died soon after their retirements. And there was no sadder death than that of Tim Aron, one of the first three instructors at Plas y Brenin, who was drowned off the Anglesey coast while trying to save life, shortly after he had moved there with his young family to take up life as a farmer.

After what has already been said, little need be added about the CCPR's finances, except that, from the start, P.C.C. set a pattern of economy and efficiency that was never altered in her time. In some quarters, the idea was current, particularly among those who had been less successful in securing statutory grant-aid, that P.C.C. had the Ministry's officials 'eating out of her hand' and got all the money she wanted by personal cajolery. Nothing could be further from the truth. Admittedly, she made good use of the close relationships she had established with the Ministry from the days of the wartime Directorate. But the records show that, from the last years of the war, she had to accept the refusal of applications for grants towards many schemes which she thought of great importance and on which she had set her heart. As has been shown, not only was no statutory assistance forthcoming for establishing the three National Recreation Centres that were set up between 1946 and 1955 through voluntary appeals or voluntary trust funds, but not a penny came from the State towards their maintenance until after the Wolfenden Committee had made its recommendations in 1960, when a financially embarrassed CCPR was able to secure a supplementary grant of £4,000 for that purpose.

Each year, at least one visit to the Ministry was paid by P.C.C., sometimes accompanied by one or more of the Honorary Officers or a colleague, to discuss with its officials the budgets prepared by the CCPR and approved by the General Purposes and Finance Committee for the ensuing financial year. And here a tribute is due to Miss Vaughan and the accountants who succeeded her, together with their assistant Miss Singleton, for the professional skill with which they prepared the budgets and advised P.C.C. and her successors in their presentation. Every item of estimated income and expenditure in fields of work approved by the Ministry was exposed to ruthless scrutiny, including all the income which the CCPR hoped to make through its own efforts – profits on sale of publications, surpluses on training events and demonstrations, fees for services to be rendered, and refunds of travelling expenses where appropriate. The effectiveness of Sir Percival Sharp's intervention when a Ministry official suggested that local education authorities should be expected to pay for any work done by the CCPR in their areas has already been mentioned, as has the similar line so helpfully taken by Sir William Alexander, Sir Percival's successor, before the Select Committee in 1956.

Every proposed increase in the number or salaries of grant-aided staff, or the rate at which they could be reimbursed for travelling or subsistence expenses had to be justified – generally by quoting what had already been granted in comparable fields – and it was by no means unusual for the Ministry to ask for much additional information, or to give a blunt 'no'.

There were periodic crises, related either to the national financial situation or the person at the Ministry in charge of the CCPR's destinies. In the Autumn of 1952, there was talk of drastic cuts in grants which led to the sending of a special letter to each member of the staff signed by the Chairman and Honorary Treasurer. Referring to the financial situation and the consequent problems, the letter continued : "We felt we would like to write personally to tell you that, when they met recently, the General Purposes and Finance Sub-Committees were unanimous in their decision to continue to treat the staff as generously as possible. They also asked us to appeal to you to cooperate by doing everything in your power to reduce the Council's expenditure on such items as postage, telephones, printing, stationery and travelling. We already know from Miss Colson, that most praiseworthy efforts have been and are being made in this direction, but feel that it may be possible to effect still further economies if every single member of the staff realises that it is his or her personal responsibility not to use one sheet of paper or one envelope unnecessarily, only to make toll or trunk calls at times of real emergency – and then to limit them to three minutes – and to keep travelling and subsistence claims to the minimum." Though the hand was the hand of the Honorary Officers, one may be forgiven for suspecting that the voice was the voice of P.C.C. !

Early the following year it was reported to the Committee that Mr. Gem and P.C.C. had had a meeting at the Ministry when they were told "it was not unlikely that their grant would be cut by as much as ten per cent in 1953/54", but that at a second meeting, at which an Under Secretary had been present," it had been decided to try to leave the grant at £74,000 on the understanding that the CCPR would plan for a progressive decrease in expenditure amounting to fifty per cent over the next four or five years, and would submit a statement how it was proposed to effect this reduction." The Committee then discussed how far it would be able to draw on the CCPR's very slender private resources to maintain the CCPR's structure but, happily, because either the financial skies lightened or there was a change of official at the Ministry, nothing further was heard of this 'understanding'.

The Ministry's grants to the CCPR between 1939 and 1946 have been given in Chapter Four and those for 1946 have been given in Chapter Four and those for 1946 to 1951 in Chapter Five. For the following decade they were : 1951/2, £74,700; 1952/3, £74,900; 1953/4, £74,000; 1954/5, £80,000; 1955/6 £82,891; 1956/7, £94,701; 1957/8, £113,040; 1958/9, £119,835; 1959/60, £134,698; 1960/61, £145,951.

After the publication of the Wolfenden Report in 1960, the

Government grant-aided sports organisations much more generously than previously – first through the Ministry of Education (Department of Education and Science from 1964) and then through the Ministry of Housing and Local Government (Department of the Environment from 1970). The CCPR's grants (excluding capital grants) increased as follows: 1961/2, £181,400; 1962/3, £214,500; 1963/4, £252,165; 1964/5, £336,852; 1965/6, £360,788; 1966/7, £396,820; 1967/8, £425,375; 1968/9, £420,014; 1969/70, £440,916; 1970/1. £495,974; 1971/72, £556,118. Part of the increase after 1964 was due to the cost of servicing Regional Sports Councils and the Sports Council.

Throughout its life the CCPR made continuous efforts to lessen its dependence upon statutory grants by raising funds from voluntary sources. Some of these have been described earlier, especially in Chapter Five. But it was always an uphill battle and any success achieved was on a modest scale. The Council had however good reason to be grateful to those who did support it, by arranging special events on its behalf or by giving donations or subscriptions. These included some of the governing bodies of sport, a number of industrial firms and newspapers, and some of its own individual members. The total amount raised for the National Sports Development Fund in the ten years ending 1972 was about £69,000.

CHAPTER THIRTEEN

The Sports Council (Advisory)—
Partnership and Adjustment: 1965 - 1971

We now return to the chronological pattern of the CCPR's history. March 1965 found the CCPR in a somewhat equivocal position. On the part of some committee members and staff there was uncertainty and even apprehension about the implications for the CCPR of the establishment of a Sports Council and the secondment of its General Secretary. The first necessity was to reassure the staff that: (1) the new developments did not mean, as some feared, a fatal weakening of the CCPR's influence and prestige; (2) the existence of an advisory Sports Council did not make any of the CCPR's work superfluous or detract from its responsibilities – indeed, it might lead to an increase in their importance and extent; and (3) that the CCPR could face with confidence any scrutiny of its activities by an outside body, if this was to be one of the functions of the new Sports Council. A letter to this effect was circulated by the Acting General Secretary to the Council's senior staff, and an early conference was called of Regional Officers and Centre Wardens at Crystal Palace. This did much to restore the staff's feelings of confidence in themselves and the CCPR's work.

Additional grounds for justifying such confidence were soon forthcoming. The Sports Council had set up four committees of its own members to consider different aspects of its work: 'Sports Development and Coaching', 'Research and Statistics', 'International', and 'Facilities Planning', under the chairmanship respectively of A. D. Munrow, Dr. Roger Bannister, Lady Burton, and Lord Porchester. In May 1965, Lord Porchester, as Chairman of the Facilities Committee, called a private meeting of representatives of the CCPR and the SCPR to put before them a proposal – which had already been submitted to and approved by the local authorities' associations – that Regional Sports Councils and Councils for Wales and Scotland should be established, and that the CCPR and SCPR should be invited to supply the executive officers for those Councils. The purpose of the Councils, which would primarily consist of representatives of local authorities, was "to facilitate the regional coordination and provision of facilities for sport and physical recreation" after initial surveys and appraisals had been made. They were advisory, not executive.

The Executive Committee agreed at its meeting in June 1965 (which was held at Lilleshall) that the complimentary invitation should be accepted. During the next few months the Minister convened meetings to inaugurate the new Councils, and in all cases the new bodies accepted the Sports Council's recommendation that the CCPR's Regional Officers and Welsh Secretary should be their executive secretaries, as being "admirably qualified, by virtue of their past experience and present terms of appointment to fulfil this important role". Though the Regional Councils consisted primarily of representatives of local authorities, provision was made in their constitutions for representation of the governing bodies and outdoor activity associations on them and their executive committees. The CCPR used its influence to see that such representation was as effective as possible. Moreover, in most regions the CCPR set up regional standing conferences of sports organisations to act as stimulating and advisory bodies to the Regional Sports Councils. In Wales, a similar part was played by the CCPR's Welsh Games and Sports Committee.

By its November meeting the Executive Committee could be told that Regional Councils had been established satisfactorily in nearly every region. At the same time the Committee was warned by its secretary that it was uncertain how much of their time the regional staff would be obliged to devote to the new Councils if their work was to be successful, and how far their new duties could be combined with their existing responsibilities. The Committee was also reminded that no less important questions were whether the staff's new role would create any irreconcilable conflicts of loyalties between their duties to the CCPR as a voluntary organisation and their duties to the Sports Council as a committee within a Government department, and also whether this closer identification with statutory bodies would subtly undermine their relationships with other bodies in the CCPR.

Another disquieting element in the situation that soon showed itself was that, though the CCPR was officially represented on the Regional and Welsh Sports Councils – in some cases through members of the Executive Committee – there was no corresponding representation on the main Sports Council, with the resulting anomaly that the CCPR's staff as secretaries of Regional Sports Councils were being given instructions by the Sports Council quite independently either of the Executive Committee or of the headquarters staff. This anomaly was not removed until the end of 1967.

The only official contacts between the Sports Council and the CCPR's staff at headquarters level consisted of the Technical Director's serving in a personal capacity as consultant to the Sports Council's International Committee, and the Acting Deputy Secretary's membership of the working party set up by the Sports Council to advise on standards and scales of provision of facilities. This working party's report, *Planning for Sport*, was published by the CCPR for the Sports Council in October 1968.

But good sense on both sides and the close personal relations that existed between the headquarters staff and the officials of the Department of Education and Science (as the Ministry had become in 1964), particularly with H. Sagar, H.M.I., and John Swindale, Assistant Secretary, prevented many frictions and misunderstandings that might otherwise have arisen. Moreover, frequent meetings were arranged at which the CCPR's national and regional staff were able to confer with W.W. and his colleagues at the Department.

What must be emphasised – not least in considering any analogies that might be drawn with the days of the National Fitness Council – is that the successful operation of the Regional Sports Councils, compared with the NFC's Area Committees, rested on two main factors – the cooperation and support given to the Regional Sports Councils by the officers of local authorities, especially their planning officers, and the skilful and efficient way in which the CCPR's staff rose to the new responsibilities. For them, it meant working at a much higher level of cooperation with local authorities than they had previously been accustomed to – or, indeed, been able to – reach. They quickly adapted themselves to the work of servicing the Regional Councils and the Technical Panels set up to produce surveys and establish regional priorities of action. They and their colleagues worked under very great pressure and managed to maintain a good programme of normal CCPR work, if inevitably reduced in certain directions. In spite of the extra load to be carried, it took some little time to persuade the Department that at least one extra Representative was required in each region to help the CCPR with its new work, and that the Regional Officers were entitled to some financial recognition for their greater responsibilities.

It was a challenging and testing time, and the technical and administrative staff well deserved the tribute paid to them by Denis Howell when he addressed the CCPR's A.G.M. in November 1965. Those qualified to judge say that, without the experience and hard work of the CCPR's staff, the Regional Sports Councils and the Sports Council for Wales could never have 'got off the ground'.

Later in the same month, Mr. Howell, accompanied by the chairmen of his Council's four committees and officials of the Department, spoke to a fully representative meeting of governing bodies and outdoor activity associations at Shell House. His introductory address was followed by a frank and valuable 'question and answer' session. One amusing incident at this meeting may be recalled. After the Minister's speech, Charles de Beaumont, the sports administrator whose preeminence in the world of national and international fencing had earned for him the cognomen of 'Mr. Fencing' and whose death in 1972 robbed not only fencing but the CCPR of a stalwart supporter, rose to say that though he was not of the same political persuasion as the Minister, he felt bound to declare that the Government, through him, had done more for sport than any of its predecessors. Whereat, Sir John Hunt – he became Lord Hunt the following year – got up to say that though he had never previously made any public avowal of his political convictions, Mr. de Beaumont's statement impelled him to announce that, for his part, he *was* of the Minister's political persuasion, a remark which drew lively cheers and counter-cheers.

Denis Howell also at this time invited representatives of the CCPR and the NPFA to a private lunch party to discuss relations between them. To his straight question as to the possibility of an amalgamation between the two bodies he received an unequivocal reply from both sides that such a course was neither necessary nor desirable, thus confirming the verdict reached in 1935 and by the Wolfenden Committee in 1960.

In 1966, Jack Longland and Peter McIntosh (a previous

member of the CCPR's Executive) were appointed members of the Sports Council, which strengthened the personal, if not the official, ties between the two bodies. Mr. Longland was, at the same time, made the Sports Council's 'observer' on the National Parks Commission, an important link which had long been missing. Relations between the National Parks Commission and the CCPR were strengthened in 1966 when the Commission accepted observer-status on the CCPR's Outdoor Activities Committee. The Secretary of the Commission addressed the Committee about the Commission's activities, and the Author spoke on the work of the CCPR at one of the Commission's meetings.

During this period it becomes increasingly difficult to detach the work of the CCPR from that of the Sports Council and the Regional Sports Councils, but a few exclusively CCPR items call for mention here.

The retirement of Kay Evans in 1966 after twenty-three years as Woman Technical Adviser left a vacancy on the headquarters staff which proved hard to fill. As no applications for her post were received from women with the necessary qualifications and experience, it was decided to readvertise it, making it open to men as well as women. As a result, Jack Barry, Regional Officer for London and the South-East, was appointed to succeed Miss Evans as Technical Adviser. At the same time, Elizabeth Dendy joined the headquarters staff as Principal Executive Officer, and the women's and girls' work previously undertaken by Miss Evans was shared between her and Olive Newson, in addition to other duties.

Since its formation, the CCPR's Finance Department had been under the control of a part-time accountant – Miss Vaughan had been followed successively by Peter Davies, George Reynolds and Gladys Tangye – but the increased volume and complexity of the CCPR's finances made it necessary to appoint a management accountant who could give his whole time to the work, and David Pond, F.C.A., joined the CCPR in that capacity in 1967.

At the 1965 A.G.M., P.C.C. had been elected to the newly-established office of Honorary Life Vice-President. The following year, a severe professional and personal loss was sustained by the CCPR through the sudden death, while sailing, of John Bradley, Principal Executive Officer, who was the Council's 'key man' in the development of outdoor activities, particularly water sports and mountaineering. Fred Briscoe was appointed to succeed him.

At the end of 1967, an outbreak of foot and mouth disease was so severe and widespread that Plas y Brenin could not be used at all for many weeks and the use of Lilleshall was also severely restricted. The December 1967 staff conference had to be transferred at short notice from Lilleshall to Crystal Palace. The outbreak cost the CCPR about £5,000 in lost fees.

During W.W.'s secondment, the Executive became increasingly restive under the continuing uncertainty about his future, since no firm reply could be obtained from the Minister as to whether W.W. would be returning to the CCPR from secondment, and, if so, when. The Acting General Secretary was due to retire at the end of 1967, but in the circumstances it was not possible to make any arrangements to appoint a successor. And the Executive were growing more critical of the lack of any official contact between the CCPR and the Sports Council, even at 'observer' level, and their concern was not lessened by the knowledge that in effect the greater part of the work of the regional staff had fallen under the control of another body. The staff themselves were unhappy at the situation, and, expressed concern at their conference at the evident weakening of the CCPR's autonomy and independence of action. They pressed for an official reappraisal of the respective functions of the CCPR and the Sports Council.

Eventually, official negotiations were initiated and a working party set up between the CCPR and the Department. This led to the Executive's approving an agreement provisionally reached with the Minister that, after the end of W.W.'s secondment, now fixed as December 1967, the CCPR's Executive should undertake at the Government's request "to provide the Sports Council with such services as might be agreed, in the administrative, technical and research fields" and, as part of those services, the CCPR's headquarters staff, augmented as necessary, would provide the secretariat for the Sports Council and its committees. W.W. would return to his position as General Secretary of the CCPR while continuing to be Director of the Sports Council.

Though this new agreement with the Minister was welcomed by the Executive both as a mark of the Government's confidence in the CCPR and as producing a more sensible state of affairs, there were some misgivings among its members about the difficulties inherent in having a General Secretary responsible to themselves who was also Director of a Sports Council not under their control. A pointed reference to this situation was made by Lord Aberdare in a Debate in the House of Lords initiated by Lord Willis on 17th February 1968. Mr. Winterbottom would be wearing two hats, he said. No doubt, as Director of the Sports Council, he would have been asked to brief the Government's spokesman in the Debate. But what would have been his position if he (Lord Aberdare), a member of the CCPR's Executive Committee, who might have some criticisms to make of the actions of the Government, had asked Mr. Winterbottom, as General Secretary of the CCPR, to brief him?

The same Debate, though containing many expressions of appreciation of the work both of the Sports Council and the CCPR, again showed wide disappointment that the Sports Council had not been made executive rather than advisory, at least one member being unconvinced by the statement that a Sports Council, incorporated by Royal Charter with a grant-in-aid, could not be set up without special legislation.

However, both parties entered upon the agreement for joint working between the CCPR and the Sports Council with good will, and from 1st January 1968 onwards the Sports Council and its committees were serviced by the CCPR. The Minister had felt obliged to insert a condition in the agreement that in any conflict of policy between the CCPR and the Sports Council, the Government must have the final decision, a proviso accepted by the Executive on the understanding that it would only apply to matters within the terms of reference of the Sports Council and not to matters of CCPR policy.

The Executive replied to the staff's representations by informing them that they believed that the new agreement was in the best interests of the CCPR, would improve its influence and status, would remove certain anomalies in the existing situation, and would in no way be detrimental to their personal or professional interests. They might have well added that, for a body so heavily dependent upon the Government's grant-aid, they had no option but to accede to its wishes in a matter of this substance.

The point is worth making at this stage that although the Ministry of Education and the Department of Education and Science had grant-aided the CCPR over so many years, they had done so while leaving the CCPR the utmost freedom to carry out its own policy within the terms of its grant, without any interference. The Author can only think of one exception to this generalisation – this is worth recording because it was in fact so exceptional.

As has been made clear in earlier chapters the CCPR had frequently been critical of what it felt was the inadequate attention paid to physical recreation and sport within the youth service generally. Fortified by finding that the Albemarle Committee and the Wolfenden Committee both took the same view as itself on the subject, and in view of the increased attention being given to the training of both professional and part-time youth leaders as the result of the recommendations of the Albemarle Report, it felt justified in preparing a memorandum for the consideration of local education authorities, specialist colleges and all other agencies concerned with the training of youth leaders, making suggestions as to the part that physical recreation might play in such training. A draft memorandum was circulated widely to test opinion, and, with minor amendments, it was approved by a very wide circle of people intimately concerned with the youth service, including the chairman of the National Association of Youth Service Officers, the secretaries of SCNVYO and of two of the principal national voluntary youth organisations, the principal of a specialist college for training youth leaders, a director of education and many of the CCPR's headquarters and regional staff. It was then circulated to the relevant sub-committees of the CCPR and finally to the Executive and approved. But when the Department were consulted it was made known to the CCPR that there was exception taken to it at a high level in the Inspectorate (not the Physical Education Inspectorate) and that there was no likelihood that any amendment to the memorandum would remove the objection. So the memorandum was never issued – the CCPR did not feel that at that time it should take any action known not to be approved of by the Department. This, however, was a unique event in the CCPR's history. No reason for the objection was given, nor was the name of the official in question quoted, but the inference was that personally he was not in favour of paying greater attention to physical recreation in the training of youth leaders.

With the return of W.W. to the post of General Secretary and the retirement of the Acting General Secretary, Jack Barry was appointed Deputy Secretary and Eric Edwards given a new post of Chief Executive Officer. Harry Littlewood left his position as Regional Officer in the South to become Technical Adviser, and in January 1970 Clinton Sayer, a former member of the CCPR's staff who had been Head of the Physical Education Department of Loughborough College for some years, and chairman of the Council's Games and Sports Committee since Lady Burton resigned in November 1967, succeeded George McPartlin as Technical Director on the latter's retirement.

During 1967, the first of a series of annual conferences of national coaches of the governing bodies of sport was held at Crystal Palace at the suggestion of the Sports Council and in cooperation with the newly-formed British Association of National Coaches, a body which became officially represented on the CCPR Council in 1970. In the same year at the request of the Sports Council the Department of Education subsidised the publication by the Council of a quarterly *Sports Development Bulletin* with a circulation of 35,000, which was produced as a supplement to its own journal, *Sport and Recreation* primarily to keep local authorities and voluntary bodies in touch with the activities of the Sports Council and Regional Sports Councils.

Under the Countryside Act of 1968, the Countryside Commission replaced the National Parks Commission with wider powers and responsibilities, including those in connection with the establishment of Country Parks and the preservation of footpaths and other rights of way, and a new Council for Environmental Education was set up by the Standing Committee of 'The Countryside in 1970' Conference under Jack Longland's chairmanship, representative of thirty national organisations, including the CCPR. The year 1968 also saw the publication by the CCPR of 160,000 copies of *The Mountain Code* a colourful sixteen-page leaflet initiated by the British Mountaineering Council and paid for by the Department of Education and Science. Lord Hunt of the BMC was chairman, and Fred Briscoe of the CCPR secretary of the working party which prepared the leaflet in consultation with over twenty national specialist and youth organisations.

The work of the Mountain Leadership Training Board was making good progress and its composition had been enlarged to include representatives of the Association of Mountain Centre Wardens and the British Association of Organisers and Lecturers in Physical Education, as well as the BMC, the CCPR, the SCPR and the Association of Scottish Climbing Clubs. By 1969, over 1,000 awards of the Mountain Leadership Certificate had been made. The BMC took over administrative responsibility for the MLTB at the end of 1972.

In a review of its first four years' work published in 1969, the Sports Council referred to the enthusiasm and efficiency with which the CCPR was servicing it. A reconsideration of the functions of the CCPR's advisory committees led in 1969 to a decision to revive the former Movement and Dance Committee under the chairmanship of Eileen Alexander, Principal of Bedford College of Physical Education and a former H.M.I. It, the Games and Sports, and Outdoor Activities Committees were given direct representation on the management committee of the National Recreation Centres most relevant to their fields of work.

The next twist in the tortuous lane of CCPR/Sports Council/ Government Department relations was provided by the promotion of Denis Howell in the Autumn of 1969. He left his post in the Department of Education and Science to become Minister of State at the Ministry of Housing and Local Government, while retaining his special responsibility for sport. Mr. Howell assured his audience at the CCPR's A.G.M. later that year that his change of Department denoted no change in the Government's attitude to sport, responsibility for which would now lie within the same Department as responsibility for the countryside, for open space grants, for parks and other leisure activities. Powers to make grants under the Physical Training and Recreation Act of 1937 had been transferred to his new Department, and the fact that loan sanctions for local authorities' projects and direct grants for voluntary projects would both come within the same Ministry should, he thought, facilitate planning. He would still have the valued advice of the Physical Education Inspectorate, and the Technical Unit for Sport, which had proved its worth, would continue to advise both the Department of Education and Science and his new Ministry.

There is no way of knowing officially which was uppermost in the then Prime Minister's mind – that Mr. Howell deserved promotion to a higher office in a different Ministry or that the development of sport and recreation ought to be the responsibility of the Ministry of Housing and Local Government. Such a transfer of responsibility for recreation policy to the Ministry of Housing and Local Government had been the main recommendation of *A Better Country,* a study produced by a Conservative Party's policy group under Christopher Chataway, M.P., and published by the Conservative Political Centre in 1966. It was also in line with the Wolfenden Committee's recommendation that the encouragement of sport for the community should no longer be the responsibility of the Ministry of Education.

The CCPR's Annual Report for 1968–69 spoke of the closer contact between the CCPR and the Sports Council as being for the benefit of both. The CCPR's store of technical knowledge, particularly about facilities, had been greatly enlarged, as had the Council's own programme of training events and conferences, and its cooperation in administering coaching courses and coaching tours. It recorded that the number of official coaching schemes of the governing bodies had increased from eight in 1948 to forty-eight in 1968, though it was not claimed that the CCPR had played a major part in all of them.

But though the partnership between the CCPR and the Sports Council had been proceeding more smoothly than many had expected, and the CCPR's staff were adjusting themselves well to the change in their role – a change particularly marked at Headquarters – both partners were constantly looking forward and examining their own future. It was realised that the partnership could not continue on the same basis indefinitely. The crucial question was in which way it should be encouraged – or allowed – to develop.

The review of its work published by the Sports Council in 1969, referred to earlier, reported that the Sports Council was giving consideration to its own future. In September 1969 a comprehensive and balanced confidential memorandum on the subject by W.W., 'The Sports Council and its Future', was circulated to the members of the Council and of the CCPR's Executive. It was also sent to the Chairmen and Secretaries of Regional Sports Councils, with an invitation to them to submit their views as to the implications of a possible change from an advisory to an executive-type Sports Council. Though opinions were not unanimous, the majority of all those consulted favoured the retention of the existing advisory status with certain modifications.

A special meeting of the CCPR's General Purposes and Finance Committee was held in January 1970 to consider the issue and, though there was some division of opinion, the majority supported the retention of the 'status quo', adding a recommendation that the links between the CCPR and the Sports Council should be strengthened, with the former officially represented on the latter. The decision was endorsed by the Executive Committee at its meeting the following month.

A two-day private conference of members of the Sports Council, the Sports Councils for Wales and Scotland, and Regional Sports Councils was convened by the Minister at Lilleshall Hall Sports Centre in March 1970, which was also attended by representatives of the CCPR and SCPR. The consensus of opinion both within the Sports Council and at this conference was that the existing arrangements were proving efficient and satisfactory in practice, and endorsed the Minister's own view that the Sports Council should remain an advisory body.

The Minister suggested that the four main functions of the CCPR (as of the SCPR) were: (1) to service the Sports Council and the Regional Sports Councils; (2) to administer the National Sports Centres; (3) to assist the coaching and development work of the governing bodies; and (4) to bring together the sports bodies at national level to provide "a voice for sport". If an executive Sports Council were set up, he could not see how the CCPR could continue in its present form, and thought that, if that happened, it might be advisable for the two bodies to merge.

After members of the CCPR's and SCPR's staff had stated that, on the whole, they found no difficulty in 'serving two masters' and dealing with both aspects of their work, the conference agreed that no case had been made for changing the existing pattern, in which in effect the Sports Council was a body with both advisory and executive functions.

In the meantime, within the Conservative Party, now in opposition, a small study group under the chairmanship of the Hon. Charles Morrison, M.P., 'Shadow' Minister for Sport, was considering the future responsibility of Government in the fields of sport and recreation. It took evidence in confidence from a number of relevant bodies and individuals, and its recommendation that an independent and executive National Sports Council should be established by statute was no doubt instrumental in securing that the Conservative Party went into the 1970 General Election pledged to "make the Sports Council an independent body and make it responsible for the grant-aiding functions at present exercised by the Government".

On the Conservative Party's return to power in June 1970 in a victory few had predicted, Eldon Griffiths, MP., was appointed Joint Parliamentary Under-Secretary of State at the Ministry of Housing and Local Government (soon to be renamed the Department of the Environment) and succeeded Denis Howell as Minister for Sport. Politics apart, the tributes to Mr. Howell's work as Minister for Sport and Chairman of the Sports Council from 1965 were genuine and widespread – his energy, enthusiasm and friendliness had won him many friends within the world of sport. Though he held forthright and combative views, he bore no grudge against those who disagreed with him, and was notably loyal to those who worked for him. He was entitled to claim that, apart from the issue of subsidising British teams to compete against South Africa, he had not allowed party politics to affect his actions as Chairman of the Sports Council.

On taking the chair at his first meeting of the Sports Council on 15th July 1970 in Edinburgh, just before the opening of the Commonwealth Games, the new Minister said : "Now is not the proper time to speculate on what form the relationship between the CCPR and the Sports Council might in the future take. We are not going to hurry. We are not going to make changes for the sake of making changes – or simply to create an impression of activity. Whatever decision we reach will be taken against a background of the fullest consultation with all interested bodies."

In August 1970, he paid his first visit to a National Sports Centre to see the match between the Arsenal and Crystal Palace Clubs in aid of the NSDF at the Crystal Palace Centre, and he was the principal speaker at the Council's A.G.M. on 4th November 1970, presided over by Prince Philip. At this meeting, Sir Stanley Rous, in presenting the Annual Report, said : "We are concerned about the uncertainty of the future and we hope that the staff will learn before long whether they are working for the CCPR or the Sports Council". In his address Mr. Griffiths spoke appreciatively of the work of the CCPR, adding : "Whatever form of organisation is decided upon, the work that the Central Council has done and is doing, will and must continue. I am sure it will continue with much greater vigour in the future". The Minister also met the CCPR's staff at their annual staff conference at Lilleshall in December 1970.

Discussion on the new situation took place at meetings of the Council's General Purposes and Finance Committee in October and December 1970. Though varying views were expressed at the prospects before the CCPR, the general conclusion was that "if the Sports Council became an executive body, the CCPR was so closely involved with its activities that it must accept some form of merger or absorption with the Sports Council, and that the main efforts of the committee should be directed towards seeing that the interests of the staff in England, Wales and Northern Ireland were fully safeguarded and that the CCPR's activities should be continued on the widest possible scale."

A meeting of the Games and Sports Committee to which members of the Outdoor Activities and Movement and Dance Committees were invited, was held on 17th February 1971, attended by representatives of forty-seven national bodies and chaired by Robin Struthers. Both the Minister and Sir John Lang were present to hear that the possibility of the CCPR's being taken over by the Government was viewed with much concern, several members making the point that the sports bodies *were* the CCPR. In the same month, the first conference of national sports administrators had also expressed concern about the future of the Sports Council and were critical at the lack of any consultation with the governing bodies on so vital a matter.

A special meeting of the Executive Committee was called on 24th March 1971 to consider how to answer an invitation from the Department of the Environment to let the Minister know its views about the Sports Council and its future, against the background of the Conservative Party's Manifesto before the General Election. The views of the General Purposes and Finance Committee were heard, and it was reported that the national sports bodies had urged that the new arrangements for the Sports Council should include some form of consultative and advisory committee structure, "a central forum to give governing bodies of sport opportunities to consider sports development as it affected them". Two important conclusions of the governing bodies had been that the CCPR should remain independent and that sports bodies should be adequately represented on the Sports Council. It was also reported that the SCPR, on the other hand, favoured complete integration of the SCPR with an autonomous Sports Council for Scotland and that a similar feeling prevailed in Wales.

Not unnaturally, in an issue so complex and one in which the CCPR could not pretend to be an entirely free agent in view of its agreed commitment to service the Sports Council and its dependence upon statutory grant, the Executive did not reach any clear-cut or unanimous decision. Some members felt that the best interests of sport required the integration of the CCPR's functions with those of an Executive Sports Council. Others wanted the CCPR to maintain its independence as a voluntary body.

In an attempt to convey the Executive's views, the Chairman wrote to the Minister on 1st April 1971 giving as the committee's majority opinion that, "as the present arrangements were proving satisfactory, the Sports Council should remain advisory but be given statutory existence, and that the CCPR should have closer links with the Sports Council – possibly by direct representation – and should continue to offer the services of its staff. If, however, the Government decided to set up a Sports Council with executive powers, while some members thought that the CCPR's functions should be integrated with those of the Sports Council, others thought that the CCPR should carry on its general rôle and continue to service the Sports Council and the Regional Sports Councils."

Reference was also made in the letter to: (1) the relationship of the CCPR over the years with its member-bodies, including over eighty specialist sports organisations, a cooperative partnership greatly valued by both sides and: (2) the practical services given by the CCPR to sport at 'grass roots' level (in addition to its administrative and technical services to the Sports Council and Regional Sports Councils) which should be maintained until they were satisfactorily provided by local authorities.

The letter concluded with comments on the position of the professional staff, the work of the National Sports Centres, the National Sports Development Fund, tributes to the individual men and women who had given many years of service on the Council's committees, and a reference to the regret that would be felt by many associated with it if the CCPR were to lose its identity by being completely integrated with the new Sports Council.

At its meeting on 4th June 1971, Sir Stanley informed the Executive that he had heard from the Minister of the Government's decision which was to be made public shortly, and that he had been invited to meet the President to inform him of the present situation. This was followed by the announcement by the Minister for Sport in the House of Commons on 10th June that the Government had decided "to enhance the status of the Sports Council, to give it executive powers and widen its responsibilities". The new Sports Council would become an independent body responsible for the grant-aiding functions now exercised by Government departments. A Royal Charter would be sought for the new Sports Council similar to that for the Arts Council. As soon as arrangements could be made, the Council would cease to be purely an advisory body and would be set up under an independent Chairman, Dr. Roger Bannister, who would serve on a part-time basis. Scotland and Wales would have their own Sports Councils. A joint working party had been set up to consider the future rôle of the CCPR, its staff and Sports Centres within the new arrangements. Governing bodies and other national sports and recreational organisations would be invited as a group to advise the Sports Council and would be given a voice on it.

Later the same day, Eldon Griffiths met the CCPR's Executive Committee in a conference room at the Treasury and emphasised that, because the CCPR was an independent body and free to decide its own course, nothing had been said about its future save that there would be consultations. He wished, however, to propose to the Executive, through the medium of the working party that had been set up, that the new Sports Council and the CCPR would amalgamate. He envisaged that the

Regional Sports Councils would have more power and more responsibility as agencies of an executive body, and added that the CCPR's staff were the heart and soul of what these regional bodies actually did. He had now visited every Regional Sports Council and all the CCPR's Centres as well, and had been enormously impressed by the dedication of the staff who carried out their jobs beyond their immediate responsibilities. Without the CCPR, he said, there would be no Sports Council. One of the arguments put forward by Mr. Griffiths for an independent Sports Council without a political chairman was that a chairman who bore a collective responsibility with his colleagues in Government for total expenditure patterns was bound to say "no" sometimes to requests for more money or more facilities. It was wrong to muzzle the voice of sport by putting in the Chair a ministerial person who had a total responsibility to curtail central expenditure.

So the decision of the Government to establish an executive Sports Council marked the end of this important period in the CCPR's history – one of partnership and adjustment. The course of the negotiations that followed and the decisions reached will be told in the next Chapter.

CHAPTER FOURTEEN

The Sports Council (Executive)—
Transfer of Staff and Assets: 1971 - 1972

For nearly twelve months after June 1971, the CCPR was engaged in protracted negotiations with the Minister for Sport, the Department of the Environment and the Sports Council as to whether, and, if so, on what conditions, the Minister's proposal for the amalgamation of the CCPR with the new Sports Council should be accepted. It would be tedious to recount every stage of the discussions on matters both of principle and detail that occupied so much of the time and energies of those who took part in them, but some of the main difficulties that had to be overcome must be recorded.

It was inevitable that there should be a good deal of resistance to the suggestion of a merger, fusion, absorption, amalgamation, integration or any other process – however euphemistically described – which would involve the virtual disappearance of the CCPR as an independent and voluntary body into the embrace of a statutory Sports Council. Though subsidised by the State over many years to give a service to physical recreation, the CCPR was in a very real sense the creation of its members, whether individuals or representatives of organisations, and many found it hard to contemplate its disappearance in the form they had known, supported, admired and served it.

History was repeating itself but with a difference. The memories of some of its older members went back to 1937, when the determined efforts of the National Fitness Council to absorb the CCRPT had been vigorously and successfully resisted. But the conditions for such resistance no longer applied. Through a series of progressive irreversible steps – 'seconding' its General Secretary to the Sports Council in 1965; allowing its regional and Welsh staff to administer the Regional Sports Councils; and agreeing that its headquarters staff should accept responsibility for servicing the Sports Council at national level in 1968 – the CCPR Executive had itself created a situation from which a retreat was impossible even if one had been desired.

The CCPR's representatives on the joint working party with

the Department of the Environment had no real power to dispute the 'take-over bid' or to suggest that it should only apply to some of the CCPR's executive activities – for to exclude, for instance, the National Sports Centres from the absorption would have been administrative nonsense because the CCPR's staff formed a single whole. What they could do – and indeed did do, strenuously and effectively – was to negotiate the best terms possible for the professional interests of the staff and to secure that the functions of the CCPR as a voluntary coordinating body providing a unique common forum for sports bodies, should continue, whether under the name of the CCPR or some other.

The negotiations proceeded throughout on a friendly and conciliatory basis and neither side made unfair use of its bargaining position. At the first meeting of the working party, the DOE said that their suggestion was that the CCPR should be voluntarily wound up as a separate body, and its staff and assets transferred to become an integral part of the new Sports Council, upon the latter's incorporation by Royal Charter. The new body would combine the functions of the present Sports Council, the additional tasks (for example, grant-aiding) arising from its new executive status, and the functions then exercised by the CCPR. It was promised that the whole work of the CCPR would continue in one form or another. Even if the CCPR ceased to operate as a separate entity, the Minister undertook that the forum it had provided would be succeeded by other arrangements, for under the Royal Charter it was to be mandatory that there should be an advisory body, representative of sport and physical recreation.

The Minister had an early meeting with the governing bodies of sport, after which he suggested that the working party might discuss the possibility of the CCPR's living on in the form of a new standing conference of governing bodies and other recreational organisations. It would be established by right alongside the Sports Council and would decide its own membership, elect its own officers, manage its own affairs and be entitled to nominate members for consideration as possible members of the Sports Council.

At its meeting on 9th July 1971, the Executive Committee accepted in principle the invitation to go into voluntary liquidation, asking at the same time that the interests of the staff should be fully safeguarded, that several members of the Executive should be appointed to serve on the Sports Council, that the existing committee structure for the National Centres should be maintained, and that the forum for consultation with national voluntary organisations for sport and physical recreation should be continued, in an independent form, serviced by the Sports Council's staff.

The membership of the new Sports Council as announced in August 1971 included three prominent members of the CCPR's Executive – Sir Jack Longland, as Vice-Chairman, Robin Brook and P. B. Lucas, as well as David Munrow and Peter McIntosh, both past members of the Executive. A little later the appointment was announced, as an interim measure, of three additional members from a list put forward by the specialist bodies concerned with sport and physical recreation : the Earl of Antrim, representing Water Sports, Mrs. Mary Glen-Haig, President of the Ladies' Fencing Union and a member of the former advisory Sports Council, and Sir William Ramsay, President of the Rugby Football Union (who died in March 1973). Later Alan Miller and Norman Collins, other members of the CCPR's Executive, were appointed members.

The CCPR's next Annual General Meeting, on 4th November 1971, was chiefly noteworthy for the fact that Prince Philip in his Presidential remarks made it known that he personally found it difficult to accept the proposal that the CCPR itself should be disbanded – that, in his words, it should commit "voluntary hari kiri". He would, however, abide by the decision of the Council as a whole. He reminded members that though the original suggestion for a Sports Council had come from the Wolfenden Committee, that body had not intended its recommendation to include the demise of the organisation which had set it up. Though prepared to accept the transfer of the professional staff to the Sports Council so that they could continue their work in sports administration, management of Recreation Centres, organising coaching schemes and other work, he could not see any reason why the CCPR should not continue to function in the capacity of the standing conference of sports which it had been suggested should be set up. Such a standing conference had been functioning within the CCPR for the past thirty-five years. Having been President for the previous twenty years, he felt he should take the opportunity of making clear his own opinion to the Council's members. The reception accorded by the Meeting to Prince Philip's remarks showed that he was not alone in his views, and among those who expressed support for them later in the meeting was Philip Noel-Baker.

In presenting the Annual Report to the Meeting, Sir Stanley Rous said that while there were those who would regret the passing of the CCPR, there were those who felt that the CCPR had achieved so much in pressing for Government recognition of sport that its absorption by a new independent Sports Council offered great opportunity for a new stage of development. It was up to the many friends and fellow-workers gathered by the CCPR in its long career to make the new Sports Council a proud and effective instrument for the expansion of sport and recreation.

In seconding the Report, Arthur Gem said he would be less than honest if he did not state his own position quite clearly. He had always opposed the loss of identity of the CCPR because he believed that an independent body could serve the people represented in the best possible way and, personally he would very much regret it if the CCPR had to cease to exist.

The President's comments were widely reported in the Press : "The Duke opposes a sports take-over" and "The Duke rides into battle with Council" were among the headlines. They strengthened the resolve of those members of the Executive opposed to a total merger to press for the continued functioning of the CCPR as the voluntary body to speak for the interests of all sport. The Executive Committee were allowed to study and comment on the proposed text of the Sport's Council's Royal Charter in confidence, one clause of which provided for the recognition of a body representative of sport and physical recreation "with the status of a consultative body to the Sports Council and the right to propose the names of persons whom our Secretary of State may consider for appointment by him as members of the Council".

Consideration was next given by the working party and the Executive to the propriety – indeed, the point – of preserving the traditional title of CCPR for a body which would have transferred its staff, its Centres, its financial assets, and its journal elsewhere, and also surrendered what some considered one of its most valuable characteristics – namely, that the members of its Executive Committee served in a personal capacity and not as the representatives of any interest, organisation or group of organisations. Attempts to find an appropriate alternative title acceptable to the Department of Trade and Industry failed, and, with due regard to the President's objections to a complete merger and winding-up of the CCPR with the consequent disappearance of its title, and the support given to his views by so evidently large a proportion of Council members, the Executive decided that the title Central Council of Physical Recreation should be retained as the name of what the Minister had referred to as "the residual CCPR".

A meeting of the Executive with the Games and Sports, Outdoor Activities, and Movement and Dance Committees, took place on 7th February 1972 at which it was resolved that the CCPR should remain in being to constitute a standing forum for sports bodies, and that the whole membership of the CCPR (with the exception of bodies operating solely in Wales or Northern Ireland) should be taken into membership at the initial stage, together with those individual members who wished to remain such, though the latter would have no voting rights.

The objects of the new CCPR would be :

"(1) To constitute a standing forum where all national governing and representative bodies of sport and physical recreation may be represented and may collectively or through special groups where appropriate formulate and promote measures to improve and develop sport and physical recreation.

(2) To support the work of the specialist sports bodies and to bring them together with other interested organisations.

(3) To act as a consultative body to the Sports Council."

A working party was set up to prepare detailed proposals about membership, committee structure, title and secretariat.

Even more difficult and lengthy were the negotiations about the conditions of service which would apply to the members of the CCPR's staff, who were being transferred to the Sports Council and becoming in effect civil servants. The members of the working party, led by Arthur Gem and fully supported by the whole Executive Committee, refused to agree to their transfer until an agreement satisfactory to the staff themselves was negotiated with the Minister and the DOE. The staff were kept fully informed of the progress of negotiations and had their own 'staff group' of which Harry Littlewood was the chairman and spokesman. That group informed the Executive that the staff were virtually unanimous that some form of merger with the Sports Council was in the best interests of sport and also of the staff themselves but they were uneasy about some of the arrangements proposed.

A process of 'job evaluation' was carried out throughout the organisation by a team from the Civil Service Department but not all its findings were acceptable. Matters at issue included salary scales and grading, assimilation procedure, pension rights, emoluments of those in residential posts, a number of anomalies, and recognition of the 'vocational element' in the CCPR's work which entailed working far longer hours than would normally be required from civil servants.

Assurances were given by the Minister that no member of the staff would suffer financially by the transfer, that all anomalies would be dealt with, and that there would be a complete review of the staff's position within two years. On 15th March 1972, the staff notified the Executive that, with some reluctance, they felt they had no alternative but to agree to the Government's proposals, without prejudice to further negotiations on some outstanding issues, including their professional status as physical educationists. The staff group added a message of very warm appreciation for all that the members of the working party and the Executive had done to safeguard their interests.

Arrangements could now go ahead for the Extraordinary General Meeting. This was held on 17th April 1972 with Prince Philip in the Chair and the meeting passed without dissent two special resolutions. The first was in two parts. It added a new 'objects clause' to the CCPR's Memorandum of Association, the purpose of which was to give the CCPR power to transfer its undertaking and assets to the Sports Council. The second part gave authority to the Executive Committee to carry out the new objects by entering into an agreement with the Sports Council in a form to be approved by the Executive Committee. The Resolution also stipulated that the transfer was to be subject to certain important conditions. One was that the assets of the CCPR – such as its Centres, its regional offices and the National Sports Development Fund – should be transferred to the Sports Council as Trustee of a Charitable Trust which had objects in accord with the CCPR's objects, and would therefore qualify for recognition as a charity, which the Sports Council itself did not. Two other important conditions were that the Executive Committee were not to implement the transfer until they were satisfied that appropriate arrangements had been made: (1) for the employment of the CCPR's staff by the Sports Council; and (2) for the continuance by the Sports Council of the CCPR's work.

The second resolution defined the future objects of the CCPR in the terms approved by the Executive the previous February, and the meeting ended with an expression of the gratitude felt by the Council to Farrer and Co., the Council's Solicitors, and in particular to Charles Woodhouse, for the way they had advised the Council and the Executive on the legal side of all the negotiations.

After the E.G.M., two meetings of the Executive were held to discuss matters relating to the transfer, particular attention being paid to the new conditions of employment for the CCPR's staff. 'Heads of agreement' were signed on 17th May 1972 by the CCPR, the Sports Council and the Sports Council for Wales under which it was finally agreed that the transfer should take effect on 1st June 1972. This document contained undertakings about the conditions of employment of the CCPR's staff and the provision by the Sports Council to the CCPR "of such resources and facilities as the CCPR might reasonably require in carrying out and implementing its new objects", so long as the CCPR was a body representing national organisations of sport and physical recreation.

So, officially, this history of the original CCPR comes to an end on 1st June 1972 and another CCPR entered upon "a new variety of untried being" on that day. Under the terms of their agreement, the CCPR and the Sports Council jointly selected Peter Lawson, one of the technical staff in the Yorkshire and Humberside Region, as the new CCPR's acting general secretary, an appointment later made permanent by the incoming committee. Arthur Gem, Alan Miller and Robin Struthers were appointed the CCPR's representatives on the management committee of the Sports Council Trust. It was agreed that the management committees of the National Sports Centres should continue on the same basis as hitherto, with certain additional representation from the Sports Council.

The three main activities committees of the CCPR had been supplemented in January 1972 by the appointment of a

National Water Sports Committee following on a national Water Sports Conference held at Bisham Abbey the previous November. It consisted of representatives of nine national bodies under the chairmanship of David Nations. Later, a fifth committee was added, that of 'interested organisations', to provide representation from non-specialist bodies concerned with physical recreation, such as the youth organisations and educational associations. It was agreed that a Central Committee of the new CCPR should be formed, consisting of fourteen members nominated by those five specialist committees, renamed 'divisions', plus four other members nominated in General Meeting, the President and Honorary Treasurer being members 'ex officio'.

An Annual General Meeting of the new CCPR was held on 21st December 1972, at which Prince Philip and Robin Brook were elected President and Honorary Treasurer respectively for the years 1972–1974. An Extraordinary General Meeting held on 9th April 1973 accepted the CCPR's revised Memorandum and Articles of Association and elected the members of the new Central Committee. At its first meeting, held later the same day, that committee elected as its chairman Denis Howell, M.P., who had been an individual member of the old Council since 1970.

Mr. Howell continuted in that post until February 1974, when, with the election of a Labour Government, he returned to his former office as Minister for Sport, a post widened to that of Minister for Sport and Recreation in July 1974. Mrs. Mary Glen-Haig was elected to succeed him as chairman of the CCPR.

An important one-day conference was convened by the new CCPR at County Hall, S.E.1, on 25th July 1973 at which Prince Philip, and, later, Denis Howell presided, and a valuable discussion took place on the future structure, activities and financing of the new body.

The recommendations of this conference form no part of this history, but this Chapter must include a reference to a most happy occasion. The CCPR and the Sports Council combined to arrange a Reception at Fishmongers' Hall, E.C.4, on 18th July 1973, at which presentations were made by Prince Philip, as the CCPR's President, on behalf of all who had worked with them, to Sir Stanley Rous and Arthur Gem, as a tribute of affection and gratitude for their unique and distinguished services to the CCPR since 1935. The event drew together from all over the country a large assembly of men and women who had worked for the CCPR over the years – members of the Council and committees, and those who had served on the staff, some in its earliest pioneering days.

And so, in the splendid hall of one of London's most ancient City Companies, the curtain fell fittingly on a memorable partnership, which in duration, loyalty and devotion to a cause, must be difficult to parallel, even in the long history of the many voluntary organisations established to promote the mental and physical welfare of the people of this country.

In the meantime, an appeal for a Fund to perpetuate the memory of P.C.C., the CCPR's founder, had been well supported. One of its objects is to provide for periodic Colson Memorial Lectures, and the first of these was delivered by Prince Philip at a conference on 'Sport and Youth', organised by the CCPR in London on 16th July 1974. As part of his personal tribute to P.C.C. the Prince said: 'No-one has ever tried harder, and few have achieved so much.'

CHAPTER FIFTEEN

Retrospect and Prospect

Looking back on its progress and achievements during the thirty-seven years of its life, no-one can doubt that the CCPR made an indispensable contribution to opinion and action on many aspects of physical recreation throughout the country, and was a powerful influence in leading successive Governments towards a constantly increasing expenditure in that field. At the start of the period, apart from the provision made through educational institutions and the Parks and Gardens Departments of local authorities, the practice of physical recreation depended entirely upon voluntary effort. By the end of the period, both central Government and local authorities were committed to the expenditure of many millions of pounds annually to provide facilities for physical recreation and promote coaching and participation. Many factors were responsible for this transformation of official attitudes but among the most important was the pioneering, experimental and propaganda work of the CCPR, including its initiative in appointing the Wolfenden Committee on Sport. The CCPR may have reflected public opinion but it also led and informed it.

The CCPR was a dynamic not a static body, mainly because of the character and personality of its founder. It had a sort of restless efficiency, which won for it the admiration and co-operation of those who were eager for reform and progress, and, at the same time, the backing of those who wanted to see 'value for money'. Though it experimented widely, it made surprisingly few mistakes or misjudgements. One of its functions was 'to work itself out of a job' – or rather a series of jobs – and it did this successfully in a number of fields of work which it initiated and either handed over to other bodies or left behind when the need had been removed or reduced by the passage of time or events.

It sought to give service and to respond to needs, rather than to gain power for itself. Much of its best work was done without publicity or recognition. The fact that it was not, and did not aspire to be, a grant-aiding body was a source of strength rather than of weakness, for it kept its relations with all its two hundred constituent organisations unsullied by any mercenary taint or suspicion of partiality. It also kept itself free from any suggestion of political influence.

Many will mourn the disappearance of the CCPR as they knew and admired it, and, reminded perhaps by this history of the ideals and loyalties that lay behind its spirit and work, may wonder whether indeed so successful and valuable an organisation ought to have been allowed to come to an end. But "the old order changeth, yielding place to new". It is a frequent event in social history for the work of a voluntary body to pass into statutory control. As Lionel Ellis, former secretary of the National Council of Social Service and of the National Fitness Council, wrote during the war, "The history of social services in this country has followed fairly consistent lines. First comes the pioneer who sees something that needs doing and proceeds to do it to the best of his ability. His example and enthusiasm infects others and a 'society' is formed to spread the gospel. With this backing the work grows and, with it, the ambition to provide for it everywhere. State help is sought, for only the State can provide nation-wide service. There is usually a period, long or short, during which the work remains on a voluntary though State-aided basis, but with each increase of grant-aid there is naturally an increase of State interest and State control. Once it is commonly realised that the service ought to be provided everywhere, the point is soon reached at which the voluntary element disappears and the State, quite logically, takes full responsibility".

So nostalgia for something precious that may have been lost must be tempered by a recognition that the Sports Council is now in a position to serve sport in a way that the CCPR with its more limited resources could not. And the spirit that animated the CCPR has not wholly disappeared. The services of the Sports Council do not supplant but supplement the voluntary effort which, happily, is still manifest throughout the world of physical recreation. While those who are now in charge remain, there are no real grounds for fears that physical recreation is about to be invaded by the giant of State control. Equally clearly, one has to look no further than the recently-published reports of the House of Lords' Select Committee on

Sport and Leisure for evidence that provision for recreation – national, regional and local – is now fully recognised as an important statutory obligation.

Though, in view of its dependence upon grant-aid, the CCPR was not in the fullest and strictest sense a voluntary organisation after 1937, it retained throughout the spirit of voluntaryism. Its general policy was controlled by committees elected from among its own members; to assist with its training and propaganda activities, it recruited the services of thousands of skilled and enthusiastic volunteers; and its professional staff showed a vocational attitude to their work far beyond the strict calls of duty.

In her oral evidence to the Wolfenden Committee in September 1958, P.C.C. said: "I think that any success the CCPR has had is mainly due to four facts: it has no vested interests; the Ministry have attached so few 'strings' to their grant; the committee have allowed the staff a very large measure of freedom; and we have been blessed with really keen and dedicated staff."

In her valedictory address at the 1962 Annual General Meeting, she claimed: "We are essentially an instrument for the use of other bodies – an instrument which is called upon to play a large number of variations on the theme of sports development ... Again and again, our staff have to advise, persuade and win over before organising one of the thousands of courses they run in cooperation with other bodies. They have, too, to be adaptability itself. When working for the Boys' Brigade, they try to see through the eyes of the Brigade; the next moment, they change their sights and become fencing, football, swimming or canoeing experts, developing the coaching scheme of the responsible governing body, and out to serve its interests."

Though the executive Sports Council as established by Royal Chart in 1972 differs in some important respects from the Sports Development Council "of six to ten persons" envisaged by the Wolfenden Committee in 1960, its existence is based on the same evidence and the same reasoning. The Wolfenden Committee recommended that the CCPR's grants should be received through the Sports Development Council, but did not suggest or foresee that the Sports Council, in order to function properly and efficiently both nationally and regionally, would find it necessary to call upon the staff and services built up by the CCPR in the post-war period. But this is what in fact happened. And some who knew her well feel that P.C.C.'s opposition to the idea of a Sports Development Council was based, not only on a reluctance to see physical recreation removed from the orbit of the Ministry of Education, but on a far-sighted if unspoken perception that the formation of a Sports Council would inevitably entail the disappearance of the CCPR as she had created it. If so, she was right in her foresight, though perhaps she failed to appreciate that, whether a Sports Council was formed or not, the CCPR could not continue indefinitely in its existing form, particularly if she ceased to control it. Its destinies had to be entrusted to "new men, strange faces, other minds".

Fortunately, the duties of a historian are to record and endeavour to interpret the past, not to predict the future. All that can be said here about the future is that the work of the CCPR has not come to an end. It will be carried on in two different ways. Its function of providing a meeting ground and stimulus for bodies concerned with different aspects of physical recreation and a forum through which the corporate views of sports and kindred bodies can be expressed to the Sports Council or Government Departments has been bequeathed to the new CCPR. This new CCPR carries forward into its life much of value from the old CCPR in terms of attitudes and relationships, on which a future of even greater service may be built. It has an important rôle to play.

But the other way in which the CCPR lives on is through the Sports Council. For the Sports Council has inherited, 'as a rich legacy', the principal assets of the CCPR, including the abilities and experience of its staff. Time will show whether the Sports Council will find it possible to preserve what was good in the CCPR, while adding to it all that the Sports Council alone can give, in terms of influence, authority, and material resources.

Those who shared Phyllis Colson's "vision splendid" of physical and mental health for the whole community through physical recreation will hope that that vision will never be allowed to "fade into the light of common day".

Appendix A

Published Tributes to Phyllis Colson

1 Obituaries

(a) Address by Sir John Wolfenden at Memorial Service in the Church of St. Martin-in-the-Fields, 12th October 1972.

We are come together to do honour to the life and work of Phyllis Constance Colson. Many of you knew her far better than I. You worked with her and for her more closely than I did. I beg you not to allow any clumsiness or inadequacy of mine to blur or diminish the sharp clear picture of her which each one cherishes.

I am not going to embark on a detailed biography, still less an obituary notice, complete with dates and jobs and honours. There are elements in a personality which trascend chronology, and it is those elements that we have in our hearts and minds today.

I first came across P.C.C. nearer forty than thirty years ago when we were both moderately young, and both connected with what was then the National Council of Girls' Clubs. (It has changed its name and its nature more than once since then – each time for the better.) It very soon became very clear that that context was not big enough for P.C.C. I do not mean that she self-consciously felt that this was too restricted a canvas for her. It simply was the fact that she was too big for it – too big in aspiration, energy, ideal, intellect, perspective.

Hence the CCPR. Nobody else could have done it. Nobody else could have fitted together the voluntary bodies and the statutory organisations into one coherent and cooperative whole. And nobody else could have persuaded all the parties concerned to recognise that this was the one answer to what each of them individually wanted.

For there were, if I may for a moment conceptualise, three qualities in her public achievement which come together very rarely in any one human being. First, there was vision – an imagination beyond the present to the future, a perception of what the needs were going to be, beyond what they currently were. Secondly, there was determination – the steely resolution to risk all for what she uncontradictably knew to be the right answer. And thirdly there was the skill and the shrewdness to get what she wanted. Without any one of these three qualities P.C.C. could not have done what she did. But she had them all, and that is why her name will live.

The CCPR was her child. Yes, I know that she had many loyal and indefatigable supporters, many of you among them. But it was her child and nobody else's. To it she gave her heart, her devotion and twice a normal working day.

But it is not for her achievements, notable as they are, that we remember her this afternoon – or even for their more wide-reaching consequences, of which she may or may not have approved. We are thinking of Phyllis Colson as a person. Of course you cannot entirely separate a person from his or her achievements. Hers stand, on their own feet and their own merits, a unique contribution to the public and voluntary services in this country and to the fulfilment which they have brought to the lives of millions of individual persons.

We are concerned with P.C.C. herself.

I shall value always three things about her as a person. The first is, obviously, her personal courage in the face of personal adversity. Progressive physical handicap was never allowed to reduce by one iota her total involvement in whatever it was that was current in her fertile mind. Secondly, I remember – and many of you must remember it more sharply than I – her complete devotion and dedication, to whatever it was that she was doing. That filled her mind, occupied all her energies, left her incapable of entertaining anything else. And thirdly, as a gloriously human attribute, lest she should seem too transcendent for mortals like us, a splendidly down-to-earth determination to get her own way, by vigorous argument (if that was the right approach), by subtle ingenuity (if that would achieve what she wanted in a good cause) or by the exercise of a combination of intellect and personal charm to which the most pompous, the stickiest and the most antagonistic had to yield.

All this being said, in my own mind and my own experience the most suitable metaphor or simile is that of (simply) a flame. She burnt abidingly bright, from irresistible inner conviction: she enveloped and destroyed opposition, trivial or important: she warmed those to whom her heart went out. She was irresistible. For her spirit was mirrored in her face – beautifully-boned, serene, fine-chiselled, indomitable.

She exercised that combination of masculine intellect (forgive me) and feminine intuition (I bow to it) which neither woman nor man could resist. Patient, persistent, if necessary ruthless, she persuaded the most improbable; a tigress in defence of her child, but equally a tireless and timeless listener to a colleague's personal distress she smiled, seemingly (but only seemingly) detached through both operations. The secret, if I may dare to presume to diagnose, was that in whatever she did she was deeply involved but yet retained that element of detachment which must be reserved by any person of integrity and self-standing. Whatever the claims from outside – and they were infinite – she remained herself. If she had not, she would not have done what she did, or been what she was.

(b) By Bronwen Lloyd Williams (Physical Education Association's *The Leaflet,* 1972).
"A mind fixed and bent upon somewhat that is good doth avert the dolours of Death ... Above all, believe it, the sweetest canticle is Nunc Dimittis ... Death openeth the gate to good fame."

A very fair epitaph surely on the life and death of Phyllis Colson. Her mind "was fixed and bent on somewhat that is good". She was reminiscent of great women and men, themselves afflicted, crippled, blinded or disabled, who, with the help and support, physical and moral, of their friends, rose to the height of fame in their professions and have left a name behind them which shall not be forgotten.

She and I were the products of the same college, not contemporary; but from the day of her entry and throughout her career, her name was on everybody's lips as an outstanding student, teacher and potential administrator – one whose whole outlook was illumined by a spirit of dedication. Such dedication means the surrender of much, of home and family ties, of other pressing responsibilities, ultimately of the teaching in which Phyllis Colson excelled. Vital, emphatic, far-seeing, on occasion ruthless, she commanded respect, admiration and awe and, in those who knew her best, affection and self-sacrifice.

Others better informed than I can tell of her professional and personal life. I knew her first as working indefatigably in Mecklenburgh Square and realised where her great attributes lay; respected her when she refused to succumb to the exigencies of war and to 'shut up shop'; but, with the help of Mr. B. L. Pearson in the then Board of Education, Mr. A. H. Gem, Sir Stanley Rous, Miss Phyllis Spafford and others of similar calibre, pursued her work with a Churchillian tenacity, facing difficulties, discomfort, criticism, even envy, with a firmness of purpose which surmounted such obstacles and established her as a great pioneer in the field of education.

That her health gradually failed over the years became evident. Still more evident was her refusal to accept disability as an ultimate bar to progress in her plans – not for herself but for the whole world of education and recreation. She had little enough time to enjoy the latter but wanted it for others; and I believe her to have spent any holidays she had in helping handicapped children and others in need, financially and personally.

It took men of big heart and generosity of spirit to serve under a woman in the earlier part of the thirties and sequent decades in this century; and it says much for those men and their counterparts among women to have served, cooperated with and supported Phyllis Colson as her physical frailty began to take toll of her physical (not mental) health.

It is doubtful whether the CCPR would have been created or would have continued without her inspiration; whether the new Sports Council would have come into being without her initial work; whether the Royal Family would have taken so much interest in recreation and the need for leisure usefully occupied; whether the distinguished Olympic athletes and other representatives of all branches of recreation would have rallied round; whether the National Recreation Centres, one by one, would have been established, furbished and maintained at Bisham Abbey, at Lilleshall, in Snowdonia, at the Crystal Palace, in Scotland, Wales and Northern Ireland, without her initiative and ambition for the welfare of others rather than for herself.

Phyllis Colson had remarkable lieutenants in people such as Kay Evans, Justin Evans, George McPartlin, Christine Tayler, Paddy Medlicott (Blanckenberg), Brenda Salkeld and others too many to enumerate; and she had firm allies in Phyllis

Spafford, Peter Sebastian and some of the Organisers of Physical Education – enemies too at times, but enmity to her could never be more than transient.

That her services were recognised by appointment to C.B.E. in 1964 and a series of awards both in this country and in Europe was a source of pleasure to all who knew her; but she never gave me the impression of desiring personal acclamation.

We were not intimately acquainted nor did we meet often, except on public occasions; but it is her right that her work should not only be remembered but that it should continue with the same flame of inspiration which burned in her. If it does not, if it flickers to a dying fire, her death will have diminished us. That should not be. If an Olympic flame can be kept alight, so surely can her light and work be kept alive. Death may have come as a relief from bodily pain; and she should be remembered as a vital, not a dying spark.

Macaulay said: "We are not much in the habit of idolising the living or the dead ... but there are a few characters which have stood the closest scrutiny and the severest tests, which have been tried in the furnace and have been found pure, which have been weighed in the balance and have not been found wanting, which have been declared sterling by the general consent of mankind."

Let that be the record of Phyllis Colson among us and among succeeding generations who will benefit from a mission she began. "Death openeth the gate to good fame". I trust that in a new world she will be rejuvenated.

(c) By Arthur Gem (Physical Education Association's Leaflet, 1972).
I wish to associate myself with the tribute paid by Miss Bronwen Lloyd-Williams:

I worked very closely with Phyllis Colson, from the formation of the CCPR to the time of her retirement and as the years passed my admiration for her great qualities grew.

She was a terrific worker – and it was lightly said by the staff that it was a question of whether P.C.C. (as she was always known) or the milkman reached the office first – and she always took an enormous pile of work home with her in the evening.

She had great administrative qualities and was quite fearless in fighting for what she considered right. The magnitude of her achievements were all the more remarkable when it is realised that she fought a continuing battle against increasing ill health.

She may outwardly have appeared authoritarian at times, but all those who were close to her knew that underneath this she was a sensitive and very kindly person who attracted outstanding loyalty from those who worked with her. It is sad to know that her last two years were clouded by the merging of the Sports Council and the CCPR; to her it was like the death of something she had created and loved dearly.

An outstanding woman has passed on, leaving behind her a record of fine work faithfully accomplished. She will long be mourned by her many friends.

(d) By the Editor, *Duke of Edinburgh's Award Journal* (9/72). Phyllis Colson died from an illness which she had fought unflinchingly for a great number of years. On first meeting her it seemed incredible that such a dynamic personality could emerge from the pain-wracked, crippled frame. But after a short while it was only the personality, the liveliness of mind, the concern and interest for others of which one was aware.

In 1935 Phyllis Colson had the vision and drive to found the Central Council of Physical Recreation and for 28 years served as its secretary.

On early retirement she became associated with the Duke of Edinburgh's Award. In 1964 she undertook a review of the operation and effectiveness of the scheme. She was advised by others but the document was justly known as the Colson Report. Reading through it now, one realises how many of the recommendations have been put into practice. Her suggestions led directly to revision of the scheme and its present form.

Phyllis Colson became a trustee in September 1965 and throughout her term of office determinedly carried out all duties though often in extreme pain.

A first-class administrator, Phyllis Colson also paid meticulous attention to detail. She had ideas, and the courage and energy to see them through to fruition. As a thinker concerned with policy-making, she undoubtedly influenced the shape and destiny of the Award scheme.

Phyllis Colson had a penetration of thought and clearsightedness which stimulated many, though it disconcerted some. Brave, almost stubbornly independent, with great charm she had an understanding and sympathy with others. It is indicative that until the last short bout of severe illness she served regularly with the Samaritans.

Phyl was someone I personally feel privileged to have known. She inspired both admiration and affection.

(e) By H.J.E., *The Times* (30th June 1972).

By any standards, Phyllis Colson, who died on June 26 ... was a remarkable woman. More than any other factor it was her creative vision in establishing the Central Council of Recreative Physical Training (later the Central Council of Physical Recreation) in 1935 that imparted a dynamic initiative towards cooperation into the somewhat amorphous worlds of sport and physical education, a cooperation which later made possible the formation of the new Sports Councils in England and Wales.

Her sense of purpose and limitless energy were allied to a rare administrative ability and an even rarer gift of securing the cooperation of a wide circle of influential people. Senior civil servants, members of Parliament, business leaders, physical educationists, heads of the governing bodies of sport and the outdoor activity organisations – all fell under her spell and did her bidding.

Feminine without being feminist ... her charm and consummate tact achieved results impossible for a mere man. Over the years, she surrounded herself with a staff of men and women who shared her ideals and soon became infected with her vocational attitude to work. She never sought personal publicity but fought like a tigress for the interests of the CCPR.

She retired from the general secretaryship of the CCPR in 1963 ... Her death, after many years of ill-health borne with unequalled courage, leaves an empty place in the hearts of all who worked with her. But she has left a lasting memorial throughout the whole world of physical recreation.

2. *Appreciations on Retirement*
(a) From *Sport and Recreation* (CCPR's Journal, 4/63).
(i) from Sir Stanley Rous, Chairman of the CCPR Executive Committee.

I was very glad to hear that this issue of *Sport and Recreation* would contain a number of tributes to Miss Colson's work as General Secretary of the CCPR over the past 28 years. During that time my associations with Miss Colson have been very close and continuous, especially since I succeeded the late Lord Hampden as Chairman of the CCPR's Executive Committee in 1945. I have therefore better reason than most to know how much the progress and growth of the CCPR to its present position of commanding influence in this country have depended on her unique energy and abilities.

The atmosphere in which the Council had its birth and infancy was well recaptured by Miss Colson in her address at the last Annual General Meeting ... The way she gained the support of Government Departments and of the jealously autonomous sport bodies and influential people was little short of miraculous. People very soon came to appreciate that the Central Council of Recreative Physical Training (as it was called for the first eight years of its existence) was not just another well-intentioned but woolly-minded voluntary organisation with a somewhat nebulous and self-imposed task of 'coordination', but an extremely efficient and businesslike body which sought to achieve practical results and was prepared to be judged by them.

It was her efficiency as an administrator and her skill in personal relations that laid the foundation stones for the subsequent rise of the CCPR to its present position. Throughout the years, in face of every obstacle, including that of the war, Miss Colson has preserved her initial vision and 'drive'. At 'making friends and influencing people' she has remained superb.

As her Chairman, I always knew that committee business would be meticulously prepared, every possible contingency provided for, and, moreover, that I would be given a very helpful private briefing on the matters to be discussed. Would that the business of more committees was prepared by people like Miss Colson! Or, on second thoughts, perhaps it would not be good for all chairmen to be 'spoiled' as Miss Colson 'spoils' me!

A public tribute cannot fully convey how much the CCPR and the country as a whole owe to the devotion with which Miss Colson has served the cause of physical recreation for so many years. Nor can it convey the unique personal gifts which Miss Colson expended so selflessly and exclusively on the Council. It is so much her creation that it will be as hard to think of it without Miss Colson as it will be to think of Miss Colson without the CCPR. But she has built well and hands over to her successor an organisation with a high and firm reputation. It is good to know that she will be retaining some form of link with our work, at least for some time to come, and she will carry into her increased leisure the deep affection, heartfelt gratitude and warmest good wishes of all who have worked with her.

(ii) from Lesley Sewell, Secretary, National Association of Youth Clubs.

Part of Miss Colson's genius has been her unique ability to hold together the many and varied strands which make up the strength of the CCPR – not always an easy task. Her intimate knowledge and experience of the voluntary youth organisations has been of the greatest value and, under her leadership, CCPR staff have helped and stimulated our programmes and assisted in the development of a large number of new activities. Many of us will wish to place on record our deep sense of obligation for the encouragement and support Miss Colson has given throughout the past years, not only to the youth organisations but to hundreds of individuals within their membership.

(iii) from A. H. Gem, Deputy Chairman, CCPR Executive Committee.

Limitation of space makes it impossible to pay an adequate tribute to Miss Colson and so I must confine myself to three of her outstanding qualities.

We all admired her tremendous capacity for hard work, not for her the modern attitude of trying to get as much as possible for doing as little as possible. As long as there was a job to do she did it, even if it meant a fourteen-hour day and a seven-day week.

The precision of ther work was outstanding. She always strove for the best and was intolerant of the second-rate and the slipshod.

Finally, she had a wonderful sense of timing; she seemed to judge instinctively the right moment to do the right thing.

Much of the progress of the CCPR is due to her skill in this respect.

She will leave with the lasting gratitude and admiration of all, and with the wish that only good things may journey with her in the years that lie ahead.

(iv) from C. L. de Beaumont, President, Amateur Fencing Association.

An indomitable will and singleness of purpose, an infinite capacity for work, sympathetic consideration of anybody's problems and considerable charm of manner are the rare combination of attributes which made Miss Colson respected and loved by the innumerable people who came into contact with her while she steadily built the CCPR to its present unique position. She commanded success and inevitably achieved it.

Her clear mind and great experience enabled her to give prescient advice to those, like myself, concerned with the development of a governing body for sport and her constant help has been invaluable to us through the years. To know her and watch her work was a liberal education.

In wishing her many years of happiness during her well earned retirement, it is good to know that her advice will still be available to the CCPR and to us its members. She is too dynamic a person to rest long on her laurels. She takes with her our affection and our thanks.

(v) from E. Major, formerly Ministry of Education Liaison Officer to CCPR.

The quality which instantly springs to mind when one thinks of Miss Colson is courage. Not only has she shown this quality to a high degree in dealing with the problems of indifferent personal health, but also when concerned with the inevitable problems of such an organisation as the CCPR. Often these problems must have seemed well nigh insoluble, but Miss Colson, with her outstanding powers of organisation and administration and her firm belief in the CCPR, has produced the solution required to enable progress to be made and the work of the Council to be developed along sound lines.

Miss Colson has been a most loyal servant of the Council and her devotion to duty has been an example to all of us. Her record of service as General Secretary has been in many ways unique, and when the history of the CCPR comes to be written no one will merit a more honourable place in it than Miss Colson.

(vi) from Sir John Wolfenden, Vice-Chancellor, University of Reading.
"Be ye therefore wise as serpents, and harmless as doves". Nobody could accuse P.C.C. of being serpentine. But wise she certainly is – and, when it suits her, dove-like. I well remember, though I am sure she does not, the first time I encountered this irresistible combination of skills. Everybody who knows her knows what I mean.

These skills, this nature, this intelligence, have for many years been dedicated (that is not too strong a word) to the service of the CCPR. She has been it: and it has been the most remarkable collection of people in the history of British co-operation.

My recent experiences as Chairman of the CCPR Sport Committee have increased, if that were possible, my respect and admiration for her. The Committee's views did not always agree with P.C.C.'s. How many people (especially women) would admit that a view different from their own, on a subject about which they felt passionately, might be right? I have met one, Phyllis Colson.

(vii) from Phyllis Spafford, formerly Secretary of the Physical Education Association of Great Britain and Northern Ireland.
Before the CCPR was formed, Phyllis Colson and I worked together on the staff of the then National Council of Girls' Clubs, and I realised at once that she was a woman in a thousand. Her organising ability and powers of observation, her vision and above all, her understanding of young people, impressed me greatly, and these gifts, developed with the years, have been largely responsible for the success of the Central Council.

Phyllis Colson's undaunted courage in the face of physical handicaps, and her refusal to be depressed in the face of set-backs in the Central Council's early days, earned her the respect of all who came in contact with her. I felt that Phyllis had an inner spiritual strength, which always supported her.

It is impossible to do justice in the short spaced allowed, to a woman outstanding in every way. I am proud to know Phyllis Colson as a friend.

(c) By C. Muriel Webster (Physical Education Association's *The Leaflet*, 4/63).

A woman with vision, organising ability and a working capacity that few can emulate – these are some of the attributes of a member of our Association to whom we wish to pay tribute – Phyllis Colson. Some of us have ideas, some work hard and there are many good organisers in our profession but rarely do we get all these qualities combined in one person. When it does happen then we see something emerge, bigger than the confines of our subject and more far-reaching than the playing fields of a school.

The work of the CCPR is well known to many of us although some may not know how the Council started. Miss Colson, in a recent article in *Sport and Recreation,* told us that she first gave birth to the concept of Physical Recreation for All when she was walking down Woburn Place one April day in 1935. That was over 25 years ago and the idea has resulted in a Council with a Royal President; offices in N. Ireland, Wales, and in nine regions of England; three national centres and now the Crystal Palace. We, as members of The Physical Education Association, are proud that Miss P. Spafford and Mr. H. Cole, who were then Secretary and Treasurer of The Ling Association, helped to launch the venture which has grown in size and repute due largely to the genius and tenacity of one woman.

I have been lucky enough to work with Miss Colson on many occasions and in different fields. I would like to cite three that may help to highlight some of her work.

At the outbreak of the war the CCPR refused to die. Instead the Council, against great odds, ran Recreational Summer Schools and many campaigns for the war effort. Keep Fit, National Dancing, Games and Sport were welcome activities after the dreary spells of waiting for sirens. Many ideas for the future were no doubt hatched under the mulberry tree in the beautiful garden of Lowther College where the Summer Schools were held. I, who had at first merely admired Miss Colson's ability to organise such excellent courses while remaining in the background herself, gradually realised how far ahead she was looking and planning.

Many of us will remember the summer of 1957 when the International Council of Physical Education and Sports for Women and Girls held its Conference in London. I was the Chairman of the Joint Committee which supposedly organised the Conference. It could have been a wearing task but not when Miss Colson was Secretary. She and some of her CCPR colleagues covered most of the backroom work while I merely graced the platform when the Conference was in smooth running. Her experience in getting in touch with the right people, in inviting and receiving Royalty, in planning excursions were all invaluable. As always, she gave her help generously and untiringly.

For six years Miss Colson has acted as Secretary of the United Kingdom Committee for International Conferences. It was not until the last meeting, when we found difficulty in finding a successor and had to trim some of our far-reaching plans, that we realised how heavily we had relied on the work of the Secretary.

These three instances of service do not give a picture of the development of what has been Miss Colson's life work – the Central Council of Physical Recreation. The history of the Council has been given elsewhere and we can find out about it by reading the beautifully produced CCPR Annual Reports.

Miss Colson must have the satisfaction of knowing that she leaves a ship that is not only safely launched but is sweeping along at full sail. Tributes have already been paid to her by Bedford College, where she was trained, by the CCPR Executive Committee and Staff, and also by other organisations. It is now our turn to record thanks to this member of our Association of whom we are justly proud. Our good wishes go to her for the future.

Appendix B

Honorary Officers, Committee Chairmen and Executive Membership (at May 1972)

(1) Honorary Officers

Patrons

1935–1936 H.M. King George V, H.M. The Queen, H.R.H. The Prince of Wales
1936   H.M. King Edward VIII
1936–1952 H.M. King George VI, H.M. Queen Mary
1952–1972 H.M. The Queen

Presidents

1935–1945 The Viscount Astor (d. 1953)
1945–1951 The Viscount Hampden, G.C.V.O., K.C.B., C.M.G. (d. 1958)
1951–1972 H.R.H. The Duke of Edinburgh, K.G., K.T., O.M.

Hon. Life Vice-President

1966–1972 Miss P. C. Colson, C.B.E. (d. 1972)

Hon. Treasurers

1935–1937 The Viscount Hampden
1937–1944 Sir Percival Sharp (d. 1953)
1944–1947 Sir John Catlow (d. 1947)
1947–1962 Sir Clarence Sadd, C.B.E. (d. 1962)
1962–1972 R.E. Brook, Esq., C.M.G., O.B.E. (later Sir Robin)

Hon. Medical Advisers

1947–1952 Sir Robert Stanton Woods, M.D., F.R.C.P. (d. 1955)
1953–1957 The Lord Webb-Johnson, G.C.V.O., D.S.O., F.R.C.S. (d. 1958)
1958–1967 Sir Arthur Porritt, K.C.V.O., C.B.E., F.R.C.S. (later Lord Porritt)
1967–1972 Dr. O. G. Edholm, M. B., B.S.

Hon. Legal Advisers
1937–1945   C. Wreford Brown, Esq.
1945–1954   Ernest S. Watkins, Ll.B.
1954–1961   Geoffrey Rickman, Esq.

(2)   Chairmen of Committees and Sub-Committees

Executive, and General Purposes and Finance Committees
1935   Sir George Newman (temporary)
1936–1945   The Viscount Hampden
1945–1972   Sir Stanley Rous, C.B.E., J.P.
(1945–1972   Deputy Chairman – A. H. Gem, Esq C.B.E., M.C.)

Technical Advisory Sub-Committee
(later called Recreative Gymnastics and Movement, and General Technical Committee)
1935–1938   S. F. Rous, Esq.
1938–1958   A. H. Gem, Esq.

Staff Committee, Staff Appointments Committee and National Test Sub-Committee (until 1949)
1940–1972   A. H. Gem, Esq.

Games and Sports (Advisory) Committee
1943–1948   Alderman H. E. Fern, C.B.E.
1948–1957   The Lord Aberdare, G.B.I., Ll.D., K.St.J. (d. 1957)
1957–1960   Sir Frederick Browning K.C.V.O., K.B.E., C.B., D.S.O. (d. 1965)
1961–1962   The Duke of Norfolk, K.G., G.C.V.O., P.C.
1962–1967   The Baroness Burton of Coventry
1967–1969   Clinton Sayer, Esq.
1969–1972   R. J. W. Struthers, Esq.

Outdoor Activities (Advisory) Committee
1943–1945   Wing-Commander J. G. Paterson, M.V.O.
1945–1960   J. B. Henderson, Esq., O.B.E. (d. 1967)
1960–1963   J. S. Edbrooke, Esq., O.B.E.
1963–1972   Sir Jack Longland

Movement and Dance Committee
1969–1972 Miss Eileen Alexander

Water Recreation Committee
1972 David Nations, Esq.

Physical Recreation in Industry Committee
(*later Industrial Advisory Panel*)
1937–1940 Wing-Commander J. G. Paterson, M.V.O.
1946–1952 The Viscount Bridgeman, D.S.O., M.C.
1952–1955 T. G. Bedwell, Esq. (d. 1973)

Sports Trade Advisory Panel
1954–1972 J. Eaton Griffith, C.M.G., O.B.E.

Mountain Leadership Training Board
1963–1972 Sir Jack Longland

Harrison's Rocks Sub-Committee
1971–1972 J. S. Edbrooke, Esq., O.B.E.

Welsh Committee
1944–1972 T. Glyn Davies, Esq., C.B.E.

Welsh Games and Sports Advisory Committee
1950–1962 Lt. Col. W. R. Hawkins, T.D.
1962–1968 H. Roy Evans, Esq.,
1968–1972 David Thomas, Esq.

North Wales Advisory Committee
1960–1964 A. M. Rees, Esq., O.B.E.
1964–1972 Geoffrey Gadd, Esq., M.B.E., J.P. (d. 3/1974)

Scottish Section, CCPR – 1945–1953
Presidents
1946–1948 Sir Iain Colquhoun of Luss, K.T., D.S.O. (d.
           1948)
1949–1953 The Lord Inverclyde

Chairmen of Scottish Committee
1945–1949 W. J. Stuart, Esq., F.R.C.S.E.
1949–1953 H. Stewart Mackintosh, Esq., Ph.D.

Northern Ireland Section
Presidents
1955–1964   The Lord Wakehurst, K.C.M.G.
1965–1968   The Lord Erskine of Rerrick, G.B.E.
1968–1972   The Lord Grey of Naunton, G.C.M.G., K.C.V.O.

Chairmen of Northern Ireland Committee
1952–1954   W. H. Smyth, Esq., M.B.E.
1954–1961   P. Smiles, Esq. O.B.E.
1961–1962   Capt. T. D. Morrison, O.B.E.
1962–1972   R. B. Hunter, Esq. O.B.E.

National Recreation Centre Committees
Bisham Abbey
1948–1961   The Lord Hampton, D.S.O.
1961–1972   J. Eaton Griffith, Esq. C.M.G., O.B.E.

Glenmore Lodge
1948–1953   H.Stewart Mackintosh, Esq. Ph.D.

Lilleshall Hall
1952–1963   J. Eaton Griffith, Esq., C.M.G., O.B.E.
1963–1972   A. J. M. Miller, Esq., D.S.C. V.R.D.

Plas y Brenin
1955–1965   Sir John Hunt C.B.E., D.S.O., D.C.L.
1965–1972   Sir Jack Longland

Crystal Palace
1963–1972   A. H. Gem, Esq. C.B.E., M.C.

Cowes
1967–1972   W. J. Borthwick, Esq., D.S.C.

Cardiff
1971–1972   T. Glyn Davies, Esq. C.B.E.

Holme Pierrepont
1971–1972   E. Major, Esq., M.B.E.

Liaison Officers with Government Departments
Ministry of Education
1935–1949   Lt. Col. S. J. Parker, O.B.E., H.M.I.
1949–1958   E. Major, Esq., M.B.E.
1959–1972   H.Sagar, Esq., H.M.I.

Ministry of Labour and National Service
1947–1961   Mrs Sybil Stuart Horner, M.B. B.Sc.

Ministry of Education for Northern Ireland
1950–1963   J. M. Benn, Esq., C.B.
1963–1970   L. Arndell, Esq.
1970–1972   J. Finney, Esq.

Ministry of Housing and Local Government
1970–1972   W. M. Schwab, Esq.

Membership of Executive Committee, May 1972

Sir Stanley Rous, C.B.E.
(Chairman)
A. H. Gem, C.B.E., M.C.
(Deputy Chairman)
Miss Eileen Alexander
W. J. Borthwick, D.S.C.
R. E. Brook, C.M.G., O.B.E.
A. G. K. Brown
Miss A. F. Bull, C.B.E.
Baroness Burton
of Coventry
N. R. Collins
H. F. David, C.B.E.
T. Glyn Davies, C.B.E.
J. G. Dunbar
J. S. Edbrooke, O.B.E.
J. Eaton Griffith,
C.M.G. O.B.E.
R. St. G. T. Harper

A. Henderson, J.P.
R. B. Hunter, O.B.E.
P. J. Liddell, D.S.C.
Miss B. Lloyd-Williams
Miss M. J. Lodge
Sir Jack Longland
P. B. Lucas, D.S.O., D.F.C.
E. Major, M.B.E.
K. B. Martin
A. J. M. Miller,
D.S.C., V.R.D.
K. K. Mitchell
Rt. Hon. P. J. Noel-Baker
AirVice-Marshal
R. A. Ramsay Rae
C.B., O.B.E.
Lt. Col. R. H. Russell
R. J. W. Struthers

Appendix C

Long-Serving Staff—
Technical and Administrative

Note – The normal qualification for inclusion in this list is a minimum of ten years' full-time service, though some exceptions have been admitted in the case of senior officers. The post stated is the final one held. Complete staff records are unfortunately not available and any omissions are greatly regretted.

AINSWORTH, CYRIL, Regional Officer, North-West, 1963–1972
ALDERSLADE, MRS. K. B. (Perry), Regional Officer, N. Midlands, 1950–1965

BAINES, ALEX, Stores and Transport Manager, Plas y Brenin N.M.C., 1958–1972
BARLOW, RHONA (later Hall), Senior Representative, North-West, 1946–54, and 1957–58
BARNETT, NANCY, Representative, West Midlands, 1942–1965
BARRY, JACK, Deputy Secretary, 1940–1947 and 1963–1972
BARTRAM, GRACE, Acting Senior Representative, Yorkshire, 1941–1951
BENNETT, HAZEL, Representative, West Midlands, 1966–1972
BIRCH, JOHN G., Senior Representative, London and S.E., 1965–1972
BLANCKENBERG, MRS. L. (later Medlicott), Senior Representative, London and S.E., 1937–1948
BLANEY, SANDRA, Assistant, Finance Dept., 1964–1972
BRADLEY, JOHN B., Principal Executive Officer, 1947–1966 (d. 1966)
BRADLEY, M. R. (Mick), Senior Representative, Eastern, 1949–1972
BRIDGEMAN, LAURIE J., Regional Officer, Eastern, 1961–1972
BRIDGES, JEAN (later Tallantire), Representative, Yorkshire, 1963–1972
BRISCOE, FRED L., Principal Executive Officer, 1946–1972
BURNS, EILEEN (née Chapman), Assistant Secretary, 1962–1972

BUTCHER, VIOLET, Manager, Bookshop, 1942–1971

CARR, JOHN, Representative, North Midlands, 1963–1972

CASSELTON, JEAN, Secretary, Bisham Abbey NSC, 1961–1972

CLARKSON, EVE, Senior Representative, South-West, 1939–1967 (d. 1971)

COGHLAN, JOHN F., M.B.E. T.D., B.A., Regional Officer, West Midlands, 1965–1972

COLBECK, A. L., M.B.E., Regional Officer, North-East, 1939–1972

COLE, HENRY A., O.B.E., Technical Adviser, 1935–1944 (d. 1957)

COLSON, PHYLLIS C., C.B.E., General Secretary, 1935–1963 (d. 1972)

COOMBER, MARY, Editor's Assistant and Advertising Manager, 1953–1970

CORMACK, GEORGE, Senior Representative, North-West, 1945–1962 (d. 1962)

COWIE, ALIX, Representative, London and S.E., 1945–1972

DAVIES, CADFAN, T. D., Senior Representative, Wales, 1957–1972

DAWSON, MOLLY, Senior Representative, Southern, 1944–1972

DENDY, ELIZABETH, Principal Executive Officer, 1966–1972

DIBLEY, G. S., Director, Holme Pierrepont National Water Sports Centre, 1955–1972

DICKINS, DAPHNE, Senior Representative, South-West, 1962–1972

DOCKING, W. MADGE, Senior Representative, South, 1939–1957 (d. 1957)

DUMMETT, BARBARA, M.I.S.T.D., Ballroom Dancing Specialist, 1940–1953

EATOUGH, MARJORIE, Representative, Yorkshire, 1961–1972

EDWARDS, ERIC A. J., M.C., Principal Administrative Officer, 1951–1972

ELLIS, HATTIE, Domestic Bursar, Lilleshall NSC, 1951–1962 and 1966–1972 (d. 1973)

EMBUREY, EILEEN, Assistant Secretary, 1941–1972

ERSKINE, PHYLLIS, Senior Representative, North-West, 1940–1963

EVANS, H. JUSTIN, O.B.E., M.A., Acting General Secretary, 1944–1968

EVANS, K.E. (Kay), M.B.E., Technical Adviser, 1939–1966

GARLAND, PAT, Senior Secretary, Welsh Office, 1958–1972

GARSIDE, COL. B. R. D., M.C., Regional Officer, London and S.E., 1968–1972

GILL, KENNETH L., Senior Representative, Yorkshire, 1959–1972

GLASGOW, L. GEORGE, Secretary, Northern Ireland, 1955–1972

GRIFFITHS, S. GORDON, Representative, Wales 1963–1972

HAMMOND, JOHN, Deputy Director, Crystal Palace NSC, 1967–1972

HASELEY, G., Assistant Maintenance Officer, Lilleshall NSC, 1957–1972

HAWKESFORD, NANCY (later Mrs Bates) Secretary, London and S.E., 1942–1953

HEATHFIELD, BERYL (née Mercer), Senior Assistant Secretary, 1948–1965

HICKLING, GEORGE, Specialist in Weight Lifting and Handling, 1945–1968 (d. 1968)

HIGGINS, MARGARET, B.A., Secretary, London and S.E., 1954–1967

HODGE, JOHN, B.A., Senior Representative, South-West, 1963–1972

HODGES, CELIA, Representative, West Midlands, 1966–1972

HUGHES, SHEILA, Executive Officer, 1963–1972

HUMPHREYS, DAVID, Instructor, Plas y Brenin NMC, 1961–1972

HUMPHREYS, RAY, Regional Officer, Southern, 1957–1972

ILOTT, DAPHNE, Secretary, Southern, 1955–1972

JACKSON, JOHN A., Director, Plas y Brenin NMC, 1957–1972

JACKSON, M. ADAIR, Representative, Kent, 1937–1944

JAGGER, BASIL F. (Joe), B.A., Representative, London and S.E., 1945–1962

JOHNSON, DOROTHY (née Collett), Secretary, North-East, 1960–1972

JONES, EMLYN B., Director, Crystal Palace NSC, 1947–1972

KEEBLE, RUTH, Senior Representative, London and S.E., 1940–1967

KEEBLE, W. B., Director, Cowes National Sailing Centre, 1965–1972

KILKENNY, JOHN C., O.B.E., Regional Officer, North-West, 1961–1968

KING, KATHERINE C., Book-keeper, Finance Department, 1947–1968

LANE, JAMES, J.P., Director, Lilleshall NSC, 1950–1972

LATTO, KAY (née Caister), Senior Representative, North Midlands, 1936–1959

LATTO, W. L., Assistant Technical Adviser, 1940–1951

LEE, BRIAN, Director, Bisham Abbey NSC, 1961–1972

LEWIS, ESMÉ, Senior Representative, North Midlands, 1943–1972

LEWIS, H. J., Senior Representative, Southern, 1946–1972

LEWIS, W. PETER, Representative, Wales, 1964–1972

LITTLEWOOD, HARRY, B.Sc., Principal Technical Officer, 1943–1972

LOADER, CATHERINE M., Senior Representative, Scottish Section, 1941–1953 (to SCPR)

LOGAN, RALPH, Regional Officer, North Midlands, 1946–1972

MACK, JUNE, Executive Officer, 1957–1972

MACKENZIE, W. S., Senior Representative, West Midlands, 1941–1965

MCKINNON, ROBERT, M.A., Editor, *Sport and Recreation* (part-time), 1958–1966

MCPARTLIN, G. A., O.B.E., Technical Director, 1945–1969

MARSHALL, OLIVIA (née McFarland), Representative N. Ireland, 1965–1972

MEREDITH, MARY, Secretary (part-time), North Wales Office, 1959–1972

MERRITT, JUNE (née Lewer), Assistant, Book Shop (part-time), 1959–1972

MITCHELL, DENISE (later Squire), M.B.E., Senior Secretary, 1956–1969

MOORE, REGINALD, Publicity Officer and Editor, 1966–1972

MOORHEAD, ANNE, Senior Representative, N. Ireland, 1961–1972

MORGAN, RITA, Representative, Wales, 1961–1972

MURPHY, ANNA, Secretary, Yorkshire, 1949–1972

NEWSON, OLIVE W., Principal Executive Officer, 1947–1956 and 1964–1972
NORMAN, W., Head of Bookings Department, 1953–1965

OAKES, HAROLD, Welsh Secretary, 1951–1972
ORGILL, ROGER, Chief Instructor and Deputy Director, Plas y Brenin NMC 1955–1972

PARK, W. D., B.Sc., Regional Officer, South-West, 1946–1969
PARRY, BRIAN, Senior Representative, North-West, 1962–1972
PARRY, SARAH, Head of Reference Department and Library, 1964–1972
PARSONS, EDWINA M., Assistant Secretary, 1938–1953
PERRY, MARY (Molly), Machine Room Supervisor, Finance Department, 1955–1967
POLLITT, KATHLEEN, Senior Representative, North-West, 1963–1972
POND, DAVID F., F.C.A., Accountant, 1967–1972
POOLE, JOAN, Domestic Bursar, Bisham Abbey NSC, 1954–1962
POWELL, V. B. V., O.B.E., M.A., Principal Executive Officer, 1956–1958 and 1965–70
PRATER, E. H., B.A., Welsh Secretary, 1946–1959
PRICE, HUW, Representative, South, 1949–1963
PRICE, IVY, Senior Representative, North-East, 1941–1965
PRYKE, KATHLEEN (later Mrs. Loveluck), Assistant Secretary 1937–1946

REVELL, D. R., Engineer, Crystal Palace NSC, 1964–1972
RICHARDS, GEOFFREY, Regional Officer, Eastern, 1939–1969
RICHARDSON, R. A. W., Representative, Eastern, 1941–1954
ROBERTS, EMRYS, Bursar, Plas y Brenin NMC, 1955–1967
ROBINSON, JOYCE (later Jarvis), Senior Representative, North-West, 1945–1955 and 1968–69
ROSS, DAVID G., M.C., International Service Officer, 1946–1953
ROYLE, J. B., Senior Representative, North-West, 1963–1972
RUSSELL, N. B., Representative, Wales, 1960–1972

SADLER, ELSIE, Assistant Domestic Bursar, Lilleshall NSC, 1957–1964 and 1967–1969

SADLER, J. M., B.A., Senior Representative, West Midlands, 1967–1972

SALKELD, BRENDA, Senior Representative, Eastern, 1940–1961

SANDERS, ANNE, Assistant Manager, Bookshop, 1949–1969

SAUNDERS, W. L., Senior Representative, North-East, 1955–1972

SAYER, CLINTON, M.A., Technical Director, 1939–1946 and 1970–1972

SCOTT, ELEANOR, Senior Representative, North-East, 1939–1964

SHOWERS, JAY N., Head of Reference Department and Library, 1945–1971

SINGLETON, KAY M., Assistant Accountant, 1940–1945 and 1946–1971

SLADER, A. D., Senior Representative, Northern Ireland, 1961–1972

SMITH, MARGARET, Assistant, Reference Department and Library, 1964–1972

STUBBS, JESS, Secretary, North-West, 1952–1970

SWANSON, GEORGE, Maintenance Officer, Lilleshall NSC, 1967–1972

SYKES, MARJORIE, Secretary, Lilleshall NSC, 1950–1966

TANGYE, GLADYS, F.C.A., Accountant (part-time), 1959–1967

TANNER, BARBARA, Head of Bookings Department, 1956–1967 (d. 1973)

TARRANT, RONALD, Shorthand Typist, 1945–1972

TATTMAN, MARGARET, Secretary, Eastern, 1951–1972

TAYLER, M. CHRISTINE, Principal Executive Officer, 1949–1963

TAYLOR, ELIZABETH, Representative, Eastern, 1961–1969

TAYLOR, JOHN, Senior Representative, Eastern, 1963–1972

TEMPLEMAN, FRANK L., B.A., Regional Officer, Yorkshire, 1946–1972

TOLSON, JOYCE, Representative, London and S.E., 1943–1951

TURNER, ALTHAM, Senior Representative, North Midlands, 1949–1962

VAUGHAN, DOROTHEA M., F.C.A., (Mrs. Magnus Pyke), Accountant (part-time), 1937–1953

WADE, DENNIS A., B.Sc., Principal Executive Officer, 1962–1972

WARD, MAUD, Assistant, Finance Department, 1966–1972

WARD, MRS. O. D., Secretary, Welsh Office, 1960–1969

WARDALE, PETER, Senior Representative, North Midlands, 1960–1972

WATT, HELEN M., Industrial Relations Officer, 1938–1946

WEBBER, R. L., Sports Hall Manager, Crystal Palace NSC, 1964–1972

WEST, IVY, Representative, London and S.E., 1940–1963

WHEATLEY, JOHN W., Regional Officer, South-West, 1954–1972

WIGGINS, C. E., Senior Representative, Southern, 1941–1949

WILKINSON, T. E., Representative, Eastern, 1963–1972

WILLIAMS, RAY, Senior Representative, West Midlands, 1956–1967

WILSON, PAULINE (later Fancourt), Senior Representative, London and S.E., 1963–1972

WINTERBOTTOM, WALTER, C.B.E., General Secretary, 1963–1965 and 1967–1972

WITHERS, K. (JANIE)., Representative, North-West, 1941–1962

WYNESS, MURIEL, Representative, South-West, 1940–1962

Appendix D

Members of the CCPR Council at May 1972

Note: The figures give the year of election.

Organisations devoted to Physical Activity in General

COMPREHENSIVE
British Olympic Association '35
National Playing Fields
Association '35

PROFESSIONAL
British Association of Organisers
and Lecturers in Physical
Education '35
Physical Education Association
of Great Britain and Northern
Ireland '35

SERVICES
Army Physical Training
Department '35
Army School of Physical
Training '41
Army Sport Control Board '35
Royal Air Force Directorate of
Physical Education '35
Royal Air Force School of
Physical Education '48
Royal Air Force Sports Board '35
Royal Marines' School of
Physical Training '35
Royal Naval and Royal Marines
Sports Control Board '35
Royal Naval School of Physical
and Recreational Training '41

MISCELLANEOUS
British Association of National
Coaches '70
British Field Sports Society '70
British Sports Association for the
Disabled '70
British Universities Sports
Federation '63
Civil Service Sports Council '35
Incorporated British Association
for Physical Training '35

Institute of Baths Management '71
Institute of Park and Recreation
Administration '62
National Council for Schools'
Sports '51
Universities Athletic Union '61
Women's Inter-University
Athletic Board '61

Specialist Organisation

ANGLING
National Anglers' Council '68

ARCHERY
Grand National Archery
Society '48

ASSOCIATION FOOTBALL
English Schools' Football
Association '49
The Football Association '35
Women's Football Association '72

ATHLETICS
Amateur Athletic Association '35
British Amateur Athletic Board '71
English Schools' Athletic
Association '35
Women's Amateur Athletic
Association '35

BADMINTON
Badminton Association of
England '47

BASKETBALL
Amateur Basketball Association '43

BICYCLE POLO
Bicycle Polo Association of Great
Britain '43

260

APPENDIX

261

MOUNTAINEERING
British Mountaineering Council '45

NETBALL
All England Netball Association '35

ORIENTEERING
British Orienteering Federation '67

PARACHUTING
British Parachute Association '67

RAMBLING
Ramblers' Association '37

RIDING
British Horse Society '38

ROUNDERS
National Rounders Association '47

ROWING
Amateur Rowing Association '55
Women's Amateur Rowing
Council '47

RUGBY LEAGUE FOOTBALL
Rugby Football League '35

RUGBY UNION FOOTBALL
Rugby Football Union '35

SAILING
National Schools Sailing
Association '67
Royal Yachting Association '58
Sail Training Association '67

SHOOTING
The Clay Pigeon Shooting
Association '57
National Rifle Association '66
National Small-Bore Rifle
Association '56

SKATING
National Roller Hockey
Association '48
National Skating Association of
Great Britain '47

SKIING
National Ski Federation of
Great Britain '49

SQUASH RACKETS
Squash Rackets Association '50
Women's Squash Rackets
Association '50

SURFING
British Surfing Association '70
Surf Life Saving Association '71

SWIMMING AND LIFE SAVING
Amateur Swimming Association '35
English Schools Swimming
Association '50
Royal Life Saving Society '35
Swimming Teachers'
Association '48

TABLE TENNIS
English Table Tennis
Association '38

TENPIN BOWLING
British Tenpin Bowling
Association '64

TRAMPOLINING
British Trampoline Federation
Ltd. '69

UNDERWATER SWIMMING
The British Sub-Aqua Club '55

VOLLEYBALL
English Volleyball Association '64

WATER SKIING
British Water Ski Federation '66

WEIGHT-LIFTING
British Amateur Weight-Lifters'
Association '40

WILDFOWLING
The Wildfowlers' Association of
Great Britain and Ireland '68

WRESTLING
Amateur Wrestling Association '35

Other interested Organisations

EDUCATIONAL
Association of Assistant
Mistresses '35

Association of Education
 Committees '35
Association of Municipal
 Corporations '61
Association of Teachers in
 Colleges and Departments of
 Education '42
British Association of
 Settlements '35
Community and Youth Service
 Association '71
County Councils Association '36
Educational Centres Association '40
Incorporated Association of
 Assistant Masters '35
Incorporated Association of
 Head Masters '35
Incorporated Association of
 Head Mistresses '35
National Association of
 Divisional Executives for
 Education '48
National Association of Head
 Teachers '35
National Association of
 Schoolmasters '35
National Association of Youth
 Service Officers '52
National Union of Teachers '35
Society of Education Officers '35

HOLIDAY-PROVIDING
The Country-Wide Holidays
 Association '44
Galleon World Travel '48
Holiday Fellowship '41

INDUSTRIAL
Coal Industry Social Welfare
 Organisation '35
Industrial Society '36
Recreation Managers'
 Association of Great Britain '69

MEDICAL AND HEALTH
British Association of Sport and
 Medicine '68
British Medical Association '35
Chartered Society of
 Physiotherapy '35
Society of Medical Officers of
 Health '65

VOLUNTARY YOUTH AND
ADULT
Air Training Corps '42

Army Cadet Force Association '42
Association for Jewish Youth '35
The Boys' Brigade '35
British Camp Fire Girls '35
British Legion '47
British Red Cross Society '43
Campaigners '45
Church Army Youth Service '43
Church of England Board of
 Education '48
Church Girls' Brigade '35
Church Lads' Brigade '35
Co-operative Youth Movement '43
Duke of Edinburgh's Award '71
Girl Guides Association '35
Girls' Brigade '35
Girls' Friendly Society '35
Girls' Venture Corps '43
Habonim '38
Jewish Lads' Brigade '35
Methodist Association of Youth
 Club '59
National Association of Boys'
 Clubs '35
National Association of Youth
 Clubs '35
National Council of Social
 Service '35
National Federation of
 Community Associations '47
National Federation of Young
 Farmers' Clubs '37
National Trust '67
Outward Bound Trust '53
Primrose League '48
Royal Society of St. George '43
St. John Ambulance Brigade
 Cadets '45
Salvation Army '35
The Scout Association '35
Sea Cadet Corps '45
Shaftesbury Society '35
Union of Maccabi Associations '43
Young Christian Workers '47
Young Men's Christian
 Association '35
Youth Hostels Association of
 England and Wales '35

Individual Members

The Rt. Hon. Lord Aberdare '61
Mrs. M. Allen '61
Mr. T. G. Bedwell '44 (d. 1/73)

Mr. R. W. Boon '69
Mr. W. J. Borthwick, D.S.C. '65
Mr R. L. Bradley, C.B.E. '60
Sir John Braithwaite 58 (d. 4/73)
Major General The Viscount
  Bridgeman, K.B.E., C.B.,
  D.S.O., M.C., '54
Mr. R. E. Brook, C.M.G.,
  O.B.E. '62
Miss A. F. Bull, C.B.E. '70
The Rt Hon The Baroness
  Burton of Coventry '54
Mr. C. J. Chataway, M.P. '65
The Rt Rev The Lord Bishop
  of Chester '61
Miss E. B. Clarke, C.V.O., J.P. '61
Mr. N. R. Collins '68
Dr. R. Cove-Smith, Ph.D.,
  M.R.C.P. '35
Mr. H. F. David,
  C.B.E. '54 (d. 2/74)
Mr. T. Glyn Davies C.B.E. '49
Mr. M. Dower '64
Dr. O. G. Edholm '64
Sir Charles Evans, D.Sc.,
  F.R.C.S. '58
Mr H. J. Evans, O.B.E. '69
Miss K. E. Evans, M.B.E. '66
The Most Hon The Marquess of
  Exeter, K.C.M.G., LL.D. '52
D. Ford, J.P. '70
Sir Charles Forte '64
Mr. C. H. Gadney, M.B.E. '62
Mr. A. H. Gem, C.B.E., M.C. '35
Mr J. Eaton Griffith, C.M.G.,
  O.B.E. '51
Brigadier E. A. L. Gueterbock, '64
Mr. R. E. Hadingham, O.B.E.,
  M.C., T.D. '68
Mr. R. St. G. T. Harper '56
Sir William Hart, C.M.G. '68
Lieut-Colonel W. R. Hawkins,
  T.D. '70
Sir Isaac Hayward, LL.D., J.P. '64
Mr. A. Henderson, J.P. '47
Mr. D. Howell, M.P. '70

The Rt. Hon. Lord Hunt,
  C.B.E., D.S.O., D.C.L., LL.D. '55
Mr. R. B. Hunter, O.B.E. '62
Mr. K. R. Imeson '70
Mr P. A. Land '70
Mrs. R. G. Lean '60
Miss C. Leitch '67
Mr. P. J. Liddell, D.S.C. '68
Lieut-Colonel H. M. Llewellyn,
  C.B.E., D.L. '69
Miss B. Lloyd-Williams '54 (d. 5/73)
Sir Jack Longland '61
Mr. P. B. Lucas, D.S.O.,
  D.F.C. '63
The Rt. Hon. Lord Luke, T.C.,
  D.L. '52
Mr. P. C. McIntosh '62
Mr. H. McMaster '57
Mr. E. Major, M.B.E. '35
Mr. A. J. M. Miller D.S.C.,
  V.R.D. '60
Captain T. D. Morrison,
  O.B.E., M.C. '62
Mr. A. D. Munrow, O.B.E. '56
Mr. H. E. Naylor '35
The Rt. Hon. P. J. Noel-Baker '44
Mr. H. A. Pawson '61
Mr. B. L. Pearson, C.B., D.S.O.
  M.C. '55
Miss S. L. Perkins '62
Sir Arthur Porritt, Bt., G.C.M.G.
  K.C.V.O., C.B.E., F.R.C.S. '64
Mr. F. N. Punchard '46
Mr. W. F. Roberts '69
Sir Stanley Rous, C.B.E., J.P. '35
Lieut-Colonel R. H. Russell 66
Mr P. M. Scott, C.B.E., D.S.C. '58
Mr. F. H. Smith '56
Miss P. Spafford, O.B.E. '36
Mr T. Stephenson '68
Sir Peter Studd, G.B.E. '70
Mr. C. J. H. Tolley, M.C. '54
The Rt Hon. Lord Wakefield '45
Mr. J. P Walker '49
Sir John Wedgwood, Bt '57
Colonel W. H. Whitbread '55
Sir John Wolfenden, C.B.E. '44

Appendix E

CCPR Publications

(Note: Where not otherwise stated, the author(s) were members of the CCPR's staff).

1935   *Twelve 'Keep Fit' Gymnastic Tables for Women's Classes*
1936   *Twelve Simple Dances*
1937   *1937 Daily Dozen for Girls and Women*
        1937 Daily Dozen for Boys and Men
        Play Leadership
        Report on an Investigation into Recreative Gymnastics for Older Women, Dr. Anna Broman and Miss V. Vulliamy
        The Use of Music for Recreative Gymnastic Classes
1938   *1938 Daily Dozen for Girls and Women*
        1938 Daily Dozen for Boys and Men
        Demonstrations of Recreative Physical Training
        Exercises and Activities with the Use of Sticks
        Recreative Gymnastic Tables for Use in Older Women's Classes
        Second Series of Simple Dances for Recreative Classes
        Second Series of Recreative Gymnastic Tables for Girls and Women
1939   *Play Leadership – Its Development and Organisation* (revised edition)
        Activities and Games for use in Girls' and Women's Physical Recreation
1940   *Suggestions with regard to the Organisation of Physical Recreation for Boys and Young Men in Recreational Centres and Clubs*
        Suggestions with regard to the Organisation of Physical Recreation for Girls and Young Women in Recreational Centres and Clubs
1941   *Eight Ball Studies for use in Girls' and Women's Physical Recreation*
        Six Simple Hungarian Dances, G. Bogyo

Films about Movement and Health

1942   *The Coordination of Music and Movement in Keep-Fit Classes,* M. Cuthbertson

Five Peasant Dances, Helen Wingrave

Activities and Games for Youths and Men

Games and Games Training for Girls and Young Women

National Character Dances, M. Webster and M. Hulme

1943   *Old Scandinavian Dances,* A. Schnitt

Rounders – Its Play and Coaching in Clubs, by M. C. Tayler

Physical Recreation Equipment – Notes on Its Maintenance and Improvisation during wartime

1944   *Ballroom Dancing in Youth Clubs*

Books on Physical Recreation – A List for Leaders, compiled by R. E. Roper

Facilities for Physical Recreation – Suggestions for Local Authorities

National Test for Leaders – Regulations and Syllabus, Specimen Questions

Physical Recreation for Mixed Groups

Pianist and Leader, Music by R. Dawes

Keep-Fit and Recreative Gymnastics

1945   *Simple Progressive Dances,* C. M. Webster

1947   *Medicine Ball Work for Women and Girls*

The CCPR Book of Stick Work (revised edition)

1949   *Skipping With Music*

Ballroom Dancing – the Class Teaching Method

1950   *A Guide to Judging and Presiding at Foil and Sabre,* by Roger Crosnier

1957   *Housework with Ease,* T. McClurg Anderson (in association with the SCPR)

1958   *Keep Fit – A Guide for Leaders –* by Joyce Jarvis

1960   *'Sport and the Community' – Report of the Wolfenden Committee on Sport*

1961   *'Sport and the Community' – the CCPR's Statement of Views'*

Safety on Mountains

Simple Continental Character Dances, Madge Baranek

1964   *Inland Waters and Recreation,* Survey by Birmingham University

Sports Facilities in Wales
Three New Keep-Fit Schemes, Madge Baranek
'Dutch Dances' and *'More Dutch Dances',* H. M. Watt
1966 *Community Sports Halls,* by G. A. Perrin (jointly with NPFA)
Water Sports Code
1967 *The CCPR – What it is; What it does*
Coaching Schemes of the National Governing Bodies of Sport, (report of an inquiry committee under the chairmanship of Peter McIntosh)
Local Sports Advisory Councils
Sport for All – The United Kingdom (a study for the Council for Cultural Cooperation of the Council of Europe) J. G. Birch
1968 *The Mountain Code*
Planning for Sport – Report on Scales of Provision (for the Sports Council)
1969 *Provision for Sport and Physical Recreation in England and Wales* (for the Sports Council)
The Sports Council – A Review, 1966–1969 (for the Sports Council)

Appendix F

Principal Sources Consulted

Apart from Minute Books of CCPR Committee and Sub-Committee Meetings, Correspondence Files and Private Memoranda, below are listed the principal books, pamphlets and other documents consulted, given so far as possible in chronological order of publication :

Annual Reports of CCRPT and CCPR, from 1935 to 1972

CCRPT News Leaflets, Nos. 1 to 3 (1935–1937)

CCRPT and CCPR National Leaders Bulletins, Nos. 1 to 18 (1941–1946)

CCPR Physical Recreation Bulletins (for International Circulation) Nos. 1 to 4 (1947–48)

Recreation Review, Joint Quarterly Journal of CCPR & NPFA (Jan. 1947 to Oct. 1948)

Physical Recreation and *Sport and Recreation,* CCPR's Quarterly Journal (Jan. 1949 to Apr. 1972)

Day Continuation Schools, Ferguson and Abbott (Bournville and Pitman – 1935)

Report of the British Medical Association's Physical Education Committee, (BMA 1936)

Physical Training and Recreation, White Paper, Command 5364 (HMSO 1937)

Physical Training and Recreation Act, 1937 (HMSO 1937)

Fitness Wins – 24 ways of Keeping Fit, (HMSO for National Fitness Council, 1938)

The National Fitness Campaign, (HMSO for NFC 1939)

The National Fitness Council, Report of Grants Committee (HMSO 1939)

The Boy, 1935–1944, Quarterly Journal of NABC (Ed. by W. McG.Eagar)

The Needs of Youth, A. E. Morgan (OUP 1939)

Young Citizen (revision of above), A. E. Morgan (Penguin Special 1943)

The County Badge or the Fourfold Experiment, (OUP 1941)

Board of Education Circulars – No's. 1445(1/36), 1486(11/39), 1529(11/40), 1543(3/41)

Ministry of Education Circular, No. 51 (6/45)

The Youth Service After the War, Report of Youth Advisory Council, (HMSO 1943)

Teachers and Youth Leaders – McNair Report on their supply, training and recruitment (HMSO, 1944)

Purpose and Content of Youth Service, Report of Youth Advisory Council, (HMSO 1945)

Youth Service in an English County, L. J. Barnes (King George Jubilee Trust 1945)

The Outlook for Youth Work, L. J. Barnes (King George Jubilee Trust 1948)

National Parks and Access to the Countryside Act, 1949

Youth Hostel Story, Oliver Coburn (NCSS 1950)

Citizens of Tomorrow, Report for King George's Jubilee Trust (Odham's 1955).

Britain in the World of Sport, (Physical Education Association, for Birmingham University 1956)

Seventh Report from the House of Commons Select Committee on Estimates, 1956/7 (HMSO)

The Challenge of Leisure, pre-Election Pamphlet (Conservative Political Centre 1959)

Leisure for Living, pre-Election Pamphlet (Labour Party 1959)

Sport and the Community, Report of the Wolfenden Committee (CCPR 1960)

The Youth Service in England and Wales, Albemarle Committee's Report (HMSO 1960)

The Training of Part-Time Youth Leaders and Assistants, Bessey Report (HMSO 1962)

Central Government Aid to Sport and Physical Recreation in Countries of Western Europe, D. D. Molyneux, (Birmingham University 1962)

Hansard, House of Commons: 26/10/54, 28/4/61, 8/5/62, 20/12/62, 17/7/63, 22/6/64, 4/12/64, 3/2/65, 19/1/68, House of Lords: 2/3/60, 15/2/61, 9/5/62, 6/11/62, 31/1/63, 22/5/63, 13/5/64, 9/7/64, 3/2/65, 8/12/65, 7/2/68

Provision of Facilities for Sport, Joint Circular by Ministry of Housing and Local Government (49/64) and Department of Education and Science (11/64) (Aug. 1964)

Inland Waters and Recreation, (CCPR 1964)

Sport in Society, Peter McIntosh (New Thinker's Library 1963)

Nine Pioneers in Physical Education, (Physical Education Association 1964)

Youth in Action – The Duke of Edinburgh's Award Scheme, 1955–1966, D. Wainwright (Hutchinson's 1966)

The Countryside in 1970 – Proceedings of the Study Conference, November 1963 (HMSO 1964)

The Countryside in 1970 – Proceedings of the Second Conference, November 1965 (Royal Society of Arts and Nature Conservancy, 1966)

Fourth Wave – the Challenge of Leisure – Civic Trust Survey by Michael Dower (*Architects' Journal,* 1965)

Leisure and the Waterways – (British Waterways Board, 1967)

A Better Country, Report of Group (Conservative Political Centre 1966)

The Sports Council – A Report (HMSO 1966)

The Sports Council – A Review (HMSO 1969)

Physical Education in England since 1800, Peter McIntosh (Revised Edn. 1968 – Bell)

A Woman's Reach, Nea Morin (Eyre and Spottiswoode 1968)

Recreations (Visual History of Modern Britain) – J. A. R. Pimlott (Studio-Vista 1968)

A Better Tomorrow, Conservative Party Election Programme (Conservative Central Office 1970)

Labour Party's Election Manifesto (Labour Party 1970)

First and Second Reports from the Select Committee of the House of Lords on Sport and Leisure (HMSO 1973)

Index

Heathfield, Beryl, 165, 166
Henderson, J. B., 80, 109, 110
H.M. Inspectors, 75, 133, 199, 214
Hickling, G., 52, 141, 201
Historic Buildings Council, 102
Hitler Youth, 22
Hockey Association, 166, 193
Hogan, J. M., 55
Holiday Fellowship, 80
Holme Pierrepont Centre, 126 sqq.
Holmes, Margaret, 42
Holt, E. J., 186
Holt, Lawrence, 55
Hookway, R. J. S., 196
Horder, Lord, 29
Horobin, Sir Ian, 91
House of Commons Debates, 156, 159
House of Commons Select Committee, 77, 91
House of Lords Debates, 156, 159, 211
House of Lords Select Committee, 232
Howell, Denis, 18, 107, 114, 120, 125, 156, 167, 187, 195, 208, 214, 217, 229
Hughes, Sheila, 165
Hunt, Sir John (later Lord Hunt), 18, 83, 85, 110, 113, 114, 142, 150, 196, 208, 213
Hunter, R. B., 141
Hutchinson, Ken, 139

I.C.I., 51
I.M. Marsh College of P.E., 66, 114
Imperial Society of Teachers of Dancing, 71, 95
Ince, Sir Godfrey, 145, 152
Industrial (Welfare) Society, 33, 52
Industry, Work in, 50, 51, 62
Information Service, 76
Inland Waters, 161
Innes, Dr. P. (later Sir Peter), 39
International Work & Conferences, 68–71, 95, 120, 134, 199
Institution of Water Engineers, 161

International Olympic Committee, 74, 75

Jacks, Dr. L. P., 29, 55
Jackson, J. A., 111, 113, 140
Jackson, Millicent Adair, 39, 92
Jackson, Rhona, 140
Jameson, Sir Wilson, 186
Jenkins, Sir William, 130
Jones, Emlyn, 72, 73, 85, 118
Joseph, Sir Keith, 114
Jubilee Trust, King George's, 22, 25, 28, 40, 48, 66, 91
Junior Instruction Centres, 19
Junior Leaders, 50
Juvenile Organisations Committees, 20

Keeble, Ruth, 49, 84, 162
Keeble, W. B., 123
Keep-Fit Association, 95, 166
Kennedy, Douglas, 27, 39
Kerr-Hunter, J. A., 136
Kilmuir, Lord, 156
King George V, 22, 27
King George VI, 21, 39, 40, 78
King George VI Memorial Foundation, 107, 108, 112, 117, 118
Knibbs, F., 33
Knight, Frank and Rutley, 102

Laban Art of Movement, 95
Labour Party's Report, 156
Lacrosse, All England Ladies' Assocn., 67
Lang, Sir John, 157, 158, 168, 195, 218
Lane, Jim, 104, 105, 201
Latto, Kay (formerly Caister), 33, 72, 92, 150
Latto, W. L., 49, 72
Lawn Tennis, 73
Lawson, Peter, 228
Leach, Johnny, 73
Lee, Brian, 100
Legion of Health and Happiness, 29
Lewis, Jim, 78, 100